THE LONDON BRIGHTON
AND SOUTH COAST RAILWAY:
I. ORIGINS AND FORMATION

The London Brighton and South Coast Railway:

I. ORIGINS AND FORMATION

JOHN HOWARD TURNER

B. T. BATSFORD LTD
London

ISBN 0 7134 0275X

Printed in Great Britain by
Butler & Tanner Ltd
Frome, Somerset
for the Publishers
B. T. Batsford Ltd
4 Fitzhardinge Street
London W1H 0AH

5801

CONTENTS

List of Plates. vii

Preface by S. W. Smart, CVO, OBE. ix

Foreword. x

Abbreviations. xv

I Introduction. 1

II The Founding of the Croydon, Brighton, and South Eastern Railways. 26

III The London & Greenwich Railway. 40

IV The London & Croydon Railway. 45

V The London & Brighton Railway: The Choice of Route — Discussion. 65

VI The London & Brighton Railway: The Choice of Route — Decision. 88

VII The London & Brighton Railway: Building the Line. 116

VIII The First Years of the Croydon and Brighton Companies. 147

IX The Opening of the South Eastern Railway and its Effects, 1842-44. 170

X The Bricklayers Arms Branch. 192

XI The Shoreham & Chichester Line. 205

XII Extensions to the East. 213

XIII Extensions to the West. 232

XIV The London & Croydon's Atmospheric Phase and the Line to Epsom. 239

XV General Developments, 1844-45. 257

XVI Events in 1845-46, and the Formation of the L B S C Rly. 269

Concise Index. 283

LIST OF PLATES
(between pages 160-161)

1   Croydon Canal: remaining section.
2   London & Croydon Rly offices.
3   Corbett's Lane Junction in 1839.
4   Corbett's Lane Junction in 1967.
5   Rockshaw Road Bridge, Merstham.
6   Ouse Viaduct.
7   Burgess Hill Station.
8   Old Tunnel under Brighton Station.
9   Brighton Station.
10 Hassocks Gate Station.
11 Kingston Bridge, Shoreham, in 1840.
12 Kingston Bridge, Shoreham, in 1945.
13 Stoat's Nest Station.
14 Arun Bridge.
15 Falmer Tunnel.
16 Original Horsham Station.

PREFACE

THE LONDON BRIGHTON
& SOUTH COAST RAILWAY

Whilst over the years a number of books have appeared
dealing with individual railways of the pre-1923 era, their
authors either have concentrated on specific subjects such as
motive power or train running, or have so summarized the
building up of the lines concerned that those seeking the
reasons for such developments are often unable to find
satisfactory answers to their questions. This absence of
adequate information has always seemed to me to be regret-
table, and I can only assume that it is partly, at any rate,
because the writers concerned have not been fortunate
enough to have really detailed personal knowledge of the
old railways. No doubt this is also the reason why errors in
earlier accounts are repeated, and why myths are sometimes
dressed up as facts.

As one who started his railway career on the London
Brighton & South Coast Railway and who retired as Superintendent of Operation of the Southern Region of British
Railways — into which the L B & S C Railway came via the
Southern Railway — it therefore gives me particular pleasure
to welcome this really authoritative account of the L B & S C
Railway. The two volumes comprising the complete work
will, I feel sure, be read with great interest not only by those
whose particular interests lie with that railway, but by others
who will perhaps see it in the larger context of one of the
many achievements of the railway era.

Eastbourne   S. W. Smart
1976

FOREWORD

An immense number of books and articles have been written
on the history of railways in the United Kingdom, apart
from a very large number of others on railways in other
countries. Most of these publications have dealt with their
subjects in a fairly broad-brush manner, and those seeking
more detailed information on a particular railway have a
relatively limited field in which they can search for the data
required.

Railways in the United Kingdom were normally founded
and built as commercial ventures, and therefore somewhat
naturally had a 'commercial-in confidence' outlook. Hence
each company tended to develop on its own unless it specifi-
cally sought information from another company, contacts
between managements and heads of departments of various
companies being more on a personal basis than on an 'official' one. In the light of this, it is not surprising that great
differences in practice grew up between various companies.

From the practical point of view, it is only necessary to
remember that every company nominally fixed its own
structure gauge, so that subsequent amalgamations of small
companies into larger ones resulted in the necessity for
composite structure gauges to be prepared, giving the
maximum dimensions within which rolling stock of the
company had then to be designed in order to be able to work
freely over the lines of the amalgamated railway. If, later, a
company or line having a structure gauge that was more
limited in any way than the composite gauge of the parent
concern, was brought into the large company, the latter
might be saddled more or less indefinitely with the need to

restrict its normal stock from running over the line having reduced clearances, and even with the need to build special stock for that line.

The insularity of railways in their formative years inevitably gave rise to the development of individual designs of permanent way — in essence, the most important part of a railway, as without the track there would be no railway — and of signalling (also a fundamental feature of railways). The differences between locomotives and rolling stock of various companies were also to a large extent no doubt due in earlier years to each company proceeding independently. Many books and articles have of course been written on the locomotives of the various railway companies, and a few on their rolling stock, but in most cases in the form of chronological or technical appraisals of development rather than in the larger sense that the sole object of locomotives and rolling stock was — and still is — to cater for the traffic as effectively and economically as possible. Locomotives and rolling stock play their part — an important part — in the general picture, but they are not the 'be-all and end-all' of railways.

This two-volume work on the London, Brighton & South Coast Railway, gives information which enables readers to understand why particular routes were chosen for various lines, instead of alternative routes. Descriptions of each line are given in sufficient detail for the work of constructing them to be understood, and for subsequent rebuilding and enlargement works to be seen in context. The complete book is therefore much more than a history of this railway, and has only been possible because of the Author's personal and extremely detailed knowledge of the L B S C Rly, of which his own recollections go back to about 1917 when he first travelled on it. Reference is only made to the lines of other companies where this is essential in order to enable the overall position to be understood.

The book has been written 'from scratch', the Author having taken the great bulk of the information, including the technical descriptions of the various lines, from his own library and records (of which the principal portion comprises official data), and from his own direct knowledge. Recourse has not, except incidentally, been made to previously-published accounts of this railway, although it has sometimes been necessary to correct oft-repeated errors of statement. The Author therefore hopes that readers will find in this book, answers to questions whose solution cannot be satisfactorily obtained from earlier publications.

Despite having in my own records most of the information and illustrations needed, some help has, of course been sought from, and been freely given by, other sources, which it gives me pleasure to acknowledge. Assistance from the British Railways Archivist, and later from the Public Records Office, in respect of references some years ago to Minute-books, etc., is greatly appreciated. Much help, for which I am particularly grateful, has been freely given by my many friends on the Southern Region of British Railways, in ascertaining or corroborating certain facts and in facilitating my reference to plans and records, as well as in encouragement. Some of the photographic illustrations came from the records of the National Railway Museum, with whose Keeper I am professionally associated as a consultant and whose permission to use these illustrations is acknowledged with pleasure.

I wish to refer by name to Eleanor Howard Turner, my wife, to Joan Eastland, and to Patrick Piper. Eleanor, herself the daughter of a station master, not only helped me with research into some of my records, but constantly typed and re-typed various drafts as I continually sought to condense the account, since limitations of space have meant that only a fraction of the information that I have has been published. In addition, she shared with Joan the typing of the final version of the book. My wife's interest has been immense, her support — including late nights galore — has been unwavering, and her patience has been inexhaustible.

Joan was born on the L B S C Rly, in the then station house at West Croydon, where her grandfather was station master at the time. Her father was also on the L B S C Rly in the Auditor's Department, and she herself had 37 years service on the Southern Railway and Southern Region before joining forces with me. Her help in sifting out, summarizing, and indexing my official data relating to signalling and engineering works changes, and in identifying and indexing information pertinent to this book, has been beyond words.

In addition, she shared with Eleanor the typing of the final version of the book.

Patrick Piper, a professional illustrator, prepared all the diagrams and line illustrations for the book, usually from my rough sketches but sometimes from early drawings cluttered with unnecessary detail. The value of his help and interest in the preparation of this book has been immense, and it gives me great pleasure to acknowledge it.

Finally, I should like to thank Messrs. Batsford, and in particular William (Bill) Waller, for publishing what I hope may be of great interest as well as being a source of reference for other historians.

Volume I traces the origins and early developments down to the Act of Consolidation which formed the L B S C Rly in 1846. Volume II, in preparation, will complete the account down to 31 December 1922, the final day of the company's separate existence.

JOHN HOWARD TURNER

ABBREVIATIONS

The following abbreviations are used from time to time in this book:

Abbreviation	*Full Title*
C M G Rly	Croydon, Merstham & Godstone Railway
L & Bn Rly	London & Brighton Railway
L & C Rly	London & Croydon Railway
L & G Rly	London & Greenwich Railway
L & S Rly	London & Southampton Railway
L B S C Rly	London Brighton & South Coast Railway
L S W Rly	London & South Western Railway
Rly	Railway
S E Rly	South Eastern Railway
S I Rly	Surrey Iron Railway
£ s. d.	Pounds, Shillings, and Pence (old British currency). There were 12 pence to 1 shilling, and 20 shillings to £1. At the time of change of currency, 1s. was represented by 5p. in new (present) currency.

CHAPTER ONE

Introduction

THERE SEEMS little doubt that the town of Croydon, which lies south of London and which existed in Roman times, became a centre of some religious importance at an early date, and as such gradually grew in size and standing. After the Norman Conquest the manor was apparently given to Lanfranc, then Archbishop of Canterbury, who is supposed to have founded the palace of Croydon. It was used from time to time as the archiepiscopal residence up to the time of the Civil War, and Queen Elizabeth I, at any rate, stayed there on occasions. Requisitioned by Parliament, it was handed back to the Church after the Restoration, the Archbishops continuing to use it until about 1780. Ultimately it became a girls school.

For a lengthy period Croydon had been bounded by large areas of forest, in which the practice of charcoal-burning grew up. The charcoal was then commonly known as 'coal'; mined coal, when it became available, was used only in districts surrounding the pits. Exposed seams on the North-East Coast resulted in coal being washed ashore, and when transported by coastal shipping to places like London became known as 'sea-coal'. The charcoal-burners, or 'coal-burners', became known as 'colliers', remembered in the name of the district of Colliers Wood near Tooting.

Before sea-borne coal began to reach London in substantial quantities, there was a demand for charcoal to supplement normal supplies of wood for domestic heating. This applied particularly in the Capital, because of its use in the cooking of luxurious foods for the banquets given by the Trades Guilds and other large bodies. In consequence

1

there was a regular movement of charcoal from Croydon to the City of London, apart from normal commerce between the two places.

Croydon was in addition a market town with days set aside for various assemblies — e.g. Thursdays were devoted to the cattle market. There was also an annual fair.

The natural topography did not assist the introduction of improved means of transport. To the south of London there is a ridge of hills, mainly of clay, running roughly in a curve from the bank of the Thames east of Greenwich, through Blackheath and Shooters Hill, to Sydenham and Streatham, and then to Putney on the bank of the Thames in the west. This ridge is cut into or through by the Ravensbourne to the east, feeding the Thames at Deptford, and the Wandle to the west flowing into the Thames at Wandsworth, between which there were one or two very small streams. Croydon lies south of this ridge of hills, but still above the level of London itself. The summit of the ridge, which is the highest point between the two places, is in the area of Sydenham Hill. When the provision of better transport facilities became practicable and economically possible, toward the end of the eighteenth century, the topography became important in selecting the best route for the means of transport to be used.

Improved methods of transport had generally been sought for many years, and serviceable roads, maintained by turnpike trusts, had been established on various routes; but the Industrial Revolution, by creating a pressing need, was a vital factor in giving a fillip to new methods. First came canals, and then railways. Part of the River Wey, in Surrey, had been improved by the construction of a Navigation, with locks, as long ago as 1651, but it was not until 1757 that the major part of the first canal in the modern sense had been opened at St. Helens. The Duke of Bridgewater's Canal from his coal mines at Worsley to Manchester was opened in 1761. Other canals soon followed, and with them the development of locks and aqueducts to enable the route to be taken over hilly ground. Apart from the building of canals for commercial purposes, the involvement of the United Kingdom in the war with France at the end of the eighteenth century gave a fillip to their promotion and construction for the movement of troops and stores for defence purposes. Where the route of a canal was close to that of a turnpike, the traffic on the road was affected, but not necessarily to total disadvantage; the heavy traffic went by water and so the reduced maintenance of the road went some way to offsetting the fall in revenue to the turnpike trustees.

Where the building of a canal would have been unnecessarily expensive, or where there was an inadequate supply of water, an alternative means of relatively large-scale transport was sought which would still be a marked improvement on the rutted and pot-holed roads then common in the absence of turnpikes. The principle of a prepared and properly maintained 'road' had been established for some thousands of years, and had been used for certain industrial traffic flows in the United Kingdom since the closing years of the sixteenth century. Iron plates had been used to strengthen wooden rails early in the eighteenth century, and such 'railways' were established in mining areas in the North East and at certain other places, over short distances and reasonably level ground, to bring coal down to water craft of various types. During the canal period a number of such 'railways' were projected as feeders to canals where the construction of branch canals could not be justified on economic grounds, and where the land was essentially level. Where major differences in level could not be avoided, inclined planes were introduced to concentrate the gradients into relatively short lengths, which were worked by special means.

The disadvantage of 'railways' in comparison with canals at that period was essentially that loads were very limited as compared with what could be taken at any one time by water, even where a number of wagons was formed into a horse-drawn train. Hilly ground involved both 'railways' and canals in heavy constructional costs, to attain a satisfactory route.

At the beginning of the nineteenth century two steps of particular importance in the history of transport were taken, which were intimately associated with Croydon. These were the decision to build a railway from the Thames to Croydon, independently of any canal; whilst at the same time, separate interests decided to build a canal from Croydon to the

Thames. Since part of the course of an extension of the railway south of Croydon, made by a separate company, was subsequently utilized for the route of the main line of the London and Brighton Railway, and another section was partly occupied by a branch line, whilst the Croydon Canal was purchased and much of its general route utilized by the London and Croydon Railway — the two main concerns subsequently combined to form the London Brighton and South Coast Railway — it is essential to include in this account some particulars both of the early railway and of the canal.

The railway was part of a much larger scheme proposed in 1799 for a horse tramway from London to Portsmouth, to avoid the risk to shipping from attacks by the French in the English Channel and the Straits of Dover. As Portsmouth lies roughly south-west of London, it was natural that the whole scheme was associated with an approach to the Thames to the west side of the City. To take in Croydon, the first part of the route was planned to run along the valley of the River Wandle, thus giving an essentially easily-graded connection between London and Croydon. The Wandle was then busy with mills and works depending on waterwheels, but William Jessop, who reported on the possibility of constructing a canal along the selected route, stated firmly that he considered that there was insufficient water available for the purpose. Accordingly the promoters (one of whom was George Tritton, a banker and part-owner of the Ram Brewery at Wandsworth) went ahead on the basis of a railway. That part of the line from the Thames to Croydon received its Act on 21 May 1801 (41 Geo. III cap. 26) as the Surrey Iron Railway Company, and the line was opened for public traffic on 26 July 1803.

The canal was promoted in 1800 to connect Croydon with the Thames at Rotherhithe, thus being planned to enable barges to go direct alongside sea-going ships on the river. The route originally proposed was largely beside the River Ravensbourne and would have approached Croydon without involving extensive engineering works. However, while the proposals were still under discussion a separate company was in the field to build a canal from Rotherhithe westward to Peckham and Camberwell, and then on to

4

Kennington, Clapham, Tooting, and Mitcham. This took the name of the Surrey & Kent Canal, later altered to the Grand Surrey Canal. Arrangements were then made for the Croydon Canal to join the Grand Surrey Canal near New Cross instead of having its own independent access to Rotherhithe, and this necessitated a change of route via Sydenham and involved a sharp fall from Sydenham to New Cross. The Act (41 Geo. III cap. 127) for the construction of the Croydon Canal on this alignment was obtained six weeks after the Act for the Surrey Iron Railway, but constructional and financial difficulties delayed the opening until Monday 23 October 1809.[1] In 1803 a scheme was launched to build a canal from Croydon to Portsmouth, but this failed from lack of financial support.

At the beginning of the nineteenth century Croydon thus became the first town in Britain which would have directly competitive means of transport, horses in both cases, of course, providing the motive power. Its population in 1801 was 5743.[2] The relative routes of the railway and the canal are shown in Figure 1.

The Surrey Iron Railway was actually a plate-way, in that the track consisted of cast-iron angle-plates with up-turned flanges so placed that the blind-tyred wheels of wagons ran on the flat surfaces and were guided by the flanges, which were between the wheels. Another flange below each length of rail acted as a stiffener between the stone blocks which carried the plates. Although the 'gauge' does not seem to have been recorded, it must have been 4 ft. 2 in. since the latter was adopted for the Croydon, Merstham & Godstone Railway (which was in practice an extension of the Surrey Iron Railway — see later). The rails were carried on stone blocks more or less flush with the ground. The line started from a place called Ram Field (adjacent to the Ram Brewery) in Wandsworth, where a basin for barges was completed on 9 January 1802, and ran to the east of the Wandle until it crossed Wandsworth High Street. The line then turned south-west, crossed over the Wandle, and then continued past various mills and works until it turned south-east again, crossing over the Wandle and also over Garratt Lane, and thence running beside the latter in a direction somewhat east of south. It then passed through

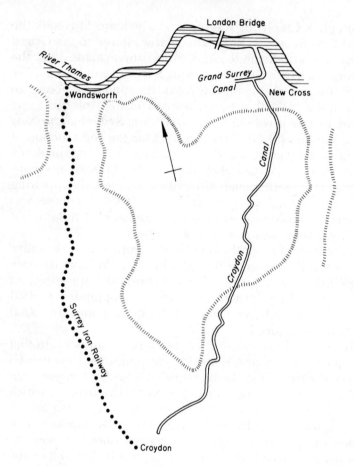

Figure 1. Relative Routes of Surrey Iron Railway and Croydon Canal.

Merton and Mitcham, and finally turned south-east over Mitcham Common to a terminus at Pitlake Meadow near Croydon Parish Church, some nine miles from Wandsworth. The Weigh and Toll House still exists, and is situated on the down side of the line from West Croydon to Sutton, a few hundred yards after leaving West Croydon station. The name 'Pitlake' comes from the words 'pytt' and 'lacu', meaning the stream in the hollow.

A branch from Mitcham to Hackbridge (then Hack Bridge) in the parish of Carshalton does not seem to have been opened until about 1 June 1804. Double track was laid on the 'main line', with 'crossovers' as necessary and turn-plates at the termini to facilitate the handling of carts. As the Surrey Iron Railway was a toll company, it had no 'rolling stock' of its own. Gradients appear generally to have been very slight as the line was never far from the Wandle. The Engineer was Wm. Jessop, with George Leather as Resident Engineer. The line cost some £60,000, and the shareholders saw little for their money. The general route of the Surrey Iron Railway and of its 'extension' the Croydon, Merstham & Godstone Railway — described later — are shown in Figure 2.

The Croydon Canal was in every way more difficult to build than the Surrey Iron Railway. A short distance after its commencement by a southwards cut from the Grand Surrey Canal in the parish of St. Paul, Deptford, in a south direction, it had to start to climb some 150 feet to the district now known as Forest Hill on the east slopes of Sydenham Hill. This rise entailed the construction of 26 locks on a some-what zigzagging alignment, in order to have as long a route as possible along which height was to be gained, after which the course was level to Selhurst (then spelt Sellhurst). Beyond Selhurst two further locks were needed to bring the canal over the little River Graveney and then to its final level at Croydon, where its basin was well sited in relation to the town as it then existed.

Proceeding southwards from its commencement at a turnout from the Grand Surrey Canal, the route, then in a very sparsely inhabited district, curved to the left for about 30 chains until it reached the first lock; half way along this length a lane (known later as Cold Blow Lane) had to be taken over the canal by a bridge. The first lock was suc-ceeded by a right-hand curve which was followed by a length of straight, the second lock being at the end of the curve, the third one midway along the straight, and the fourth one at the end of the straight. The main road to Deptford — now New Cross Road — was taken over the canal at the fourth lock, which was some 22 chains beyond lock No. 1.

On leaving the fourth lock, the route turned fairly sharply to the left for about 7 chains and then continued straight for some 17 chains. The left turn avoided high ground on the right. Locks Nos. 5 and 6 were on the first

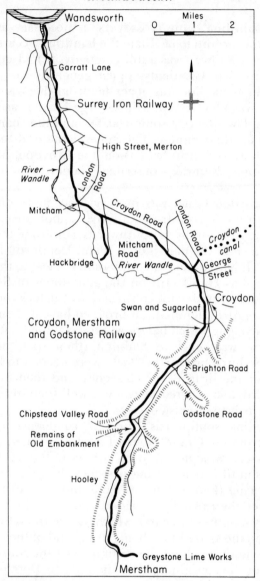

Figure 2. General Route of Surrey Iron Railway and Croydon, Merstham & Godstone Railway.

curved stretch, and No. 7 at the end of it, whilst Nos. 8 and 9 were on the straight. At the end of the latter the tenth lock marked the start of a sharp right-hand bend about 14 chains long. There followed about ½ mile of level involving easy

left and right bends, with a left-hand one at the end leading
into the eleventh lock. Beyond Cold Blow Lane bridge and
as far as the first lock, the canal was made on land owned by
the Trustees of Sir William Langham, and from there to the
fifth lock it ran across land owned by the Haberdashers
Company. After passing over relatively short lengths of land
in various landlords' hands, the canal was taken over part of
Deptford Common to the eleventh lock. There were two
bridges carrying roads over the canal between locks Nos. 10
and 11, one (now represented by Vesta Road) some 5 chains
beyond lock No. 10, and the other (now represented by Endwell Road) just over ¼ mile farther on. It was at lock No. 11
that the real part of the climb began.

In the next 55 chains there were no less than nine locks,
many of them separated by pounds only 70 or 80 yards long.
The alignment was straight, except at the extreme south
end, where a right-hand curve started just before lock No.
20. The first part of this straight length lay in the Parish of
St. Paul's Deptford, and the major part in the parish of
Lewisham. About half-way along this straight the canal ran
over land held by the Governors of Christ's Hospital. The
right-hand curve starting at lock No. 20 continued through
locks Nos. 21 and 22, and the canal then entered another
straight some 35 chains long, on which were locks Nos. 23-26
inclusive, the last one some 25 chains along the straight.
Much of the land along this length was owned by Lord Eliot.
It will be seen that the 26 locks were situated over a length of
only just over 1½ miles. The top of the climb, at No. 26 lock,
was roughly where Honor Oak Park road now crosses over the
railway immediately south of the present Honor Oak Park
station, but the canal was to the west of the railway's alignment and some 30 feet above the level of the present railway,
which is itself in a deep cutting at that point. There were four
bridges carrying roads over the canal on this climb, over
locks Nos. 17, 20, 22, and 26, the first two represented today
by Dalrymple Road bridge and Brockley Way bridge (the
latter commonly called Brockley Jack), and the last one by
Honor Oak Park bridge.

The canal now continued level until nearly the outskirts
of Croydon, but it followed a sinuous course to avoid undue
earthworks and expense in acquiring property. On leaving

lock No. 26, some 10 chains of straight were followed by a left-hand curve which got steadily sharper until the direction of the canal had turned through more than 90°. This turn was immediately followed by another in reverse, to bring the direction back to a line parallel to that through lock No. 26 but some 330 yards to the east. The whole of this meander was on land owned by Lord Eliot.

After some 17 chains of straight, the canal again started to curve left, and at a distance of about 70 chains beyond lock No. 26 it was proceeding in a direction nearly at right angles to its previous course. A few chains of straight then led to a right-hand bend, this length covering in all about ¼ mile. At this point the site of the canal was roughly where the fore-court of the present Forest Hill station is situated, the canal's approach from the New Cross direction being along the line of what is now Devonshire Road. There was a bridge over the canal at this point, carrying what is now London Road on its former alignment straight down the hill. About 65 chains from lock No. 26 was an enlargement on the outside or west side of the bend, into which there was the first intake of water. Continuing past what is now Forest Hill, the canal once again curved left and then right for a distance of about ½ mile, with the second intake, on the right, at the left-hand bend and the third intake, also on the right, at the end of this length.[3] The two curves enabled the line of the canal to clear a reservoir on the west or right-hand side, which was known as Sydenham Reservoir and was dug for the purpose of supplying water to the canal. The necessary deviation involved acquiring a small parcel of land from Mr. M. W. Mayow (whose name is remembered today by Mayow Road, not far away). The remainder of this stretch of the canal was over Sydenham Common.

Beyond the third intake the alignment was roughly straight and in the general direction of Croydon for nearly a mile to Penge Common, there being two bridges. The first carried Sydenham Street over the canal (now represented by Sydenham Road bridge) and the second carried Beckenham Hill over the canal (now represented by the underbridge immediately on the London side of Penge West station: the relevelling of the road to pass under the railway, whereas it had passed over the canal, is very clear). The bridge carrying

Beckenham Hill was just over 2½ miles beyond lock No. 26.
The corresponding distance by the railway is 2 miles 27 chains,
the extra distance along the canal being due to the meander-
ings of the latter. The land over this length was owned by a
number of private persons. A wharf was provided by the
right-hand side of the canal immediately before it passed
under Beckenham Hill bridge. This wharf, erected by Mr.
John Scott, was intended to serve Beckenham, Bromley, and
other parts of Kent, and formed the subject of a painting.[4]

Beyond Sydenham Hill bridge, the canal followed an
exceptionally sinuous course for over 1¾ miles to Norwood,
in order to make the best use of the ground and to avoid
unnecessary earthworks. Immediately beyond Beckenham
Hill bridge, it curved to the left and then at once to the right,
until it reached a point some 25 chains beyond the bridge;
here there was an intake from the right and the canal then
turned sharply left. Passing another intake on the right and
continuing itself to turn left, it eventually straightened out
after a change of direction considerably greater than a right
angle. The general left turn was along the line of what are
now Trenholme Road and Ridsdale Road. The two intakes
were fed from a reservoir to the right of the canal. This
reservoir was dug to supply water to the canal, and still
exists as South Norwood Lake. The straight was extremely
short and was followed by a very sharp right-hand bend of
just over a right angle, which was succeeded by some 25
chains of straight. A bridge at the end of the sharp right-
hand bend carried what is now Anerley Road over the canal.
At the end of the straight there was a left-hand bend of some
45°, followed by some 16 chains of straight leading to a bridge
under the road from Penge to Croydon. All trace of the latter
seems to have disappeared, but it appears to have been near
where the Bromley Junction to Beckenham Junction railway
crosses *over* the road from Penge to Croydon. The portion of
the canal between the bridges carrying Beckenham Hill and
the present Anerley Road, ran through what was then called
Penge Forest, and was later known as Penge Wood.

After the canal had passed under the Penge to Croydon
road, it turned still further left and then immediately made a
bend to the right through nearly 180°. This led into a short
straight followed by a left-hand bend to bring it once again

11

into the general direction of Croydon. At the end of this left-hand bend, the road from Norwood to Woodside (now called Portland Road) crossed over the canal. The difference in levels was so small that a swing bridge had to be used to enable barges to pass. The distance by water from Beckenham Hill bridge to the swing bridge was 1¾ miles; by railway between the same places it is about 1¼ miles.

Beyond the swing bridge the canal followed a south-south-west line between China Hall and Sellhurst Farm (then so spelt), but then curved slightly left and then more distinctly right, to enter the lock to carry it over the River Graveney. Having crossed the latter by a bridge, it entered a second lock to bring it down to ground level again, and then proceeded straight in a south-westerly direction for ¾ mile until it finally curved left to finish in the basin at Croydon. The distance to the far end of the latter was nearly 2 miles from the swing bridge at South Norwood. There were three bridges over the canal south of where it crossed the Graveney, about ¾ mile south of the swing bridge: they were at 27 chains, 41 chains and 63 chains approximately beyond the Graveney bridge, and carried what are now known as Gloucester Road, Sydenham Road, and Whitehorse Road. The two former are thought to have been swing bridges, as the level of the road was in each case very little above the level of the Canal. What is now called Sydenham Road was then known as Middle Heath Lane. The general route of the Canal is shown in Figure 3, on which modern names of relevant roads have been shown to assist identification.

Lock-keepers' houses were provided at two places. The first was on the east side of the canal nearly 25 chains south of lock No. 10; it was immediately to the north of the present alignment of Endwell Road, and hence was roughly opposite the London end of the down platform of the present Brockley station (although actually away from the railway as at this point the latter is some little distance to the west of the route taken by the canal). The second lock-keeper's house was on the west side of the canal beside lock No. 26; it was immediately to the south of the present alignment of Honor Oak Park road, itself south of the present Honor Oak Park station; and was away from the railway as at this point the latter is some little way to the east of the route taken by the

12

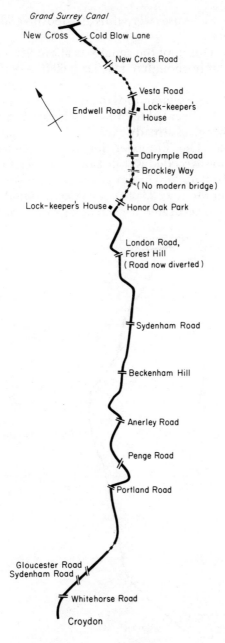

Figure 3. General Route of Croydon Canal, showing locks and bridges.

canal. The two houses were thus at opposite ends of the main flight of locks.

The total length of the canal was about 9⅝ miles, and the locks were large enough to take craft 60 ft. × 9 ft.; there was 5 feet of water. The Canal Company's act allowed them to operate steam-driven pumps to take water from the Thames, but it was later decided to build reservoirs at Sydenham and South Norwood, as already explained, with a pumping station at Croydon. The Engineer for the promoters was John Rennie, who succeeded Ralph Dodd, but actual construction was carried out under Dudley Clark as Engineer. The opening festivities on Monday 23 October 1809 included a ceremonial trip by barge, decorated for the occasion, from Sydenham to

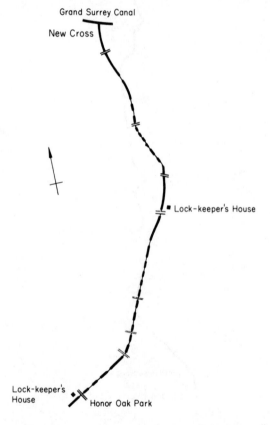

Figure 4. Detailed Route of Canal, New Cross to present Honor Oak Park.

Croydon. Only the two locks at the Graveney crossing had to be negotiated, therefore, by the proprietors' barge. The Chairman, Edward Smith, then presided at a dinner at the Greyhound, Croydon, at which, in addition to the usual toasts, Mr. T. Welsh (one of the proprietors) sang a song beginning:

> All hail this grand day, when with gay colours flying,
> The barges are seen on the current to glide,
> When with fond emulation all parties are vieing
> To make our canal of old England the pride.

The shareholders saw little or nothing for their money, however, partly from shortage of funds to run the canal properly (it had cost about £127,000 to build compared with an authorised capital of £50,000 with powers to raise a further

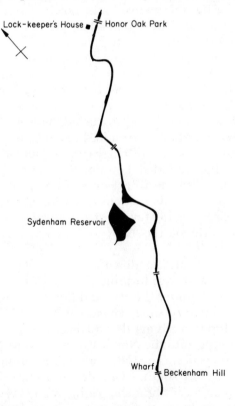

Figure 5. Detailed Route of Canal, present Honor Oak Park to present Penge.

£30,000) and also, undoubtedly, on account of competition from the railway[5] The northerly parts of the canal are shown in more detail in Figures 4 and 5.

The Surrey Iron Railway had not been opened when consideration was given to establishing a separate undertaking to extend it southwards from Croydon to Merstham and Reigate, with a branch from Merstham to Godstone. Among those particularly interested in the extension were Colonel Hylton Jolliffe and his brother, Rev. William John Jolliffe. The younger Jolliffe had given up his calling in order to manage the family estates, and both brothers had become magistrates. The proposed extension to the railway would pass over part of the Jolliffes' land and if built the line would be able to serve the chalk and stone quarry owned by Colonel Jolliffe and situated to the north of Merstham. A new company was therefore formed to be responsible for the extension, the board consisting of the Surrey Iron Railway directorate together with the two Jolliffes.

The Act for the extension was in fact obtained on 17 May 1803 (43 Geo. III cap. 35), over two months before the Surrey Iron Railway was opened. Extensions to Portsmouth and elsewhere were also being discussed, as well as a new line running from the Surrey Iron Railway to Lambeth and thence via the proposed Strand Bridge (finally opened as Waterloo Bridge) to the intended London Railway (a line from the London Docks to the wharf on the Canal at Paddington). These proposed further extensions were never built, but the line from Croydon to Merstham was opened on 24 July 1805, under the title of the Croydon, Merstham & Godstone Railway.

To the south of Croydon there is a ridge of chalk hills running east and west forming the North Downs, the chalk emerging from under the clay and the resulting 'spring line' being the source of small rivers, such as the Wandle. The northern slope is fairly gentle, and there is, south of the town, a valley running into the North Downs for several miles in a southerly direction. The Caterham Valley branches left from this some distance south of Croydon and a mile further south the Chipstead Valley branches right. With this exception the North Downs form a continuous ridge from where the valley of the Mole cuts through them some 12 miles south-west of Croydon, to the Darent Valley, also through the Downs some 12 miles east of Croydon. Several points on the North Downs exceed 500 feet above sea level.

The only practicable route for the line south of Croydon was therefore up the long valley already mentioned, south of the town. After leaving Pitlake Meadow where it connected with the Surrey Iron Railway, the Croydon, Merstham & Godstone Railway ran for about 4½ miles adjacent to, or close to, the Brighton road and on the west side of the latter, climbing gradually as it made its way up the valley. Where the Chipstead Valley forked right, the line continued to the west of the Chipstead Valley Road until it had gained a sufficient height above the latter to turn left and cross over it in a south-easterly direction by means of an arched bridge. Having reached the east side of the Chipstead Valley, the line later turned right and again ran parallel to, and on the west side of, the main Brighton road, which was now climbing more steeply than further north as the valley floor was rising comparatively rapidly towards the south. Eventually the levels of the line and the road coincided, and the Croydon, Merstham & Godstone Railway was then taken across the main road on the level to run south to Merstham on the east side of the road. At Merstham, the line turned eastwards into the Greystone Lime Works, where it finished. Its cost was £45,000. Extensions to Reigate and Godstone were never made. At dates, variously given as 1809 and 1811, a short branch was built at Pitlake (Croydon) to the south side of the basin of the Croydon Canal, this branch being the property of the Canal Company[5] The 'gauge' was 4 ft. 2 in[6] and the Engineer was Edward Banks under William Jessop. The permanent way was of a similar type to that used on the Surrey Iron Railway. Neither the latter nor the Croydon, Merstham & Godstone Railway seem to have given any proper return to the shareholders[7] The general route is shown in Figures 6 and 7, including the connection with the Surrey Iron Railway at Croydon, with relevant modern roads but excluding the reconstruction of central Croydon and the M23 motorway.

The main traffic of both the two railways and the canal was sea-borne coal to Croydon; chalk, stone, and Fuller's earth to London; and miscellaneous freight. The railways and the

canal continued in business without any real financial benefits, but more up-to-date means of transport—namely
railways in the modern sense—eventually caused both to
cease trading.

The Surrey Iron Railway was the first publicly-owned
'railway' in the world, and also the first to serve London,

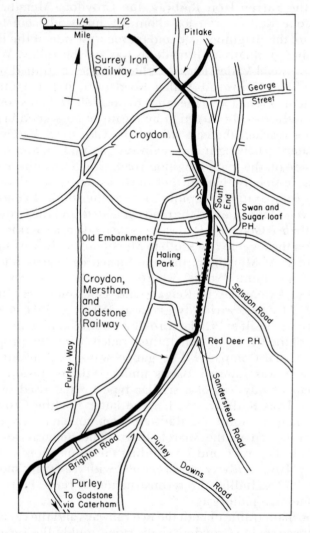

Figure 6. Detailed Route of Croydon, Merstham & Godstone Railway:
Croydon area.

but it was essentially an operating company on which traders could, on payment of toll, run their own horse-drawn vehicles — provided, of course, that the vehicles would fit the gauge. Other than being publicly-owned, it was therefore similar to many other lines already in use elsewhere in the Country. The Croydon, Merstham & Godstone Railway was

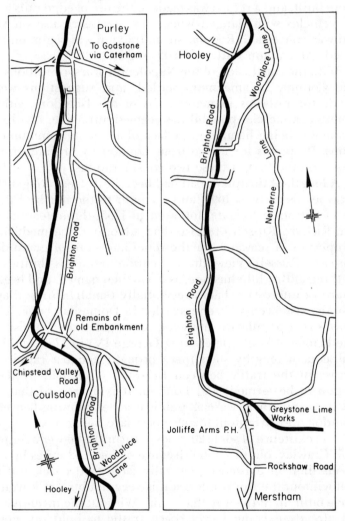

Figure 7. Detailed Route of Croydon, Merstham & Godstone Railway: Purley — Coulsdon and Coulsdon — Merstham.

19

also a toll company. The regular acceptance of fare-paying passengers by railway had commenced as early as 25 March 1807 on the Oystermouth Railway or Tramroad (the fifth such railway to receive its Act of Parliament), using a horse-drawn vehicle provided by a contractor paying tolls to the railway company. Over the next few years other railways were built, and a return was made to the use of edge rails and to vehicles with flanged wheels for exclusive use on the railway concerned. Regular steam traction was begun on the Leeds-Middleton Railway on 12 August 1812.

With the conclusion of the Napoleonic wars, conditions in the Country became more settled, and suggestions were made for railways in many parts of the Kingdom, either where commercial possibilities seemed attractive, or where trade was being hampered by lack of adequate communications. Proposals for a line from London to Brighton were based on the first of these two considerations.

A length of turnpike road had been built from Reigate to Crawley as early as 1696, and a length to the north of this, from Sutton to Reigate, followed in 1755, three years after Dr. Richard Russell of Lewes had advocated the medicinal properties of seawater for the relief and cure of glandular diseases. Russell's views drew attention to the possibilities of bathing at Brighthelmstone, as it was then named, and began to arouse interest in what was essentially a small fishing village whose existence had been recorded in Domesday book. The town's real popularity, however, commenced after a visit of the Prince of Wales (later King George IV) in 1783; and his subsequent lengthy stays there brought about a rapid increase in the traffic between Brighton (as it had by then begun to be termed) and London. It is on record that, as early as 1819, there were 52 public coaches running between London and Brighton, the cheapest fare being 6/-.[8]

The existence of some 20 miles of turnpike between Sutton and Crawley, out of a total distance of some 52 miles by the roads then in existence, naturally facilitated coach traffic, but without the Royal interest it is very doubtful if it would have built up in the way that it did. Without the incentive of an already-existing heavy coach traffic to hold out good commercial prospects there would not have been the same urge to build a railway between London and Brighton, whose main justification has always been passenger traffic.

The earliest serious proposal for a railway from London to Brighton seems to have been made by William James in a plan dated April 1823. James was something of a visionary, and suggested that a railroad operated by steam locomotives should be built from Waterloo Bridge in London to Tooting to join the Surrey Iron Railway, which would be improved and altered to take locomotives. South of Croydon, the Croydon, Merstham & Godstone Railway would be similarly modified, and a new line built from Merstham to New Chapel north of East Grinstead. Here it would join a line running direct from Strood across to Portsmouth, with a branch from Holmbush (in St. Leonard's Forest), south-west of Crawley, down the Adur Valley to Shoreham and then along the coast to Southwick for Brighton. A modern diagram based on James's plan is given in Figure 8.

James's proposals were before their time, but in 1825 there were two further schemes for a line to Brighton, one proceeding more or less south from Croydon and the other from Nine Elms via Wandsworth, Dorking, and Horsham, thence down the Adur Valley as in James's scheme. These proposals were put forward by a concern entitled the Surrey, Sussex, Hants, Wilts & Somerset Railway Company, whose Engineer was John Rennie (later knighted). Rennie himself surveyed the 'direct' route via Croydon, and employed Charles Vignoles to survey the Dorking route. Neither scheme came to anything, and a later one of 1829 similarly failed to attract interest. Yet another attempt was made in 1833 to use the 'direct' route, which was again surveyed under Rennie's control, the actual work being done by Francis Giles; this got as far as plans being deposited in Parliament, but was abandoned. These schemes, and others, are dealt with in more detail in Chapters V and VI. In the 1820s there was a national economic crisis, with a depression in agriculture, so that rural communities were suffering from high prices, low wages, and unemployment.

Attention was not, however, limited to a line from London all the way to Brighton, and a line to Croydon was also under discussion. Moreover, after a concern known as the Kentish Railway had failed to attract public support, a scheme for a line initially from London to Greenwich was proposed in

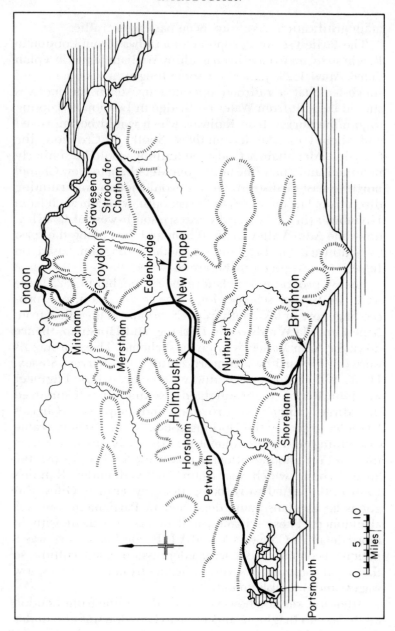

Figure 8. James' Proposals for Railways in Surrey, Sussex, Kent, and Hampshire, 1823.

1831 as the first stage of a route to Dover. The new London Bridge built by Rennie had been opened on 1 August in that year, and the London end of the projected line was therefore planned to start near the south end of that bridge. To avoid large numbers of level crossings over existing streets and alleys adjacent to London Bridge, it was proposed that the railway should be built on a viaduct and that that general elevation should be maintained for some distance before coming down to ground level; later, the decision was made to continue the viaduct throughout to Greenwich. The general route of the London & Greenwich Railway is shown in Figure 9. The London & Greenwich Railway received its Act on 17 May 1833 (3 Will. IV cap. 46).

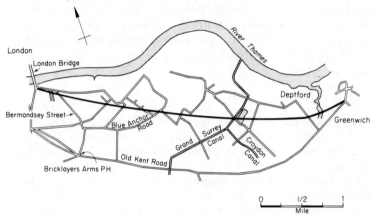

Figure 9. General Route of London & Greenwich Railway.

The London & Greenwich line was planned essentially as a passenger-carrying railway, and it was all along intended that London Bridge station should be the starting point of a line through Kent to Dover. While the line was under construction, a number of schemes were proposed for railways from London to the south and south-east, the proposed line in each case having a physical connection with the London & Greenwich Railway. Some of these schemes came to nothing, but one received its Act before even the first part of the London & Greenwich was opened, and two others received Acts before the Greenwich was completed. The first of these was the London & Croydon Railway (enacted on 12 June

23

1835), the second the South Eastern (or London & Dover) Railway (21 June 1836), and the third the London & Brighton Railway (15 July 1837). The Croydon and Brighton Companies, with others, subsequently amalgamated to form the London Brighton & South Coast Railway with which this history is concerned, whilst the South Eastern Railway became intimately associated with the working of certain parts of the line used by the London Brighton & South Coast Railway trains, and ultimately took over the Greenwich line on a perpetual lease.

The importance of the Greenwich line in the development of railways to the south and south-east of London, together with the effect of the South Eastern Railway on the London Brighton & South Coast Railway and its predecessors, therefore, necessitates extended references to both of these companies in order that the development of the London Brighton & South Coast Railway itself may be properly understood.

NOTES

1. Contemporary account in the Morning Chronicle, Friday 27 October 1809 stated that the opening was 'on Monday last'. The usually-quoted date of 22 October (which was a Sunday) is therefore incorrect.
2. The Croydon Natural History & Scientific Society Limited, *Croydon: the story of 100 years.* 1970, 4.
3. One of these two intakes was discovered in 1930, in the form of a tunnel 5 ft. in diameter, passing under the present four running roads about 10 ft. below rail level.
Southern Railway Magazine, VIII (1930), 435.
4. Reproduced in *Southern Railway Magazine,* XXIV (1946), 77, but incorrectly identified therein by being described as having been at the site of the present Sydenham station.
Again reproduced, to a larger size, and with improved clarity, in *British Railways Magazine,* Southern Region, 3 (1952), 76.
5. Further data on the Croydon Canal will be found in:
Hadfield, Charles. *The Canals of South and South East England.* David & Charles, 1969, 109 *et seq.*
Warwick, Alan R. *The Phoenix Suburb: A South London Social History.* The Blue Boar Press, 1972, 45 *et seq.*
6. Report on a section of track excavated early in 1967 at Quarry Dene Farm, Merstham, by Mr. W. G. Tharby, and specially examined by Messrs. S. B. Hamilton and Chas. E. Lee on 10 March 1967.

Railway Magazine, 113 (1967), 465.

AUTHOR'S OBSERVATION:
In a subsequent article by Mr. Tharby not published until 1971 but
referring to the 1967 excavations at Merstham, the gauge is given as
4 ft. 6 in. instead of the correct 4 ft. 2 in. Since Mr. Tharby himself
sponsored the special examination of the Merstham relics, it can
only be assumed that error in his 1971 article was due to a misprint.
See Tharby, W. G. The Surrey Iron Railway.
Surrey (The County Magazine), 6 (No. 3), 100-101 and 104. The gauge
is referred to on page 104.
7. Further data on the Surrey Iron Railway and on the Croydon,
Merstham & Godstone Railway will be found in:
Hill, Thomas. Contemporary Observations on the Surry (sic)
Tramroad, contained in *A Treatise upon the Utility of a Railway from
Leeds to Selby and Hull.* Wood and Sands, Leeds, 1827.
Bing, F. G. *The Grand Surrey Iron Railway.* The Croydon Public
Libraries Committee, 1931.
Lee, Chas. E. *The Evolution of Railways.* The Railway Gazette, 1944.
Townsend, Charles E. C. *Further Notes on Early Railways in Surrey.*
The Newcomen Society, 1950.
Numberous other books and articles make reference to these two
early railways, but they do not contain any data of substance which
are not found in Bing, Lee, Townsend, the special *Railway Magazine*
report at (6) above, or Tharby.
8. Cook, Hartley Kemball. *Over the Hills and Far Away,* George
Allen & Unwin, 1947, 122-123.
Mr. Cook was quoting Mrs. Fitzherbert, who had been secretly
married to the Prince of Wales.

CHAPTER TWO

The Founding of the Croydon, Brighton, and South Eastern Railways

IT HAS already been explained that neither the Surrey Iron Railway nor the Croydon Canal was a financial success. The former probably always suffered because its 'London' end was so far west of the City and the docks for sea-going vessels. The Croydon Canal, with its 'London' end connected to the docks at Rotherhithe, was undoubtedly the more logical link with Croydon, but suffered from the heavy capital expenditure involved in construction over a fairly difficult route, and also from lack of adequate supplies of water.

Just over 24 years after the Acts for both these concerns had been made, the Stockton & Darlington Railway was opened on 27 September 1825. The Act for the Canterbury & Whitstable Railway was given that same year, and authorized three methods of traction — horses, steam stationary engines, and steam locomotives. The following year — 1826 — the Act for the Liverpool & Manchester Railway was granted, and on this were held the famous Rainhill trials in 1829 which established steam locomotives as the most satisfactory means of traction then available. Whilst the Canterbury & Whitstable was opened on 3 May 1830 and used a steam locomotive, it was the opening of the Liverpool & Manchester Railway on 15 September 1830 that was the real landmark in development, both passenger and freight traffic being handled by steam locomotives on a double-track railway from the opening day. The Liverpool & Manchester Railway, connecting two important centres, gave a very satisfactory financial return from the start, and stimulated the many concerns that were promoted over the next few years.

Early in the field was a new railway from London to

Croydon. The promoters of the proposed railway based their scheme upon two main points:

(a) to utilize as far as practicable the route of the Croydon Canal, which was now almost, if not quite, moribund, and which would be purchased for the purpose; and

(b) to continue the line northwards from the end of the canal to a junction with the London & Greenwich Railway (then under construction) about 1¾ miles short of the latter's London Bridge terminus, to which the Croydon trains would run over the Greenwich metals.

A survey of the suggested route was made in 1834 by Joseph Gibbs, whose report was accepted by the board of the proposed railway. Discussions were opened with the canal company on the terms under which the latter would accept purchase by the railway, before the latter obtained its Act, but had not reached a satisfactory conclusion when application for the Act was made. The railway had originally offered £30,000, but the canal people demanded £40,000; the railway increased its offer to £35,000, but this was again rejected (it had cost about £127,000 to build). During the ensuing deadlock the railway company received its Act (5 Will. IV cap. 10) on 12 June 1835, empowering it to construct its line from the south up to a junction with the London & Greenwich, near where that line crossed Corbet's Lane (later normally spelt as Corbett's Lane) (see Figure 10). The date of the Act has been

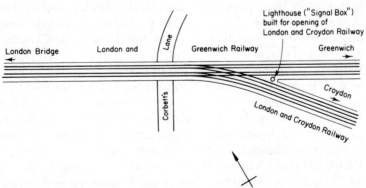

Figure 10. Junction of London & Croydon Railway with London & Greenwich Railway (L & C Rly 1835 Act).

erroneously given as 5 June.[1] The Greenwich Company at that date was still constructing its line, of which the first part, from Spa Road (about ¾ mile north of the junction at Corbett's Lane) to Deptford was not opened until 8 February 1836, 8 months later. Experimental running of Greenwich trains started on 8 June 1835.

The latter date marked an important step. Not only was the London & Greenwich the first railway, in the modern use of the term, to serve London, but Spa Road became the first London station. The Greenwich Company's line was extended to Bermondsey Street, just south of London Bridge station, on 10 October 1836, passengers proceeding on foot to and from the latter; and to the terminus on 1 December 1836. London Bridge then became the first terminus in the Capital.

Reverting to 1834, two further routes were proposed for a line to Brighton, by Vignoles and by Nicholas Cundy respectively. Vignoles' proposed route was via Croydon, then generally south-west until it entered the Adur Valley, down which it went to Shoreham. Cundy's scheme involved using the London & Southampton Railway (authorized in that same year) as far out as Wandsworth, and then proceeding via Dorking and the now well-considered route down the Adur valley to Shoreham. Early in 1835 the Rennie 'direct' proposal was again brought forward. The London & Brighton Committee asked Robert Stephenson to advise on the best of the competing routes; he advocated Cundy's, but said that the latter's detailed proposals were unsatisfactory. Robert Stephenson then proposed that G. P. Bidder should put forward a scheme along this route. Other proposals were put forward by Joseph Gibbs (of the London & Croydon Railway), Henry Palmer, and John Vallance. Of these Vallance's was the most original in that he proposed to blow or suck trains through a continuous tunnel, his scheme thus being somewhat analogous to an atmospheric line. Henry Palmer was acting for a company interested to reach Dover as well as Brighton; his proposed route was therefore from Croydon southwards and then south-east up the Caterham Valley to Oxted, whence one line would have gone to Dover. At Oxted, the Brighton line would have turned south-south-west towards Lindfield and on to Brighton. The first part of Palmer's route, as far as Oxted, was afterwards

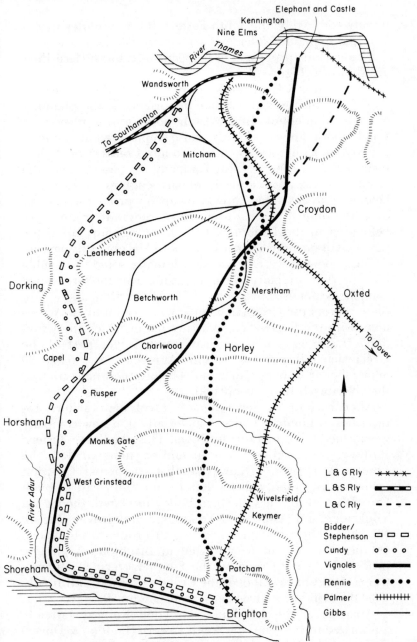

Figure 11. Brighton Surface Line Proposals of 1835.

largely adopted by the South Eastern Railway under its Act No. 1, as explained later.

The various proposals in being in 1835 for surface lines are shown in Figure 11.

The London & Croydon Railway's Act contained a Section (No. 135) which was of extreme importance to the planning and development of railways to the south and south-west of London for many years. This clause empowered the London & Croydon Company to enter into any Contract or Agreement with any other railway company for passage over the London & Croydon Railway of any engines or carriages belonging to any other railway company, or for the passage over any other line of railway of any engines or carriages belonging to the London & Croydon Company, upon the payment of such rates and tolls as should be mutually agreed.

These powers were of course originally sought to enable the Croydon company to run its traffic over the Greenwich company's metals above Corbett's Lane Junction, and within these powers the Croydon company entered into an Agreement with the Greenwich company under which the Croydon's traffic was for some years carried over part of the Greenwich railway's tracks. This Agreement was dated 30 September 1835, over four months before the first section of the Greenwich line was opened.

After certain earlier schemes, involving various approaches to London, had not materialised, a new company was formed to build a line to Dover. This, the South Eastern Railway, proposed to make an end-on junction with the London & Croydon Railway at that company's Croydon terminus, and then, curving left, to run south-east through Croydon and up the Caterham Valley to Oxted, thence via Tonbridge and Ashford to Folkestone and Dover (Figure 12). One of the reasons for selecting this route was to enable another line to run from Oxted to Brighton, as already proposed. Above Croydon, the South Eastern Company's trains would have run over the Croydon railway and finally over the London & Greenwich into London Bridge.

Apart from the London & Croydon Railway (already authorized in 1835) and the South Eastern (London & Dover) Railway (which included a line to Brighton but was not yet authorized), schemes for a separate line to Brighton were

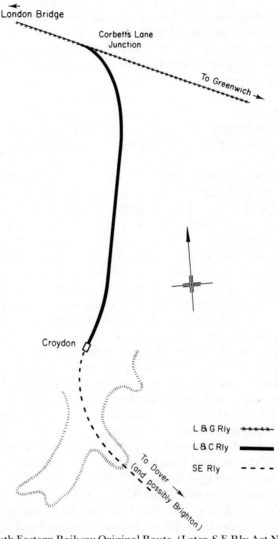

Figure 12. South Eastern Railway Original Route. (Later, S E Rly Act No. 1).

reaching finality. Eventually four were left — a 'direct' route by Rennie, and three routes via the Adur Valley (by Vignoles, Cundy and Stephenson/Bidder respectively) — and were hotly debated in Parliament and out of it during 1836, with one of Rennie's variants of his 'direct' scheme gradually becoming the most favoured.[2] In the meantime the South Eastern obtained its Act on 21 June 1836 for a line to Dover

31

only, when the Greenwich line was still open only as far as Spa Road. This Act (6 Will. IV cap. 75, later known as South Eastern Railway Act No. 1) contained a Section (No. 138) similar to that in the Croydon company's Act concerning running over other companies' metals, and permitting other companies to run over South Eastern metals.

Realizing that the Greenwich company's terminus at London Bridge, when it was finished, would be inadequate to handle all the traffic now expected to come over the Croydon line as well as the Greenwich line's own traffic, the Croydon company obtained powers on 14 July 1836 (6 and 7 Will. IV cap. 12) to build an enlarged terminus of its own at London Bridge. The Croydon company thereupon made arrangements with the Greenwich company to purchase from the latter an area of ground which the Greenwich company had already bought and cleared. This land had been acquired in order that the London & Greenwich Railway could build a large station to accommodate the trains of all companies using the terminus, which was its original intention and which had caused the London & Croydon to make no provision in its estimates for any accommodation of its own at London Bridge. The Greenwich company's finances were by 1836 in such low water, however, due to the need to overspend on the viaduct, that it offered to sell the unused land at London Bridge to the Croydon company for £18,000, the latter then being free to erect its own independent station. The offer was accepted.

The land concerned lay on the north-east or river side of the area to be used immediately by the Greenwich company. The positioning of the new station on the north side of the Greenwich line when the Croydon line came in from the south at Corbett's Lane, was later, as will be explained in due course, the cause of difficulty and eventually of an exchange of ownership of the two sites between the Croydon and Greenwich companies. Still later, however, the South Eastern, who had leased the Greenwich, must have been thankful that it then held the 'north' station, as its site was used for the start of the extension to Charing Cross and later to Cannon Street. Further reference will be made to these matters later.

The Greenwich line was opened to London Bridge on 1 December 1836.

The report of the Parliamentary proceedings in 1836 relating to the alternative routes to Brighton, is extremely important, not only because it emphasizes much of the natural
lack of knowledge of laymen but also because it reveals the
attitudes of the engineers concerned. The report is therefore
covered in considerable detail in Chapters V and VI.

On 3 July 1837 the South Eastern Railway was authorized
(7 Will. IV and 1 Vic. cap. 93) to abandon its end-on connection at Croydon with the London & Croydon company,
and instead to form a junction with the latter at Penge, about
a mile north of the point where the London & Brighton's
junction was intended to be, and then to run parallel to, and
on the east of, the Brighton company's line for some distance to near the present Purley station (South Eastern Railway Act No. 2, Penge Deviation). The arrangement is
shown in Figure 13. The 1836 South Eastern Railway Act
now became known as Act No. 1 for that company.

As the Brighton company's Bill was before the Select
Committee of the House at the same time as the South
Eastern's second Bill, the Committee considered that it was
expedient that the South Eastern's line should start at Redhill some 10 miles south of Croydon, and thus 12 miles south
of the proposed junction at Penge, rather than partly dupli-
cate the Brighton's line for some 5 or 6 miles. From Redhill,
the South Eastern would be able to run nearly east towards
Dover along easy country, to rejoin their authorized route
via Oxted at Chiddingstone (between Edenbridge and
Penshurst). The Parliamentary Committee's reasoning was
that as the South Eastern company was first in the field south
of Croydon, they should be given the option of purchasing
the Brighton company's line from near Penge to Redhill
(which itself involved heavy engineering works through the
North Downs), instead of constructing their own line which,
once it turned south-east up the Caterham Valley, would
also involve heavy works through the North Downs. If the
South Eastern took up this option, duplication of railway
facilities north of the present Purley station would be avoided
and there would be less disturbance of the countryside, but
the South Eastern's route to Dover would be lengthened by
some 9 or 10 miles.

The London & Brighton Railway received its Act on 15

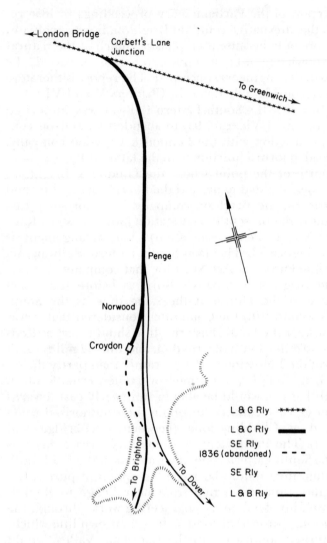

Figure 13. Penge Deviation Act. (S E Rly Act No. 2, Penge Deviation).

July 1837 (1 Vic. cap. 119). This empowered it to build a line from a junction with the London & Croydon Railway at (South) Norwood to Brighton under the Rennie scheme of that year, with branches to Shoreham, Lewes, and Newhaven, and additionally gave authority (Section 40) for the Company to purchase the Croydon, Merstham & Godstone Railway so as to be able to utilise part of its route. The Act also contained a Section (No. 23) similar to those in the Croydon and South Eastern Acts, concerning running over other companies' metals and permitting other companies to run over the Brighton company's lines. The promoters of the Brighton company in fact made an agreement on 19 January 1837 with the Croydon company for the passage of its traffic over the Croydon and Greenwich lines, while the Brighton company's Bill was still in Parliament. As a result of the Select Committee's view that Redhill should be the point of junction between the South Eastern and the Brighton companies, a Section (No. 135) was inserted in the Brighton company's Act which required that, if within 2 years from the passing of the Act the South Eastern company elected to alter its point of junction to Redhill, the Brighton company should be required to sell to the South Eastern company, at cost price, the whole of that part of the London & Brighton line which lay north of the new point of junction with the South Eastern line — that is, the length between Penge and Redhill.

After the granting of the South Eastern company's Act No. 2, an Agreement was entered into between the Directors of the two companies, and was dated 25 April 1839. This Agreement provided that if the South Eastern relinquished its right to purchase the whole of the Brighton's line north of Redhill, and if the former company were authorized by any Act passed before July 1841 to divert its line so as to start from Redhill, the South Eastern company should be entitled to an absolute transfer to itself of the southern part of the London & Brighton line lying between the points of junction with the Croydon and South Eastern companies. In this event, the northern part would remain in London & Brighton ownership. The Agreement further provided that each company should run over the other company's section without payment of toll.

Accordingly, the South Eastern, in pursuance of this Agreement, obtained an Act on 19 July 1839 (2 and 3 Vic. cap. 79) empowering it (Section 2) to alter the junction of the line from Penge to Redhill. This became known as South Eastern Railway Act No. 3, Redhill Deviation. This Act repealed the clause in the London & Brighton railway's Act requiring that company to transfer to the South Eastern company the whole of the former's line north of Redhill, and gave the South Eastern power to purchase only the southern part of the Brighton's line north of Redhill. This resulted in the Brighton company having to construct the whole length from Norwood to Redhill (apart, of course, from building its own line onwards to Brighton), and retaining the first 6 miles down to Coulsdon; the second 6 miles on to Redhill being transferred to the South Eastern company at half the cost of the whole 12 miles (see Figure 14).

While all this was going on, the Croydon company obtained an Act on 11 June 1838 (1 Vic. cap. 20) authorizing it to enlarge the station that it was constructing at London Bridge under its 1836 Act. Such an enlargement was clearly necessary in view of the amount of traffic that would shortly begin to move along the Croydon company's line, and so on to the Greenwich line. The London & Greenwich Railway was itself opened through to Greenwich on 24 December 1838, thereby increasing its own business.

In 1839, the year in which the London & Croydon Railway was opened for traffic (see later), a Select Committee was appointed by the House of Commons to enquire into the state of communication by railways. After referring to the necessity of avoiding accidents in conveying the traffic of the Croydon, the Brighton, and the South Eastern Railways along the Greenwich company's line from Corbett's Lane to London Bridge, the Select Committee reported that the traffic of the four companies should not be allowed to be conveyed along the Greenwich line until some arrangements had been made to eliminate the danger. As will be explained in Chapter VIII, both the Croydon and the Greenwich companies then presented Bills, but the Greenwich company was given an Act on 7 August 1840 (3 and 4 Vic. cap. 127) empowering it to widen the viaduct above Corbett's Lane, the widening being on the south-west side and to be able to take two extra tracks which were to be allocated solely to the trains of the Croydon company and to the Brighton and South Eastern companies' trains passing over the Croydon's metals. This Act was extremely important, its provisions dictating all future plans for the area for many years. The arrangement is shown in Figure 15.

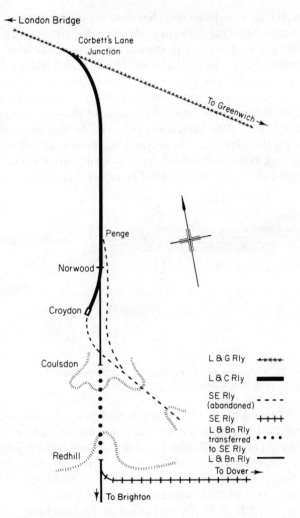

Figure 14. Ownership of Line between Croydon and Red Hill. (S E Rly Act No. 3, Red Hill Deviation).

Two other Acts of 1840 relating to London Bridge station must now be recorded. One was obtained by the Croydon company, and the other by the Greenwich company. The Croydon company's Act (3 and 4 Vic. Session 1840, dated 10 August) empowered it to provide additional station accommodation in anticipation of the expected traffic of the Brighton and South Eastern companies, not then opened.

This Act also empowered (Section 17) all four companies to enter into agreements with each other for the apportionment among themselves of the stations at London Bridge, for the execution of the works, and for the use and management of the station, and also of any additional lines of railway which the Greenwich company was authorized or required to make for the accommodation of the traffic of the other three companies. This latter provision referred to the two additional lines on the Greenwich company's viaduct already recorded as having been authorized by that company's earlier Act of 1840 and shown in Figure 15. The other Act was an additional

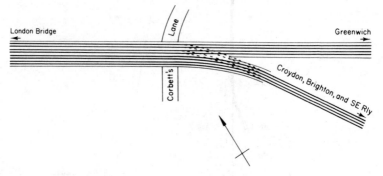

Figure 15. Widening of Greenwich Viaduct, completed in 1842, and Use of Roads. (L & G Rly 1840 Act).

one obtained by the Greenwich company in that same year (3 and 4 Vic. cap. 128) enabling them to provide a station at St. Olave (London Bridge), south of the existing station, for the accommodation of the traffic of the Croydon, Brighton, and South Eastern Companies. The works involved in each of these Acts of 1840 will be described later.

Reverting to 1837, the inclusion in the Brighton company's Act of powers to construct branch lines from Brighton to Shoreham and to Newhaven via Lewes was, of course, to make provision for trade with the Continent, since Brighton itself has never had a commercial harbour. Shoreham is at the mouth of the River Adur but there was no town of major importance farther up that river. Newhaven, however, is at the mouth of the Ouse which, a few miles before, has flowed past Lewes, the County Town of East Sussex and always a place of considerable standing and importance. The Ouse in earlier days was, in fact, navigable for barges as far as the Wealden area south of Balcombe, and its estuary may have been used by the Romans. It was only after a severe storm at the end of the sixteenth century had caused the river to enter the sea near the village of Meeching instead of at Seaford, farther east, that Meeching began to be called the 'new haven', and eventually Newhaven. The respective merits of Shoreham and Newhaven as ports for trading with the Continent, in the light of the commercial viability of railways promoted to serve them, are considered further in Chapter XII.

Before proceeding with particulars of the Brighton company's line, which was completed in 1841, it is necessary to return to 1834 to give a brief resumé of the Greenwich company's line, and to follow this with details of the building and opening of the Croydon company's line.

NOTES

1. Banister, F. D. Engineer of the London Brighton & South Coast Railway. Official Report entitled 'Historical Notes' and relating to relations with the London & Greenwich and South Eastern Railways, 1888.
See also Dendy Marshall, C. F. *A History of the Southern Railway,* Southern Railway Company, 1936, 43. *and* 2nd Edition, revised by Kidner, R. W., Ian Allen, 1963, Vol. I, 38.
2. Further data on the Parliamentary and other discussions of the various competing schemes for a railway from London to Brighton will be found in:
Long, Montague F. 'The Genesis of the London Brighton and South Coast Railway', *The Railway Magazine* xxiv (Jan. to June 1909) 392 and 479.

CHAPTER THREE

The London and Greenwich Railway

THE London & Greenwich Railway, as already recorded, obtained its Act on 17 May 1833. The line was to run on a viaduct and bridges throughout, starting from a terminus a short distance south-east of the southern end of London Bridge (after which the terminus was named), the object of elevating the railway being to avoid numerous level crossings in the vicinity of London Bridge, and others farther out. As the route lay largely over level marshy ground which was subject to partial inundation at extra high tides in the Thames, the Engineer, Lt. Col. G. T. Landmann, R.E., planned the line to be carried on arches, with bridges where necessary. The average height of the rails was to be 22 ft. above ground, and the arches were to be mostly of 18 ft. span and 20 ft. high. The overall width was to be 28 ft. and on each side of the viaduct there were to be 'boulevards' for pedestrians. In all, 851 semi-circular arches were needed for the entire length through to Greenwich, together with 27 skew arches. The principal skew arches were at Bermondsey Street, at Neckinger Road (now Abbey Street), at Spa Road, and over the Surrey Canal. The former three are between Corbett's Lane and London Bridge. The particulars of Bermondsey Street bridge were stated to be as follows:[1] the skew was 38° and there were six cast-iron ribs each 58 ft. long, extending over a central carriage-way 17 ft. 6 in. wide and over two foot-pavements each 6 ft. 6 in. wide. Each rib was supported on each side of the carriageway by cast-iron columns, 16 ft. high. Spa Road bridge had a similar appearance, but the main arch was in brick. Its skew was about 45°. Subsequent reconstructions of bridges were undertaken as necessary.

The bricks used for the viaduct came from Sittingbourne, in Kent, by water to the Grand Surrey Canal, and construction started near Corbett's Lane (about the midway point on the line) on Wednesday, 5 February 1834. The contractor was Hugh McIntosh of Bloomsbury Square, London.

Foundations were obtained by excavating the marshy ground and tipping in ballast, lime and cement, which formed concrete footings on which the piers were built in brickwork. The first brick was laid on Friday 4 April 1834 near Corbett's Lane by Col. Landmann. Work proceeded rapidly, and by May about 100 piers had been erected east of Corbett's Lane. By September 52 arches had been completed. Progress westwards of Corbett's Lane (i.e. towards London) was not so rapid as possession had to be obtained of the property already existing along the route. At London Bridge an inclined plane or ramp had to be built across a burial ground, to give access to the station. Another ramp at Deptford enabled locomotives and rolling stock to be put on the line, the first locomotive arriving in February 1835. The first experimental trains, to which the public were admitted free, were run between Corbett's Lane and the Grand Surrey Canal on Whit Monday 8 June 1835. Four days later, on 12 June, the London & Croydon's Act was passed, to bring that line into the London & Greenwich at Corbett's Lane, Section 5 authorizing the junction to be immediately south of the bridge over that road. It has been stated[2] that the junction was originally proposed for the country end of the Greenwich company's bridge over the Grand Surrey Canal, and that an agreement between the two companies dated 23 July 1836, (i.e. 13 months after the Act was given) resulted in the junction being made east of Corbett's Lane bridge. This would appear to imply that the Croydon was exploring the possibility of seeking an amendment to their Act, but no mention of any such thoughts is made in the London Brighton & South Coast Railway Engineer's report of 1888.[3]

Construction of the Greenwich line continued steadily and the first section to be completed for fare-paying passengers was between Spa Road and Deptford, opened on Friday 8 February 1836. Completion to London Bridge took place on Thursday 1 December 1836, the hold-up being essentially caused by delay in the completion of the Bermondsey Street bridge immediately south of the station, the ironwork for which had been made in Dudley and was slow in reaching the site. Trains had been coming as far up as the bridge from 10 October, passengers walking along the viaduct for the short distance to and from London Bridge. Completion of the 'country' end of the line, from Deptford to Greenwich, was also delayed, largely due to the lack of agreement on how best to cross Deptford Creek (the mouth of the River Ravensbourne). The public opening throughout to Greenwich took place on Monday 24 December 1838.

The station at London Bridge involved a widening of the viaduct to 60 ft. Three tracks were laid thereon. There were originally no platforms on the London & Greenwich Railway, the carriages having lower steps instead. There was no end wall at London Bridge and the railway offices were on a detached site. Spa Road was even more primitive; access was by means of a flight of steps on the south side of the viaduct, with a booking office at ground level. There were no spaces for passengers to stand clear of traffic on either side, and they had either to stand in the '6 ft.' space, in which a short 'platform' was subsequently provided, or on the staircase. The number of passengers dwindled when the line was opened to London Bridge, and Spa Road was closed at the end of 1838, it being however re-opened in September 1842 after improvements had been made (see later). At London Bridge a fourth track was put in during 1837.

The line was laid out for normal left-hand running and operation, with trailing crossovers at stations and at certain intermediate points. When initially opened between Spa Road and Deptford only (at both of which places there were only the two running lines), it was however decided to adopt a system of fly-shunting to get a train into a platform road and thus avoid the need for a second engine either to re-lease the incoming engine or to work the train away. On approaching Spa Road or Deptford it was planned that the engine-driver would check his engine so as to enable the front guard to release the coupling by means of a rope. Having uncoupled the train, the driver would then have to give his engine steam again while the train would be braked by the guards. Hence the engine would be able to run forward over a set of points which could then be changed to allow the train to enter another road. To do this with left-hand running would have necessitated the laying of new facing crossovers. Hence the simple expedient was adopted of using right-hand running, for which all crossovers now became facing.

In more detail, a train without an engine would be waiting on the 'south' line at Spa Road, and the 'north' line would be clear when a train approached from Deptford. By fly-shunting the incoming train, the engine would be crossed to the 'south' line through the crossover, and coupled to the waiting train thereon, whilst the stock of the incoming train would be brought to a stand on the 'north' line. The engine and train on the 'south' line would then depart (right-hand running) for Deptford, where a similar procedure would take place, ready for the next up train to come back to Spa Road on the right-hand line. On departure of a train the stock of the incoming service would be transferred to the other road, so as to leave the arrival road again clear. It is not known for certain how this transference of stock was done, but it may have been by means of a small stationary steam engine at each temporary terminus. Although this method of working was no doubt 'Hobson's choice' when the first part of the line was opened, as there were only two locomotives (one being serviced while the other was in traffic), right-hand running became accepted as a matter of operating convenience. When the extensions to London Bridge and to Greenwich, with terminal facilities, were opened on 1 December 1836 and 24 December 1938 respectively, the practice of right-hand running was so well established that it was not altered to left-hand running until April 1839, some 3 months before the Croydon company's trains started using the line between Corbett's Lane and London Bridge on 5 June 1839.

Tow-roping took the place of fly-shunting about 1837.

The Greenwich company did not convey freight traffic.

The original permanent way of the London & Greenwich Railway consisted of 50 lb. foot-rails carried in chairs for stability, which were mounted on granite blocks with a layer of felt under each chair. Rail-ends butted in a common chair. The track was arranged at such a level that at the crown of each arch the granite blocks rested directly on the brickwork, except where packing by sand had to be done to preserve a proper level. Originally the ballast was relied upon to maintain the gauge, but tiebars had later to be provided for that purpose.

The extension from Deptford to Greenwich, opened in 1838, was laid with 85 lb. double-headed rails in chairs, mounted on longitudinal timbers and cross-sleepers. This was because experience had shown that the original form of construction not only led to excessive vibration and to the formation of cracks in the arches through which water seeped, but also was so rigid that it caused high maintenance costs for locomotives and rolling stock, with occasional broken axles.

In addition to experience having dictated an alteration to the type of permanent way, it also showed the need to asphalt the viaduct throughout. This work began in 1838, but was not completed until the summer of 1843. The Croydon started to run their trains over the viaduct in 1839, and the Brighton also did so from 1841, but both those companies' trains were diverted on to the widened part of the structure from 10 May 1842. This lengthy period from 1838 to 1843 was due to the fact that operations could only be carried out each summer, and had largely to be done at night to avoid possessions holding up traffic. The asphalting work will be referred to again later in this history.

NOTES

1. Ritchie, Robert, *Railways, their Rise, Progress, and Construction.* Longman, Brown, Green, and Longman. 1846. 186.
2. Thomas, R. H. G., *London's First Railway; the London & Greenwich.* Batsford, 1972. 111.
3. Banister, F. D., Engineer of the London Brighton & South Coast Railway. Official Report entitled 'Historical Notes' and relating to relations with the London & Greenwich and South Eastern Railways, 1888.

CHAPTER FOUR

The London and Croydon Railway

THE London & Croydon Railway, as has been recorded, was still negotiating with the Croydon Canal for the purchase of the latter when the Railway Company received its Act. Eventually agreement was reached that the price should be settled by an independent jury; the latter assessed the canal as a navigation rather than as the value of its land and materials, and fixed the sum at £40,250. This had to be accepted by the London & Croydon Railway, and the purchase was completed on 21 July 1836. The canal was stopped on 22 August 1836, but the water was not drained off for some time and the railway company had to face the consequences when the canal overflowed near New Cross (probably below lock No. 11) on Thursday 26 January 1837 after heavy rain. The result was that over 200 homes were flooded in parts of the parish of St. Paul, Deptford. The Canal Company's branch to the Croydon, Merstham & Godstone Railway at Croydon was closed on 22 August 1836, the day when the canal itself was stopped.

It has already been explained that the railway company's intention was basically to follow the route of the canal, and only to purchase land outside the boundaries of the latter where this was essential in order to ease curves and to make reasonable gradients. A satisfactory alignment necessitated the elimination of the various zigzags and meanders of the canal, and this entailed virtually a new course from Beckenham Hill bridge to the swing bridge at South Norwood — despite what has been said to the contrary in numerous earlier accounts. It also involved a new route between the sites of Nos. 6 and 11 locks, and another between No. 24 lock and the third canal intake approaching Sydenham. North of No. 6 lock the railway was to have been largely on embankment in order to maintain the necessary height between that point and the junction on the Greenwich company's viaduct at Corbett's Lane; the best way to construct this embankment was to make it alongside, rather than on top of, the canal. Only south of the Graveney crossing was the old canal bed itself to be used for the railway formation, as was the basin at Croydon — a total distance of about a mile.

The only difficulty in making a workable ruling gradient was that of ascending from New Cross to a suitable elevation in order to continue to Croydon. A balance had to be struck between the capital cost of making the railway and the subsequent operating cost, and the conclusion was reached that a limitation on capital costs was the more important of the two. Hence the planning was based on a gradient of 66 ft. to the mile (i.e. 1 in 80) and on the use of assistant engines over this stretch. A deep cutting was in any case needed immediately south of New Cross, where a satisfactory alignment could only be obtained by going through some of the high ground to the west of the canal (as has already been explained (Chapter I), the canal had been taken to the east in this vicinity in order to avoid very large earthworks; the canal itself was in a cutting). From where the railway cutting would finish, however, some 300 yards before lock No. 11 and near the site of the occupation road now represented by Endwell Road, it was found possible to ascend at 1 in 80 to reach the approximate level of the canal some 25 chains beyond lock No. 26 (the last of the flight of locks) without involving heavy cuttings; in fact the alignment chosen entailed some embankments on this length. To the south of the top of the 1 in 80 bank, the line was to be level but slightly higher than the canal, involving small amounts of cutting and filling at various inequalities in the ground which the canal had generally avoided by its meanders. Raising the level of the railway slightly above that of the canal along the 'top' stretch was done to enable the line to cross over Beckenham Hill road (lowered for the purpose) instead of passing under it as the canal did; to pass over what is now Portland Road at South Norwood whereas the road passed over the canal by a low swing bridge, as already explained; and to allow the line to cross the River Graveney by means of a culvert where the canal crossed it by two locks.

The plan and section deposited in the Parliamentary Office were drawn up accordingly under the direction of Joseph Gibbs, who was Engineer to the Croydon company, and were accepted when the Act for the construction of the London & Croydon Railway was passed on 12 June 1835. It will be remembered that at this stage negotiations were still proceeding for the acquisition of the canal, and clearly little could be done by the railway company until purchase had been completed, which was not until 21 July 1836, over 13 months after the Act had been passed. While the extra land needed was being obtained, the unemptied canal overflowed, as already recorded. A week before the latter mishap, an agreement had already been made with the London & Brighton company (whose Act had not then been granted) for the passage of the Brighton company's trains over the Croydon company's lines — and also, of course, over the Greenwich company's lines in order to reach London Bridge. Associated with this agreement, and the earlier passing of South Eastern Act No. 1 (on 21 June 1836), came the need to reconsider the gradients and curvature of the London & Croydon, in order to accommodate the traffic of what would be essentially 'main line' railways.

As a result, it was decided to ease the gradient of the bank south of New Cross from 1 in 80 to 1 in 100, and to improve the alignment at various places. The bank would now start at New Cross as before, but would continue on the same general alignment to a point about 1000 yards beyond that originally proposed for the summit, and in fact to where Forest Hill station stands today. This in turn would involve deep cuttings along part of the bank, with other shallower cuttings and a small amount of fill. Beyond the summit the alignment would be improved by inserting straights connected by curves of larger radius than those originally intended. A further adjustment of levels would take place between Sydenham Road and Beckenham Hill overbridge, in order to give increased headroom for road traffic under the latter, and, farther on, slightly improved clearance over the Norwood to Woodside Road at the site of the existing swing bridge over the canal.

The extra expense was considerable on account of the heavy cuttings at the New Cross end of the line, not only because of the large amount of extra material to be excavated, but also because more land was needed to keep the slope of the cutting sides at a reasonable angle (mainly 1 in 2). All this virtually meant redesigning much of the railway, and was obviously the basic reason why it was not until 1838 that construction of the line started in earnest.

The work involved the removal of all the locks on the canal, and the preparation of the new alignment with its cutting of up to 80 feet in depth. The water had, of course, to be drained off all those parts of the canal that would be encroached upon, or would be close to, the formation of the line, but it was left in other stretches. One of these was the right hand curve between the second and third intakes (both from Sydenham Reservoir), where the alignment of the railway was well to the west of that of the canal, about half way between the present Forest Hill and Sydenham stations. Another consisted of three adjacent lengths forming the first major series of meanders west of Beckenham Hill bridge, where the alignment of the railway twice cut across that of the canal and the latter was merely dammed up by the fill needed to form the low embankment for the railway; the middle of the three lengths thus formed was that which had the two intakes from South Norwood Reservoir, whilst the south length was that which curved sharply round to the right and went under what is now Anerley Road as it resumed the general direction of Croydon. The remaining section of the canal which was left undrained was a little farther south and included the bridge under the Penge to Croydon road and the '180°' bend leading nearly to the swing bridge at Norwood. Sydenham Reservoir seems to have been filled in as part of the changeover, no doubt being used as a dump for material excavated nearby. South Norwood Reservoir remained, however, and eventually became an ornamental sheet of water known as South Norwood Lake.

All these stretches of canal seem to have been left not only to save money in draining and filling them in, but also as a move to attract traffic to the railway by describing them as beauty spots. Anglers were encouraged by stocking the stretches of water with fish. Eventually, however, all but one of them disappeared, either by widening works on the railway or following disposal of the land to other owners. The section which remained is immediately south of the bridge now carrying Anerley Road over the site of the canal — i.e. part of the third length of the second stretch referred to above. The land to the east of this length forms Betts Park, and there is a short length of the canal formation therein. About 1934 the then Penge Council decided that this length should be cleaned and provided with a concrete bed and concrete walls, as a public amenity.[1] This was done, and the result may still be seen in Betts Park.[2] To the west of this isolated length the land is in private ownership, and the back gardens of houses stretch down to, but are higher than, the canal. The Author's recent photograph is reproduced as Plate 1.

As finally built, the junction with the London & Greenwich Railway at Corbett's Lane led into a brick viaduct about 800 feet long, starting parallel with the Greenwich company's viaduct and gradually curving right towards the south. This was followed by an embankment on a rather sharper curve as far as the bridge over the Grand Surrey canal, which was crossed at a height of some 20 ft. Beyond the bridge, another embankment, almost straight and on the east side of the Croydon canal, led to New Cross, the first station on the line and some 1¼ miles from Corbett's Lane. As far as this the gradients were negligible. The station was immediately to the north of the overbridge carrying New Cross road, and the platforms extended under the bridge. As soon as the railway emerged from under the bridge, it commenced to rise at a nominal 1 in 100 (for many years, at least, this bank has started with about 10 chains of 1 in 85, no doubt a residue of the originally — proposed gradient of 1 in 80). After about ¼ mile of straight along which the line crossed to the west side of the canal, it entered a right-hand curve of some 1½ mile radius about 50 chains long, at the end of which the course of the canal was close to the east side of the railway. Brockley station was later built at this point.

The railway now ran straight for about 30 chains with the canal alignment close by on the left (or east) side, but then entered a right-hand curve of about 1 mile radius and extending for about 30 chains. The canal continued straight where the railway commenced to curve, so that the alignments started to deviate, this being at canal lock No. 17 where the bridge now known as Dalrymple Road crosses the line. As already recorded in Chapter I, however, the canal itself changed direction to the right just before lock No. 20, and the effect of this was to cause the alignment of the railway, which had by now become straight, to cross that taken by the canal at lock No. 24, some 12 chains north of the present Honor Oak Park road overbridge. Shortly after this the canal reached its upper level at lock No. 26, from which it ran steadily southwards with many meanders. The railway, here some 30 feet below the level of the canal, continued to rise at 1 in 100 on a straight alignment during which it crossed twice under the line of the canal. At the end of the straight length, some 70 chains long, the railway entered a left-hand curve of about 1 mile radius and some 50 chains chains long; rather less than half-way around this the 1 in 100 rise ended and was succeeded by a level length of 34 chains. The old route of the canal approached from the right (or west) side at this point, but then deviated again.

About 6 chains beyond the top of the 1 in 100 rise from New Cross, was placed the second station on the line. It was named Dartmouth Arms, after a hostelry which still exists on the west side of the railway directly opposite the site of the station (which was, however, later rebuilt nearer to New Cross). Dartmouth Arms station was placed immediately south of where the canal came nearest to the railway at this point, its course having been along the line of what is now Devonshire Road and across the forecourt of the recently-rebuilt Forest Hill station, before it continued south for about ¼ mile to a left turn by one of the intakes from Sydenham Reservoir. The level length on which the station was situated continued on a left-hand curve which led into 35 chains of right-hand curve with a fall at 1 in 2591. This in turn led to about 30 chains of straight on which the next station, Sydenham, was built on the north side of Sydenham Road overbridge.

Soon after the start of the curve approaching Sydenham, the railway crossed the route of the canal, which came in from the right where it had turned at the first reservoir intake and before it reached the second similar intake. At the latter the canal turned right and was then close to the east side of the railway as far as Penge, the fourth station and situated immediately south of Beckenham Hill underbridge. That portion of the canal around the right-hand turn was left filled with water for a time, as already noted. Leaving Sydenham the railway entered a short left-hand curve and then curved right into a straight past Penge, all rising at 1 in 660 from Sydenham for 1¼ miles. This part of the alignment was subsequently altered, as noted later. The rise obviated the need for too steep a fall to be given under the reconstructed underline bridge at Penge (Beckenham Hill Road having formerly crossed over the canal, as already explained).

After Penge the line became level for 46 chains with a left-hand curve of about ¾ mile radius part-way along its length. Along this stretch it crossed the canal twice, the first time where the latter turned right about 18 chains after Beckenham Hill bridge and the second time after its short turn to the left by the two intakes from South Norwood Reservoir. Shortly after crossing the canal for the second time in this locality, the railway had to cross the road which is now called Anerley Road, the latter being raised to go over the line. The local landowner, a Scotsman named Sanderson, is reputed to have given his consent to the line being taken over his property provided that a station was provided for his use. This station, the fifth on the line, was named Annerley (later contracted to Anerley) because Mr. Sanderson apparently said that his was the 'a n n erley hoose' (only house) there. Just east of where the railway crossed the canal, the latter itself turned right and also crossed under Anerley Road to enter what is now Betts Park, and then continued so as once again to approach the railway on the east side of the latter before it took another long meander to the east prior to reaching South Norwood.

From the point where the canal came up to the railway on the east side but did not cross it, the railway ran straight for over a mile to the bridge at South Norwood, where it crossed the line of the road from Norwood to Woodside some yards to the east of the canal and at a slightly higher level than the latter. The public road falls to the east towards Woodside, and was rebuilt at a lower level when the railway was

constructed. Hence a difficult crossing for the canal (involving a very low swing bridge over it, as already recorded)
became a straightforward crossing for the railway, involving
only an underbridge. The present Grosvenor Road is approximately on the site of the canal in this area. About ¼
mile south of this underbridge a right-hand curve of about
1¼ mile radius started. The gradient over the whole of the
straight length and around the curve, which led to the
culvert over the Graveney, was falling at 1 in 660. The road
from Penge to Croydon, which had crossed over the canal on
its long detour north of South Norwood, had to be diverted
as it approached South Norwood, and taken over the railway
about 11 chains north of that carrying the road to Woodside
(now known as Portland Road). The sixth station was built
between these two bridges, and was named Jolly Sailor, after
an inn which still stands adjacent to the site, and which at the
time of the canal stood on the west side of the latter with its
garden backing on to the canal. This station was about
170 ft. above sea level.

About half way between Jolly Sailor and the Graveney
culvert, the railway again departed from the line of the
canal, the latter diverging slightly left and then curving
right, whereas the railway curved right as already explained.
As a result, the railway culvert over the Graveney was a few
yards north-west of the point where the canal had crossed it
by the two locks. The two alignments then again coincided
after a separation of 60 chains in length. After the Graveney,
the line rose at 1 in 823 for 41½ chains and was then level for
the remaining 41 chains to its terminus (the seventh station)
at Croydon. There was some right-hand curvature immediately after the Graveney culvert, but the remainder of
the line was straight except for a 20-chain left-hand curve as
it entered Croydon station.

The general alignment of the railway in relation to the
canal is shown in Figure 16.

Subsequent widenings (referred to in due course) have
obscured the position of the two original lines, but it must be
recorded here that, once clear of the junction at Corbett's
Lane, the two original lines were on the site of the present
Down and Up Fast roads as far as the underbridge carrying
Cold Blow Lane under the line north of New Cross. From

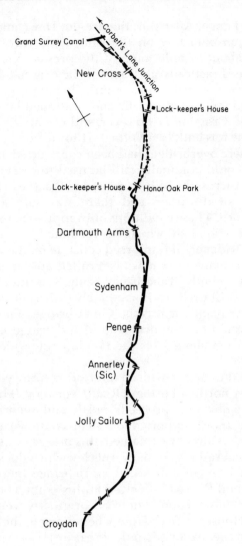

Figure 16. Alignment of London & Croydon Railway in relation to Croydon Canal.

this point southwards, the present Up Fast and Up Slow occupy the sites of the original roads to near Forest Hill. A complete deviation of the original alignment south of Sydenham in 1853-54 prevents any comparison being made between the original roads and those now existing, nearly as

53

far as Penge. After this, the present Down and Up Fast lines are approximately on the side of the two original roads until about ½ mile south of the present Norwood Junction station. Practically all traces of the original alignment have now gone over the next ½ mile, having been obliterated by alterations started in 1862 and continued later. The final ¾ mile to Croydon is, however, still essentially as it was when the line was built (see Volume II for details).

Where overbridges had been constructed across the canal, these could nominally still be used to carry the roads concerned across the railway provided that the bridge abutments were not disturbed and there was sufficient width and clearance. These conditions only applied to the last bridge at the Croydon end, which has remained unaltered except for being widened in reinforced concrete on the London side. It has for many years now been called Spurgeon's bridge, and less frequently Tabernacle bridge, as the West Croydon Baptist Church is immediately adjacent to the bridge; another name for it is the Canal bridge. The brick arch on the station (or country) side of the bridge is original, and dates from about 1808; the London-side widening was done in 1928.

Another bridge with an interesting history is that over the railway north of Portland Road, Norwood. The road past the Jolly Sailor inn proceeds north and thence over a skew bridge (now supported on steel columns) on the way to Penge. As already explained, this bridge crossed the straight length of railway south of Anerley which does not follow the original course of the canal, and a bridge therefore had to be made and the road diverted at this point when the line was under construction. The road originally went near the old Goat House, or Deer House, belonging to the archiepiscopal lord of the manor when the great forest of North Wood (the origin of the name Norwood) still existed. An inn named after the Goat House stood beside the road. It still exists in modern form, and gives its name to the bridge.

In the section between New Cross and Dartmouth Arms there were six overbridges south of New Cross Road. All of them spanned the deep cutting already mentioned. Figure 17 illustrates the bridge for an occupation road on Deptford Common, and was stated to have been typical of those across

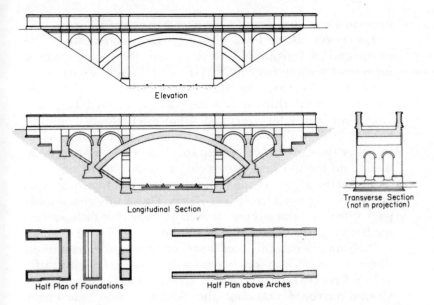

Elevation

Longitudinal Section

Transverse Section
(not in projection)

Half Plan of Foundations

Half Plan above Arches

Figure 17. London & Croydon Railway: Typical Occupation Bridge
(probably that carrying the present Endwell Road, Brockley).

the cutting.[3] All these bridges had to be reconstructed and
the two inner piers abolished when the line was widened, and
two were subsequently redesigned in connection with the
building of intermediate stations, but the general appearance
of the arch itself is unchanged in the two that remain in this
general form — namely Dalrymple Road and Brockley Way
bridge (colloquially known as Brockley Jack (the name of an
adjacent inn) or Nunhead Path (the right of way which was
the reason for the bridge)) — although the side arches have
been filled. Judging by the height of the cutting side, the
bridge shown in Figure 17 must have been north of that now
known as Dalrymple Road, and so was that which carried
what is now called Endwell Road. This bridge has since been
reconstructed. Of these six bridges, the first four and the
sixth still stand. The fifth, carrying Courtrai Road over the
line about 1 mile 50 chains south of New Cross, was removed
about 1914; the down-side footing still stands.

The overbridge immediately south of New Cross was
constructed of cast-iron ribs on brick abutments, as apparently
were the overbridges south of Dartmouth Arms, except for

those at Goat House and Croydon (Spurgeon's).

There were three level crossings over roads; one at the north end of Dartmouth Arms station; the second over a farm road leading from Sellhurst Farm (then so spelt) to the canal about 18 chains on the London side of the Graveney culvert; and the third over what was then called Brighton Road but was later renamed Gloucester Road, some 27 chains south of the Graveney. The farm road continued in use after the canal was stopped, so a level crossing had to be made; but the low bridge carrying Brighton Road over the canal did not allow sufficient head room for the railway, so a level crossing was established there. There was also a footpath crossing taking Five Bell Lane over the railway immediately north of New Cross station.

It is thought that the intention even during the promotion stages of the railway was to deal with London freight traffic at New Cross (which was readily accessible to London via the Grand Surrey Canal and the Thames), only passenger traffic continuing to London Bridge. When, as already explained, the London & Greenwich Railway's financial position in 1836 caused that company not only to shelve action to provide a large terminus at London Bridge for all the companies planning to use their station, but also to agree to sell to the Croydon company some of the Greenwich company's land at London Bridge, it was clearly confirmed that it would not be economic to any of the companies intending to use London Bridge, to consider handling much freight traffic there. A diagram of the layout at London Bridge on opening of the Croydon station in 1839 is shown in Figure 18. It appears to be incomplete, in that no means are shown for disposing of arriving trains: they could hardly have been cleared by setting back in the facing direction on to the up road, before being shunted.

In view of the foregoing position on freight traffic, fairly extensive sidings were provided by the London & Croydon Railway at New Cross (then only a hamlet in the parish of St. Paul, Deptford) as well as an engine house, a carriage shed, and coke ovens. The engine house was behind the Up platform and at right angles to the running lines; access to it was by means of a turntable. Water was available from the Grand Surrey Canal. The carriage shed was provided on the Up

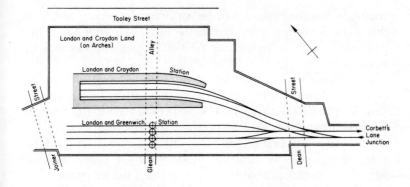

Figure 18. London Bridge Station: Layout (apparently incomplete) in 1839.

side north of the engine house. The coke ovens were also on the Up side, farther north than the carriage shed on that side and immediately south of the underbridge carrying the running lines over Cold Blow Lane. Coal was brought in by barge from the Thames via the Grand Surrey Canal. The name Coke Siding survives today for the road to the west of Millers' sidings at this point. In all, some 2¾ acres of ground were occupied. Establishment of the locomotive department at New Cross was also intended to facilitate working up the bank to Dartmouth Arms.

Dartmouth Arms, Sydenham, Penge, Annerley, and Jolly Sailor were apparently ordinary two-platform roadside stations. From later information it seems that only Dartmouth Arms had siding accommodation, on the Down side south of the station.

At Croydon there was fairly extensive accommodation, the whole area covering nearly 5 acres, but the only details that seem to have survived are shown on a plan prepared in connection with alterations to Pitlake Road, and approved by the Croydon Board of Highways on 6 June 1846. The changes then approved were shown on an existing plan for that part of Croydon signed 10 May 1845. A further complicating factor is that the introduction of 'atmospheric' working to Croydon must have involved some changes in the layout there not later than the summer of 1845. Finally, it must not be overlooked that a Board of Surveyors for what would now be considered as a local authority dealing with road alterations, might not be sufficiently concerned with the track layout at the station to notice whether what appeared on their plan for any particular period, was still up to date.

On balance the Author considers that the plan, undoubtedly of great interest and reproduced in outline in Figure 19, should be used with reserve when considering the railway facilities that were provided when the London & Croydon Railway was opened to traffic in 1839, although any alterations to the railway facilities made between June 1839 and May 1845 would probably not have been major ones.

The company's offices were at Croydon. They subsequently became the station master's house for West Croydon station (Plate 2), and were pulled down after the Southern Railway was formed in 1923.

John Francis stated that the London & Croydon Railway was 'remarkable' for nothing save its huge cost[4] (the expense of constructing the line having been £615,160 instead of the estimated £180,000, later increased to £195,000). When Francis made his criticism, he may well have had in mind that the canal had cost only £127,000, but such a comparison does scant justice to the task of construction, of which by far the heaviest work was in the length from New Cross to Dartmouth Arms. It also failed to take account of improvements to reduce curvature, made to help the London & Brighton to run their trains over the Croydon's line, for which the increased estimate was made. Nearly all the New Cross-Dartmouth Arms length, some 2½ miles, was in cutting in clay, and a vast quantity of material had to be taken out as well as the 26 locks of the canal cleared away. Some of the material was used to make the embankment between the end of the viaduct south of Corbett's Lane and New Cross, and for filling and levelling the ground there. A small amount more was needed for the relatively low embankment south of Annerley. The balance had to be disposed of, and to avoid the purchase of a considerable area of land for use for this purpose it was decided to place surplus material on top of the cutting sides, which it was thought would stand satisfactorily. This was not a very wise procedure with a clay soil in any event, but the position was undoubtedly worsened by the fact that a lot of water must have been contained in the

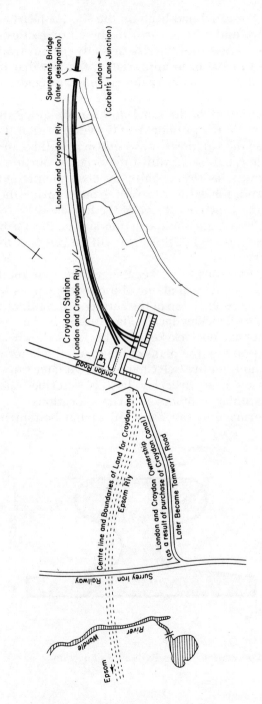

Figure 19. Croydon Station: Probable Layout in 1839 (from Plan dated 10 May 1845).

soil after the canal had been on the site for nearly 30 years. Minor slips and falls of earth in the cutting sides occurred from time to time, but the risk of really serious trouble does not seem to have been appreciated; the fact that it did not occur for 3 or 4 years after the cutting was made, no doubt induced complacency.

Few reminders of the canal now remain along the line of the railway. At the present West Croydon station the retaining wall on the Up (north-west) side may well be, in part, the wall of the canal basin, whilst the original portion of Spurgeon's bridge nearby has already been mentioned. At the London end, the area of broken ground inside the railway fence on the Down (east) side of the line about ¼ mile south of New Cross Gate station, is the site of the former canal locks Nos. 5, 6, and 7; this area will be referred to later in this history.

It has at various times been suggested that another relic still exists, in the form of one of the lock-keeper's houses on the Up (west) side on top of the cutting just south of Brockley Way bridge ('Brockley Jack'). The Author doubts the validity of this, in that no lock-keeper's house is shown anywhere near that point on the plans of the canal, the latter detailing two such houses only (see Chapter I). On later railway plans the building near Brockley Jack is described as 'railway cottages', similar to others at various locations.

The permanent way consisted of flat-bottom iron rails

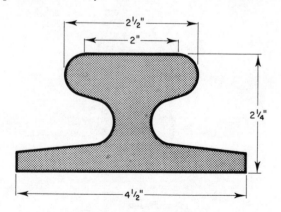

Figure 20. London & Croydon Railway Rail Section.

60

laid on longitudinal timbers of Memel fir, themselves carried on ordinary oak cross-sleepers. Beams and sleepers were Kyanised. The flanges of the rails were drilled to take a type of coach-screw, these going into the longitudinal timbers at an angle as the holes in the rails were at right angles to the tops of each side of the flange. Originally felt pads were placed between the rails and the timbers, but were later removed due to rotting having occurred. On road laid at ground level and in cuttings, drainage was provided by a rubble-filled gulley along the '6-ft.' space, with cross gulleys at intervals discharging into open cesses on each side of the line. On embankments, the cesses were at the foot of each slope. Ballast was up to the tops of the longitudinal timbers, so that the cross-sleepers were completely buried; Thames shingle was probably used. The rail section employed is shown in Figure 20, and the general arrangement of the track is shown in Figure 21.

Whilst the cross-sleepers below the longitudinal beams were 9 ft. long, a length commonly adopted by many standard-gauge railways later, it would appear that the reason for not using a shorter length of cross-sleeper was because the London & Croydon was watching events of the GWR, where Brunel had adopted a 7 ft. 0¼ in. gauge also carried on longitudinal beams. Dendy Marshall quoted a report[5] submitted to the half-yearly meeting in March 1838 which stated that sleepers 9 ft. long had been ordered in order that a gauge of 6 ft. or 7 ft. could be adopted if expedient and if all other railways did the same. As laid, the rails were at 4 ft. 10 in. centres, giving the usual 4 ft. 8½ in. gauge.

Signalling seems to have been by means of round discs painted a red-orange colour which were mounted on vertical posts and could be rotated through 90°. To stop a train, the board was presented full-face to the driver; when presented edge-on and thus nearly invisible, it signified 'proceed'. For night working hand lamps were employed. Traffic was in any case partly run 'on sight', the driver of a following train being expected to keep off the tail of the proceeding one. Similar day signals were introduced on the Greenwich line when the Croydon trains began to use part of the latter; lamps had already been introduced for night working on that line. The use of a red-orange colour for the disc signals must have

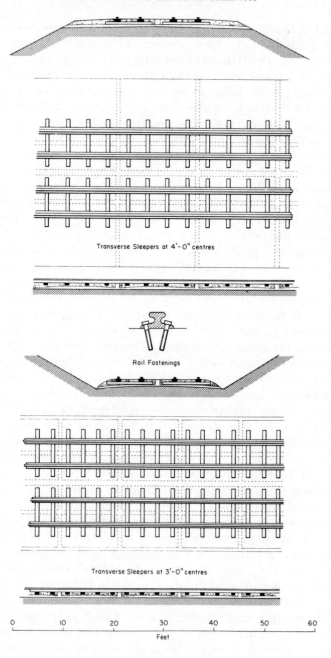

Transverse Sleepers at 4'-0" centres

Rail Fastenings

Transverse Sleepers at 3'-0" centres

Figure 21. London & Croydon Railway Track Formation.

been one of the earliest attempts to obtain good visibility.

What has been described as the forerunner of all signal boxes was built on the south side of the Greenwich viaduct, and in the fork of the junction, at Corbett's Lane for night use — apparently at the Croydon company's expense but obviously with the agreement of the Greenwich company, who staffed it. This structure was in the form of an octagonal 'lighthouse' and contained two gas lamps working with parabolic reflectors. It is stated that when the switches were set (by a switchman on the track) for the Greenwich traffic, a white light was shown towards London as well as towards Deptford and towards New Cross; and that when the switches were set for the Croydon traffic, a red light was shown all three ways. The regulations did not apparently cover the case of a train proceeding from London Bridge to Greenwich simultaneously with one from Croydon to London Bridge; perhaps the train from Croydon had to wait, although such a hold-up would not have been necessary. By day, a disc signal was turned edge-on to give the right-away to Greenwich traffic, and full-face to signify 'clear' to Croydon traffic. Hence both day and night signals at Corbett's Lane were solely intended to indicate at a distance which way the road was set, and were not used to regulate following traffic.

A similar 'lighthouse' was erected outside London Bridge, under similar agreement and working arrangements. This showed a white light when the switches were set for a Greenwich train, and a red light when they were set for a Croydon one; a red-orange disc was turned edge-on for the Greenwich traffic, and full-face for the Croydon traffic, thus giving similar indications to those at Corbett's Lane.

Both sets of signals were thus used as 'route indicators' rather than to control traffic in the ordinary sense.

Most of the constructional work on the London & Croydon Railway was done in 1838, and does not seem to have been attended by any incidents worthy of record. There was, however, difficulty in making the junction with the London & Greenwich Railway at Corbett's Lane, due to differences between the two companies on the matter of the purchase by the Croydon company of the Greenwich company's land. This land was that then occupied by the boulevard alongside the south side of the Greenwich viaduct. The London &

Croydon Railway was ready in April 1839 to construct the junction, but was unable to do so because the Greenwich company would not allow their piece of parapet wall concerned to be taken down until the dispute about the land had been resolved. It took a threat by the Croydon company to ask Parliament to intervene, to make the Greenwich company allow the parapet to be demolished so that the work could be completed. On 22 April one road was completed and enabled a special train to run from Croydon to London Bridge with the Croydon company's directors, and a further special train was run on 23 May, conveying the London & Brighton directors. The junction was completed on 31 May and the line formally opened throughout to Croydon on Saturday 1 June, the directors of the Brighton, South Eastern, and Greenwich companies being present as well as the Croydon directors. Public traffic commenced on Wednesday 5 June 1839.

An artist's impression of Corbett's Lane Junction in 1839 is reproduced as Plate 3. One wonders who the worthy pair, depicted with their luggage in the fork of the two railways, were; and also how (and why) they came to be there, nearly a mile from the nearest station. The Author, in 1967, took a photograph from what was, as far as he could judge, a similar position to that selected for the 1839 view; this is reproduced as Plate 4. There is no longer an actual junction at this point.

NOTES

1. Southern Railway Magazine, XII (1934), 327.
2. Ibid. XVII, 255.
3. Brees, S. C. *Second Series of Railway Practice.* John Williams, 1840, 13.
4. Francis, John *A History of the English Railway.* Longman, Brown, Green & Longman, 1851, Vol. 1. 241.
5. Dendy Marshall, C. F. *A History of the Southern Railway,* Southern Railway Company, 1936, 44.
Also 2nd Edition, revised by Kidner, R. W., Ian Allan, 1963, Vol. 1, 38.

CHAPTER FIVE

The London and Brighton Railway: The choice of route – discussion

CERTAIN salient points regarding the London & Brighton Railway have been mentioned briefly in Chapter II, mainly insofar as the relationships with the London & Croydon, London & Greenwich, and South Eastern Railways were concerned. It is now necessary to revert to 1836, when various schemes for a line from London to Brighton that had been put forward over more than a decade were finally being assessed to ascertain the one that should be adopted. By this date, four schemes were still under active consideration, the engineers being Sir John Rennie, Nicholas Cundy, Charles Vignoles, and Robert Stephenson respectively. The background to these schemes must therefore be explained.

Sir John Rennie had been knighted in 1831 at the opening of the then new London Bridge over the Thames, of which work (planned by his father) he had been engineer. He was in fact the second son of a very distinguished engineer who had constructed many large works. Rennie the younger had been retained as early as 1825 by the Surrey, Sussex, Hants, Wilts & Somerset Railway Company, which proposed to build a line from London to Brighton, thence along the coast through Shoreham and Portsmouth, to Southampton, and on to Salisbury, Warminster, and the Bristol coalfields. In connection with that Company's scheme, Rennie the younger had himself examined various alternative routes for a line from London to Brighton, and additionally had employed other engineers and surveyors to examine other possible routes. Among the routes concerned were (1) a 'direct' one south through Croydon (examined by Rennie himself);

(2) a variant of it to the east, using the Ouse valley down to Lewes, and on to Newhaven, with a line to Brighton from somewhere near Ardingly down to Clayton and a line across from Brighton to Lewes (examined by an experienced surveyor named Jago who had been trained under Rennie senior); with another to Portsmouth from the Red Hill gap (then often so spelt) and down the Arun valley (also surveyed by Mr. Jago); and (3) an entirely different route from Nine Elms via Wandsworth, Epsom Common, the valley of the Mole, Dorking, Capel, Horsham, and the Adur valley to Shoreham, thence along the coast eastwards to Brighton (examined by Mr. Jago from Nine Elms to near Wandsworth, and from there to Brighton examined by Charles Vignoles). These 1825 schemes came to nothing, but the promoters tried again, and other proposals were made in 1826 by Messrs. Elms and Cundy, and possibly others. Rennie the younger then employed Francis Giles to reexamine the various summits, including a possible route via Oxted, and others via Dorking and via Guildford; again the whole scheme came to nothing, due largely to Rennie's view that the complete system could not be built for less than £6½ million.

Towards the end of 1829 Rennie the younger was retained by largely the same promoters to report on the feasibility of a route to Brighton only, and on the advice of his father he employed Hamilton Fulton, lately returned from a period as principal engineer to the state of South Carolina, to undertake the work. Fulton's proposals on Rennie's behalf were again for a 'direct' route, but rather more to the west than hitherto, and nearer to the western Brighton road past Bolney, the approach to Brighton being through the gap in the South Downs at New Timber (then so spelt). Again, nothing matured as the subscribing public generally did not wish to support the scheme.

In 1833 a further attempt was made to build a line to Brighton, once again with the promotion of at least some of those who had been associated with the various schemes since 1825. Some of the promoters apparently favoured a line through Dorking and Horsham, whilst others preferred a 'direct' line. Robert Stephenson was then asked to look at the various plans. The merits of the 'direct' route were considered to outweigh those of going via Dorking and Horsham, and accordingly Rennie the younger (by now Sir John) was once again asked to resurvey the country for a 'direct' line. Rennie employed Francis Giles, as he had done in 1826, as well as others, but the promoters' committee deferred the scheme in December 1833 because of difficulty in raising the capital.

In 1834 yet another attempt was made to establish a company, and as the promoters' committee wanted to decide whether they should concentrate on a 'direct' line or on one via Dorking, they asked Nicholas Cundy to take up a Dorking route whilst Sir John Rennie was asked to take up a 'direct' route. Charles Vignoles also proposed a variant, using parts of each route – via Croydon and then to the west of Merstham, then south-west towards Charlwood and on to West Grinstead, thence down the Adur valley to Shoreham and along the coast to Brighton. Vignoles' route was thus quite different from the one that he had surveyed for Rennie in 1825. Other schemes were current, including two by Joseph Gibbs (then the assistant engineer of the London & Croydon Railway), and one by Henry Palmer. One of the Gibbs' routes would have been a virtual end-on extension of the London & Croydon Railway, south west to Betchworth (between Reigate and Dorking) and thence to Rusper and Horsham, reaching Brighton via the Adur valley and Shoreham; it would have involved very heavy engineering work between Croydon and Betchworth. In connection with this route, Gibbs proposed a branch to Sutton, Epsom, and Leatherhead, leaving the 'Main Line' somewhere near Waddon. Gibbs' other route would have started somewhere near Norwood and then have run via Merstham and to the east of Newdigate to reach Horsham, proceeding to Brighton as before. Palmer's company was concerned to reach Dover as well as Brighton, and his route was from Croydon to Oxted, from which the line to Brighton would have gone near Crowhurst, west of East Grinstead, near Horsted Keynes, and then to Lindfield; from thence it would have gone to Brighton along the route finally adopted for that part of the London & Brighton Railway.

Those routes going through Croydon had various approaches from London: Rennie's started from Kennington and went through Streatham; Vignoles' started from the Elephant & Castle and went through Brixton; Palmer's started from Nine Elms and went through Wandsworth and Tooting; and Gibbs' of course started from Croydon (although he also proposed a line from Wandsworth to Croydon along the general route of the Surrey Iron Railway, reaching Wandsworth from Nine Elms over the London & Southampton Railway (which had received its Act on 25 July 1834 (5 Will. IV cap. 88)). Cundy's route was the only one which did not pass through Croydon; it started from Nine Elms over the London & Southampton Railway to Wandsworth, and then ran via Leatherhead, Dorking, and Horsham, and down the Adur valley to Shoreham, thence along the coast to Brighton. Of all these routes, only those of Rennie and Cundy had been prepared at the request of the same promoters. 'Direct' route proposals included a branch from Brighton to Shoreham to serve the harbour there.

To assist them in deciding which of these two routes should be adopted, the promoters again approached Robert Stephenson late in 1834 to assess them and to give his recommendations. It seems that the London Committee made available to Robert Stephenson the essence of Sir John Rennie's plans and of Mr. Cundy's, but certainly without the consent of Sir John, who was then abroad, but who had, before going overseas, prepared a modified scheme with more severe gradients in order to reduce the lengths of the tunnels, apparently at the request of certain parties among the promoters. On Rennie's return to the United Kingdom, his elder brother George told him what had been happening, and eventually he was given a copy of Stephenson's report on the two schemes. The ethics of their actions seem not to have been appreciated by the promoters, but they resulted in very strained relations between the eminent engineers concerned, especially as Stephenson's report, made early in 1835, was in favour of the general route proposed by Cundy but did not accept the latter on the detailed levels and quantities. In order to enable him to give a balanced opinion, Stephenson then proposed to the committee that G. P. Bidder should prepare a properly-calculated line broadly along Cundy's route, which he (Stephenson) considered was superior to Rennie's route. Stephenson furthermore eventually allowed Bidder's detailed proposals to go forward under Stephenson's name and authority. Much play was made of Stephenson's action by those opposed to the 'Dorking' route, and until the circumstances were fully explained it did not place Robert Stephenson in a good position professionally.

Interest waned in Vignoles' line, and Gibbs' proposals were withdrawn, whilst Palmer's company ceased being a contender by concentrating on a line to Dover only. The other three — Rennie's, Cundy's and Stephenson's (Bidder's) — were then made the subject of the most searching enquiries, with the emphasis concentrated on the 'direct' route of Rennie (now to start from a junction with the London & Croydon Railway) versus the 'Dorking' route of Bidder on Stephenson's behalf.

Stephenson, working off Bidder's detailed examinations and calculations, proposed two separate termini at Brighton; the main one in Brunswick Square and a subsidiary one to serve the north of the town; the latter station would have been at the end of a single line branch nearly 1½ miles long. His route involved a tunnel through clay at Epsom Common (some 600 yards long), a second through chalk under Norbury Park, Mickleham (about 100 yards long), a third through sand near Dorking (just over 600 yards), and a fourth through chalk on the single-line branch at Brighton (about 900 yards). There would have been no major works on the London side of the first tunnel at Epsom Common, the material from which would have been deposited on the common, then regarded as inferior land. The cutting beyond the tunnel would have been succeeded by an embankment, to be formed by material from that cutting. Material from the other tunnels and cuttings to the Dorking area would similarly be used to form adjacent embankments. After climbing to Capel, the highest point on the proposed line, the route would have descended over a long embankment, involving some 660,000 cubic yards of fill, and then reached Horsham, after which there were no major works before reaching Brighton. The embankment on the London side of Horsham would have been formed by material from cuttings in the vicinity of Capel. Tunnels would have been 25 ft. high to crown, and 22 ft. 6 in. wide, the same dimensions as those on the London & Birmingham Railway. The single-line branch tunnel at Brighton would also have been 25 ft. high, but only 15 ft. wide. Stephenson's line would have been 49 miles 50 chains in length from Wimbledon to the 'depot' in Brunswick Square, the branch starting 55 chains before the latter and being about 1 mile 33 chains long. Nine Elms to the proposed junction at Wimbledon was about 5 miles 20 chains, giving a 'main line' 54 miles 70 chains long from London to Brighton (Brunswick Square). To the branch terminal it would be 55 miles 48 chains. The steepest gradient would have been 1 in 330, and the sharpest curve 120 chains (1½ mile) radius. Excavations would have totalled nearly 6,000,300 cubic yards, of which 1½-2 millions were not required for embankments. The second terminus at Brighton was included at the behest of the promoters' Committee, who considered that it would meet the wishes of a section of the populace of Brighton; Stephenson himself felt that the main terminus proposed for Brunswick Square would be adequate.

Sir John Rennie's route involved tunnels at Merstham (2,180 yards), Balcombe (800 yards), Cuckfield (1,450 yards), and Clayton Hill (1,730 yards). There would have been no major works south of Croydon until the enormous cutting in chalk before Merstham tunnel. This cutting involved 1,400,000 cubic yards of excavation, all but 200,000 cubic yards of which would have to go to spoil; the cutting would have a maximum depth of about 115 ft., and near-vertical sides sloped at 4 in 1. At the south end of Merstham tunnel there was to be a cutting with a maximum depth of about 80 ft., involving 310,000 cubic yards of chalk excavation, 160,000 of which Rennie thought could be sold as hearthstone. After passing through Red Hill gap, in which there would have been a cutting in sand, the line would have been carried over a 3½ mile long embankment past Horley requiring 617,000 cubic yards of fill; the material for this embankment would have come in part from the cutting south of Merstham tunnel (150,000 cubic yards of chalk), in part from the cutting at Red Hill (150,000 cubic yards of sand), and in part from the cutting north of Balcombe tunnel (317,000 cubic yards of various materials). The latter cutting would have been through greensand and ironstone intermixed with beds of hard shale with occasional clay fissures, and an overburden of about 18 ft. of sand and clay intermixed; the total quantity of excavation in this area was about 896,000 cubic yards for a length of nearly 2 miles, since Rennie based his calculations on slopes of 1¼-1½ horizontal to 1 vertical. Beyond Balcombe tunnel there would have been a relatively shallow cutting leading on to an embankment requiring 348,000 cubic yards of fill, succeeded by another needing 750,000 cubic yards with a maximum height of 61 feet.

The second embankment led on to a viaduct over the river Ouse, 80 ft. high, followed immediately by a short cutting leading to Cuckfield tunnel. This cutting would have had a maximum depth of about 98 ft., through similar material to those north and south of Balcombe tunnel, and have involved 360,000 cubic yards of excavation. The spoil from the cutting north of Balcombe tunnel not appropriated for the Horley embankment would have been used, together with the excavations from that tunnel, from the cutting south of it, and from the cutting to the north of Cuckfield tunnel, to form the two embankments north of the viaduct over the Ouse. South of Cuckfield tunnel there would be a cutting having a maximum depth of about 96 ft. and entailing about 775,000 cubic yards of excavation. An embankment was planned to follow near St. John's Common, and also a viaduct, with height up to 69 ft. and requiring 1,120,000 cubic yards of fill. This would have been the largest embankment on the line. Rennie proposed to obtain about 700,000 cubic yards from the cutting south of Cuckfield tunnel, a large quantity from the cutting north of Clayton tunnel, and the balance from side-cutting an adjacent hill. Some 577,000 cubic yards would also have been needed for another embankment up to 50 ft. high, before reaching Clayton Hill. The fill would have come from Clayton Hill. The cutting north of Clayton tunnel would have had a maximum depth of 92 ft. and have needed 232,000 cubic yards of excavation, whilst that to the south of the tunnel, 88 ft. deep at the maximum, would have have involved about 770,000 cubic yards of excavation; both cuttings and the tunnel would have been through ground consisting of solid chalk with an overburden of 2-9 ft. of earth, flints, and chalk. Similar near-vertical cutting slopes were proposed. Beyond the south cutting at Clayton Hill there were not intended to be any major earthworks. Tunnels were to be 25 ft. high to the crown, and 24 ft. wide. Rennie's line would have been 39 miles 25 chains from Croydon to Brighton, to which had to be added 8 miles 62 chains over the London & Croydon Railway and 1 mile 61 chains over the London & Greenwich Railway; together, there would therefore be a 'main line' 49 miles 68 chains long from London to Brighton. The steepest gradient would have been 1 in 264 and the sharpest curve 80 chains (1 mile) radius except for two very sharp ones associated with the station at Croydon, and for one of 40 chains to avoid Major Payne's property at Patcham: Rennie considered that this latter curve could be realigned to 80 chains within the limit of 100 yards generally allowed by Parliament for the difference between plans and the work actually carried out.

Rennie proposed to alter the course of the turnpike road at Hooley (north of Merstham), and his route required the construction of 54 bridges over or under roads, as well as at least 50 accommodation bridges and a number of culverts. His route, including the Shoreham branch, entailed excavations totalling 8,010,000 cubic yards, of which 2,957,000 were not required for the construction of embankments.

It will be seen that Rennie's direct route saved 5 miles 2 chains on the overall distance from London to Brighton as compared with that of Stephenson's 'Dorking' route, but at the cost of very large engineering works, somewhat steeper gradients, and less easy curves. Rennie's route involved the construction of only 39 miles 25 chains of new railway (from Croydon to Brighton), together with 6 miles for the Shoreham branch which Rennie intended should join the main line about ¼ mile before Brighton — a total of 45 miles 25 chains of new construction. Stephenson's route involve the construction of 49 miles 50 chains of new line (from Wimbledon to Brighton), together with 1 mile 33 chains for the branch at Brighton — a total of 51 miles 3 chains. The House of Commons Committee which examined the two schemes from the engineering point of view in the spring of 1836 clearly had these differences in mind.

The examination started on Wednesday 16 March, Robert Stephenson being called first before the Committee. He was followed on Monday 28 March by George Parker Bidder, who, as already stated, had been employed at Stephenson's recommendation, to make calculations of the quantities involved (Stephenson himself had been unable to undertake the detailed work, due to his engagement on the London & Birmingham Railway, then under construction). Sir John Rennie was called on Thursday 14 April, and was followed on Monday 25 April by Joseph Locke as an independent assessor of Rennie's line. The statements made before the Committee are of extreme importance, and demonstrated the lack of knowledge of laymen as well as revealing the attitudes of the engineers themselves.[1]

Robert Stephenson's examination was undertaken by Mr. Serjeant Merewether, who, after the preliminaries, questioned Stephenson on the circumstances under which the latter came to be connected with the proposals for a line from London to Brighton. Stephenson confirmed that he had been approached at least as early as 1833 to look at some plans for a railway to Brighton, and agreed with Serjeant Merewether's suggestion that he (Stephenson) had also been examined both in the House of Commons and in the House of Lords on the Great Western line to Bristol, and on the London to Southampton Railway, while both those Companies' Bills were before Parliament. Stephenson went on to confirm, as has already been stated in this chapter, that he had again been employed in 1834 to consider a route to Brighton, and yet again in 1835; as a result he had decided that the best means of reaching Brighton was via Dorking, and had recommended that that general route should be explored in detail by George Parker Bidder for the purpose of its being adopted. Bidder had a reputation for making calculations, and had been employed under Robert Stephenson on the London & Birmingham Railway.

After Stephenson had said that, if ventilation troubles occurred in the tunnel on the northern branch at Brighton, he would use a stationary engine to draw trains in and out of the terminus of that branch, Serjeant Merewether concentrated his questions on the reasons why Stephenson preferred the 'Dorking' route to the 'direct' route. Robert Stephenson stated that the initial cost of making the line via Dorking would be lower than that of any other route, and that such first costs were more important than the subsequent costs of operation and maintenance.[2] Merewether then said:

> Now, having asked you whether the expense of the formation of the line and the expense of maintenance are not the important points; I would ask you whether, considering in comparison with their directness and shortness of line, they bear any comparison in respect of importance?

Robert Stephenson replied:

> They are to be compared, and one is to be placed against the other. The view that I have taken all along in laying out railroads, has been rather to go round them than to go over high ground.[3]

Stephenson agreed that there was a limit to the detours that could be compared with the expense of going over high ground, but went on to say that 'usually a level through (sic) a circuitous course is better than an undulating direct one'. He further stated that the Adur Valley was the only gap in the South Downs.

On the relative commercial prospects of the two routes, which Stephenson said that he had taken into account, he added that there would have had to have been a very large increase in the population along the 'direct' route over and above the figures then current, to have influenced him to select the 'direct' route in preference to that via Dorking. He added that in his opinion the commercial prospects of the Dorking route were greater than those of the 'direct' route.[4] From the point of view of duration of the journey, Stephenson considered that the ordinary average timing for his route from Nine Elms to Brighton would be 2 hours, and went on to say that the reduction in distance of a less circuitous route would not result in any reduction in the journey time as the more severe gradients involved would result in slower running. In answer to a specific question from Serjeant Merewether, Stephenson said that:

> I have no question, from experience, that the cheapest line would be that which has the lowest gradients, in spite

of the additional distance, referring especially to this case.[5]

Asked for amplification of this point, Stephenson stated that the cheapness would arise by reduced operating and maintenance costs. This statements was not necessarily at variance with what he had stated earlier. In answer to a further question about working the traffic over inclines on his proposed route, Stephenson stated that neither stationary engines nor assistant engines would be needed.

Stephenson was then cross-examined by Mr. Joy, appearing for Sir John Rennie's line and the land-owners on Stephenson's route. Mr. Joy started by questioning the relative merits of the two termini for Brighton, and Stephenson made it clear that the northern one, to be reached by the single-line branch, was included at the behest of the promoters' committee to satisfy local opinion. Joy then said:

> Do you happen to know whether there was not a very great majority of the inhabitants of Brighton, an immense majority of the inhabitants of Brighton, who objected to your line altogether, and preferred another?

Stephenson replied:

> I have not mixed myself up with the question; I confine myself strictly to the engineering consideration of the question.[6]

Joy then said:

> But you say that your Committee thought it necessary to defer to the general opinion of Brighton, as to the terminus; do you happen to know whether, in adopting such line, they have gone counter to that general opinion?

Stephenson answered:

> I have heard so; but that does not alter my view of my line at all.[7]

Mr. Joy then turned to the matter of Robert Stephenson's personal position, and established that the latter had been invited to pronounce on the relative merits of the lines proposed by Rennie (and his brother George) and by Cundy. In answer to a somewhat hostile question Stephenson made it clear that Cundy's line confirmed his (Stephenson's) impression that the general route taken by Cundy was better than that taken by Rennie, 'but that there were evident blunders in the section, and to such an extent that I could not give a decided opinion as to the precise location of the line being adjusted properly.'[8] Mr. Joy then questioned Stephenson's wisdom in proposing gradients of 1 in 330 instead of using easier gradients for much of the route, with relatively short inclined planes, instancing the GWR's adoption of this practice through Box tunnel, which had been supported by Stephenson. Stephenson's reply was to the effect that the Box tunnel example was a special case which did not exist on his (Stephenson's) route to Brighton.

Opposing counsel then reverted to his previous subject and went deeply into the circumstances under which Stephenson had selected the Dorking route and had put forward his line on the basis of Bidder's detailed work, his brief being clearly to try to show that Cundy's work had been pirated. The exchanges between Joy and Stephenson on this aspect are of very considerable historical importance, as Stephenson's personal position and his part in the schemes for a line from London to Brighton were made very clear to the Parliamentary Committee. Space unfortunately does not allow the passages concerned[9, 10] to be reproduced in full, but the four essential points are:

(1) Stephenson, having been asked by the promoters' committee to give them his opinion on the relative merits of the Rennie ('direct') and Cundy ('Dorking') schemes, was in no doubt at all that the better route was via Dorking;

(2) Cundy's plans deposited with the Clerk of the Peace for the purpose of being brought before Parliament, were sufficiently in error that Stephenson could not make any objective comparison between the two routes;

(3) Stephenson was therefore asked by the promoters' committee to carry out a detailed survey of the best route via Dorking, so that an objective comparison with Rennie's scheme could be made; and

(4) Stephenson explained to the promoters' committee that his (Stephenson's) full-time engagements on the

London & Birmingham Railway would not allow him to do so, and therefore he recommended to that committee that Bidder should undertake the task (the promoters' committee of course concurred and arrangements went ahead).

The commercial aspects of the traffic potential at the London end were then considered, Mr. Joy implying that a terminus at London Bridge would be preferable to one at Nine Elms (Vauxhall), whilst Robert Stephenson considered that many passengers for Brighton would wish to travel from the west parts of London, and that goods could move by river barges between the docks and Nine Elms. On the question of relative times, Stephenson thought that the gradient of 1 in 80 then shown on the plans for that part of the London & Croydon Railway south from New Cross to Dartmouth Arms, would be the cause of sufficient delay due to the need for assistance to trains, together with the delays inherent in using the Greenwich company's line and the Croydon company's line, that the overall journey time from London Bridge to Brighton would be as long as that from Nine Elms to Brighton, since in Stephenson's opinion there would not be much delay on the London & Southampton company's line.

Robert Stephenson was questioned closely on various other aspects, mainly of detail, concerning both his line and his assessment of Sir John Rennie's line. One series of these questions is now of particular importance in helping to present a balanced picture. Mr. Wood said to Stephenson "A good deal of inquiry has been made into your connection with the present line; when were you first called in to express any opinion upon any of the plans proposed to Brighton?" Stephenson replied that it was in the latter end of the year 1833. The following dialogue then took place —

Who called you in upon that occasion? — It was a committee of gentlemen in the City.

It was in October or November, was it not? — Yes.

Mr. Routh, whose name has been mentioned,[12] and Mr. Jones and Mr. Goldsmid, were part of that committee? — Yes they were.

Had you known any of these gentlemen before you were

77

called in?—I had never seen any of them in my life.

Then you had reason to suppose that you were called in from your reputation as an engineer?—I suppose so.

What was the first step that was taken in submitting the plans to you?—I was introduced to Sir John Rennie, for the purpose of getting the information from him that was necessary to enable me to form an opinion.

Were any other lines submitted to you at the same time?—No.

In that year it was Sir John Rennie's?—Yes, entirely.

Had you frequent communications with Sir John Rennie upon the subject?—I had two or three times, not more.

And certain plans were submitted by him to your inspection?—Yes, they were submitted to me, not in a state, however, to enable me to give a decided opinion upon it, excepting upon some one or two points."

Mr. Serjeant Merewether then took over, and the following ensued—

Was one of the points upon which you had an opportunity of forming an opinion, with reference to the time it was likely to take?—Yes; I was immediately struck with the magnitude of the works, and the length of time that would be necessary to complete them.

Will you say, according to your judgment, what time will Sir John Rennie's take to execute?—I do not think that it can be well done under five years, or even more.

Is that the time which the present plan would take, and would the plan which you first gave take longer?—The plan which I first gave would have taken seven.

And the present, you think, would take five?—Yes; I will explain that answer: that it had always reference to the ordinary mode in which engineers go to work in making the cuttings, in making the embankments, and so on, making an enormous quantity of side-cutting and of spoil; it is possible to expedite things and reduce the time, but not very materially; in that case it was not so.

78

And you think that the first plan would take about seven years, and the present plan is amended in some degree, is it not?—Yes.

Is it amended in any of the particulars that you pointed out at the time?—Yes, the gradients are improved.

Was that one of the objections that you made to the line as it originally stood?—I suggested to Sir John Rennie that the gradients, I thought, were objectionable.

And they have been improved?—Yes.[13]

Earlier, under cross-examination by Mr. Joy, Stephenson had given it as his opinion that the amount of cutting on Rennie's line would approach 11,000,000 cubic yards. On being asked for the basis of his opinion, Stephenson replied that his calculations 'are made upon such data as I am always in the habit of taking for my estimates'. Counsel asked Stephenson if the latter would stake his credit on a figure approaching 11,000,000, and Stephenson replied "Yes, I do".[14] As has already been stated. Rennie's total excavation was given as 8,010,000 cubic yards, Rennie himself confirming this figure during his own subsequent examination and saying that it was absurd to suppose that the figure would be nearly 11,000,000 cubic yards.[15]

Towards the end of Robert Stephenson's examination, certain other points were made which must be recorded as bearing upon some of the personalities involved. Serjeant Merewether, during his questioning on Friday 25 March, adverted to the position of Mr. Routh junior, whose father was a member of the promoters' committee. Opposing counsel (Mr. Joy) had previously sought to show that Stephenson had acted irregularly by influencing the promoters' committee as Routh's son was one of Stephenson's pupils.[16] The following dialogue between Stephenson and Serjeant Merewether took place—

You were asked with respect to Mr. Routh's son; in point of fact, had not all been settled, with respect to the line, before Mr. Routh's son became connected with you?—Everything when I gave my opinion upon those lines; I did not know in point of fact, that Mr. Routh had a son.

And it was not till after this was settled that the connexion took place between you and Mr. Routh's son? — Certainly.

With respect to the matter itself, is it any thing more or less than this, that for a premium he has come to perfect himself as a civil engineer under you? — He came to me under the same circumstances as others, and paid me the same premium.

In the ordinary course? — Yes.

And whether Mr. Routh's son, or any other son came, he would have come on the same terms? — Precisely.[17]

Serjeant Merewether later asked Stephenson various questions concerning his (Stephenson's) grounds for recommending that Rennie's line should be rejected. Stephenson's replies were that his adverse report on Rennie's line were founded on the magnitude of the work, on the unfavourable nature of the gradients, on the expense of construction and subsequent working, on the time needed to build the line, and on the length of tunnelling needed.[18]

Merewether's final points related to Stephenson's earlier actions and to his (Stephenson's) own position. The opening questions and answers, referring to the later-abandoned 1833 schemes, were as follows —

'I think it was in October 1833, was it not, that Sir John Rennie agreed that his line should be surveyed by you? — Yes, it was about that time.

It was distinctly understood that Sir John Rennie's plan was to be submitted to you for your inspection? — Yes, I believe it was, I was present.

You were present when Sir John Rennie agreed to that inspection? — No, not exactly; but I afterwards met Sir John Rennie in consequence of that arrangement by the Committee.

Did Sir John Rennie at that time postpone the investigation of his line to the following November? — Yes, he did, I think.

That was about a month? — Yes.

That would have brought the time close up to the period for depositing the plans? – Yes.

Of course it would be very inconvenient to consider the plans in so short a time before they were to be deposited? – Certainly.

Do you happen to know whether the arrangement between the Committee and Sir John Rennie was, that his line was to be adopted and paid for, if it was deposited for Parliamentary purposes? – I have understood that this was the arrangement.

When you did look at the plan, and examine it, did you, or did you not find that the estimates that were made were insufficient for the work? – Yes, and I told Sir John Rennie so.

That they were insufficient? – Yes.

When you looked over the work with Sir John Rennie, you told him that the estimates were insufficient? – Yes.

Did you at that time discover that there would be those great works in embankments? – Yes.

The difference between his and your works is the difference between 45 and 80 or 90? – Yes.

Did you mention that to him? – I mentioned to Sir John Rennie the length of time that would be required to complete some of the works on his line, and I had seen the prospectus of the Committee, in which they stated that the work would be completed in two years, or two years and a-half, somewhere about that time, and I differed entirely from him in opinion upon it, and we had some conference; in the end I think he agreed that it would take a longer time than had been stated.

That the period that had been talked of, two years or two years and a-half, would not be sufficient for the completion of works of such magnitude? – Yes.

How much longer did you state that it would take? – I said that there were some of the embankments at that time that would take six or seven years to complete with great

81

exertion.

And that you stated at that time? — Yes.

Did you not also object at that time to there being five tunnels upon the line? — I mentioned it as an objection to it.

Were those objections that you made to Sir John Rennie's Line before you were employed to suggest any line yourself? — They were distinctly, a long time, several months before'.[19]

Merewether's next questions linked Stephenson's views on Rennie's 1833 scheme with his (Stephenson's) position in 1834-1835, regarding the schemes before Parliament in 1836.

'Those objections that you then made are the same that you now make to the line, are they not? — Yes, they are; I am not quite clear whether it was not a twelvemonth before that I made those suggestions.

Having at that time been called in by the (promoters) Committee to consider the lines that had been projected by Sir John Rennie, by Mr. Gibbs, by Mr. Cundy, and Mr. Palmer, and the rest, had you any reason whatever for believing that you would be employed to recommend a line yourself? — Not the least; I had not the least idea of it'.[20]

A member of the Parliamentary Committee then asked the circumstances under which Stephenson had reviewed Gibbs' proposals. Stephenson replied that Gibbs had written to him and asked the former if he would report on his (Gibbs') line at the same time as he was reporting on Rennie's and Cundy's line. Stephenson went on to explain that he had no orders from the promoters' Committee to report on Gibbs' line, but that he had had particulars of Mr. Gibbs' line copied on to the Ordnance map as well as having examined Mr. Gibbs' section which had been delivered to the offices of the London & Croydon Railway. Stephenson went on to say that he had not reported on Gibbs' line because he had found that the features of the country were altogether misrepresented. Stephenson continued that, in spite of this, Mr. Gibbs contended that his line was dependent upon accurate levels and that he had made an estimate, and compared it with Sir John Rennie's, and he (Gibbs) made the cuttings on Sir John Rennie's line to be eleven or twelve million of cubic yards. Stephenson then said that on the section which Gibbs showed him, it was two millions and a-half; Stephenson added that he had taken that section home with him and had had the country levelled, which showed that the proposal did not fit the facts.

One last quotation from the report of Robert Stephenson's examination must be made. Serjeant Merewether asked Stephenson about the readiness with which Sir John Rennie had made his (Rennie's) data available to him—

> 'With respect to Sir John Rennie's Line, when you were called upon to advise the (promoters') Committee with respect to Sir John Rennie's Line, did you find that Sir John Rennie gave you readily the information which would enable you to examine the estimates, and to test the line in all the ways that you were called upon to report? — No, at first he did not.
>
> Did you find that Sir John Rennie was disinclined to supply you with the information? — He was apparently so.
>
> In point of fact, did you get the information as soon as you wanted it? — No; the opinion that I was called upon to give was postponed in consequence.
>
> In consequence of your not getting the information, which was necessary to enable you to examine the line? — Yes.
>
> In point of fact, did you get the information which you wanted for the purpose of examining the line till after the plan was deposited? — No'.[21]

George Bidder's examination was started on Monday 28 March by Mr. Talbot. In reply to early questions, Bidder stated that he had been employed by 'all the most eminent engineers particularly that have been concerned in railways', and that his estimates for the London & Birmingham Railway had been borne out by the contracts. The following then ensued—

'When did you first take any part in the projected London and Brighton Railway of Mr. Stephenson? — In the beginning of last year, 1835.

For what purpose were you employed particularly? — When Sir John Rennie's Line and Mr. Cundy's were referred to Mr. Stephenson, I took out the quantities for him previous to examining them himself.

Do you mean that that was a process of calculation chiefly? — Yes, entirely so.

Do you remember a tabular statement that was made by the sub-committee of the original committee at Brighton? — Yes.

It was supposed that you had a hand in framing that statement, and the intrusting this line to Mr. Stephenson arose from that cause; what was your connexion with it? — The sub-committee was formed of Mr. Hallett, Mr. Wood, and Mr. Wright of Brighton. When they were about to meet to abstract all the answers that had been given in by the different projectors of railways from London to Brighton, they applied to me. I think it was Mr. Hallett: he said 'You are quick in calculation; I think you may render us a little assistance.' The amount of assistance that I rendered can be checked because it appears upon the tabular statement itself. Some of the engineers had given in their rise per mile without their proportion of gradient; and I said, if it is sixteen feet a mile, that is one in 330; some had given in their gradient without their rise in the miles; and if they said it is one in 400, I said then it is 13 feet 3 inches a mile.

Then they appear to me to have used you as they may have used Mr. Babbage's calculating machine? — In no other capacity.

Did you have a hand in any inference that might be supposed to be drawn, or did you merely substantiate facts? — I merely substantiated facts, and any person taking up that tabular statement, could check that I did.

It was after that Mr. Stephenson directed you to survey the country? — It was after that I was directed to make the Parliamentary survey.

84

Having received those directions, did you go upon the ground yourself? — I did.

Did you take the levels? — The Parliamentary section was taken altogether by myself, with the exception of one small portion, which was checked three or four times.

Independently of this small portion, which was checked three or four times, have your levels been checked by other persons, and by Mr. Stephenson? — The levels have not been checked by Mr. Stephenson, because of course he does not level now; but they have been checked by three independent parties.

But the line that has been laid down upon those levels that has been checked? — Mr. Stephenson laid the line down himself.

Upon the section which you furnished him? — Yes.

Mr. Stephenson has stated that every thing that you did was checked at your own desire, was that so? — Yes, it was strictly the case.

With respect to the preliminary instructions which you received from Mr. Stephenson as to the nature of the line that you were to find, if possible? — I suppose you allude to the instruction I received before the proceedings at Brighton to examine the country generally. The instruction I received from Mr. Stephenson was to get all the facts I could. I had Sir John Rennie's section, and Mr. Cundy's, and Mr. Gibbs (*sic*); I had also certain information from the South-eastern (*sic*) Company, who at that time were projecting a railway to Dover, in connexion with a railway to Brighton; and my instruction was without any reference to any party whatever, or any interest whatever, to take that line which would suit the interest of Brighton and London, which would provide for their interests in the best manner; and I did so without reference to any local interest.

Were you restricted to any particular rise per mile? — Not in the first instance; my instructions were to ascertain the best possible rise the country could afford'.[22]

Bidder then stated that he first walked over the country with all the different plans in his hand, and then discussed his observations with Mr. Stephenson; and he (Bidder) then received instructions from Stephenson to take levels in certain directions. On Bidder bringing all these levels to Stephenson, the latter decided that a line of 16 ft. a mile could be obtained between London and Brighton. Bidder went on to say that he was then directed by Stephenson to lay out the detail of the line with a rise of 16 ft. to a mile, and that this line was the one now before Parliament.

Mr. Bidder's cross-examination by Mr. Harrison on behalf of the promoters of Sir John Rennie's line, established Bidder's own position –

'When were you first applied to by Mr. Stephenson to undertake the examination of this line? – After Mr. Stephenson had made his report upon Sir John Rennie's Line and Mr. Cundy's, the Committee applied to him to make a survey to ascertain if a better line could be had, and Mr. Stephenson declined taking it, saying that his engagements would not admit of it; they then asked if he had any gentleman about him that he could recommend; at that time I was employed on the London and Birmingham, and he asked me if I had any objection to take charge of that survey, and I said I should be very glad to do it'.[23]

The rest of Bidder's evidence was essentially technical and need not be referred to in this history.

NOTES

1. Minutes of Evidence taken before the Committee on the London and Brighton Railway Bills: Engineering Evidence. James & Luke G. Hansard & Sons Ltd.
2. *Ibid.* 10.
3. *Ibid.* 11.
4. *Ibid.* 12.
5. *Ibid.* 13.
6. *Ibid.* 16.
7. *Ibid.* 16.
8. *Ibid.* 17.
9. *Ibid.* 26-30.

NOTES – *continued*

10. *Ibid.* 34-36.
11. *Ibid.* 52-53.
12. *Ibid.* 34-35 (during Stephenson's cross-examination by Mr. Joy)
13. *Ibid.* 79-81.
14. *Ibid.* 66.
15. *Ibid.* 190.
16. *Ibid.* 34-35.
17. *Ibid.* 97.
18. *Ibid.* 103.
19. *Ibid.* 104-105.
20. *Ibid.* 105.
21. *Ibid.* 106.
22. *Ibid.* 122-123.
23. *Ibid.* 145-146.

CHAPTER SIX

The London and Brighton Railway: The choice of route –decision

SIR JOHN RENNIE'S examination started on Thursday 14 April. Mr. Harrison opened, and was followed by Mr. Pollock. After the usual preliminaries, and the establishment of Rennie's connection with proposed lines to Brighton since 1825, counsel asked if Rennie remembered any report upon the subject in January 1835. He received an affirmative answer, and in reply to a further question the following exchanges took place —

I heard it stated that a report had been made by Mr. Robert Stephenson, upon the direct line of the Brighton railroad as proposed by us, and that proposed by Mr. Cundy. I certainly was never a party to that report being made by Mr. Stephenson, because I never would have submitted my plan to Mr. Stephenson; I did not conceive that he was a proper judge of those plans myself.

Then your plan had been submitted to Mr. Stephenson without your previous consent at all? — Certainly without my consent.

What was the plan that you had furnished to the promoters' Committee at that time, with reference to tunnels? — I can hardly state now the length of the tunnels, but the gradients were increased by (sic) 1 in 180, and the tunnels were very considerably shortened; I now allude to that modification of the direct line, as deposited for Parliament the latter end of 1834.

What was your object in increasing your gradients, as you have stated, and diminishing the tunnels? — The object was, as there was objections made to the length of the tunnels, to reduce the length of the tunnels.

And therefore you were desirous to shorten them as much as possible?—Yes? not because I formed any objection myself to tunnels.

You say that the plan that was in the hands of the promoters' Committee at the time Mr. Stephenson reported in January 1835, had the gradients reduced to 1 in 180?—Or rather increased, I mean.

In order to avoid the length of tunnels?—Yes.

Does that plan at all correspond with your present plan?—It certainly does not.

Is there any gradient of one in 180 upon your present plan between London and Brighton?—None whatever.

Then with reference to Mr. Stephenson's report, it would not apply to your present plan?—Certainly not.[1]

Counsel then turned to the circumstances under which Robert Stephenson's report was seen by Sir John Rennie. The latter stated that only the Brighton Committee, and not the London Committee, had sent him a copy of the report, which he thought he had received towards the end of February 1835. In answer to further questions, Rennie said that he had no objections to his plans being submitted to impartial engineers, but that it was not his practice to submit them himself. He said that several consulting engineers had been mentioned when a line to Brighton had been proposed in 1833—Messrs. Giles, Tierney Clarke, Jessop, and Robert Stephenson, but that no application had been made to him to refer his plans to any of those gentlemen. Rennie went on to say, however, that supposing that a fair disinterested commission of engineers were appointed, he would have been prepared to have submitted his plans to them, although it would have been 'contrary to my own practice of constituting any body as umpire over me'. Mr. Pollock then asked 'before any reference to your plans was made to any disinterested engineer, did you expect to be applied to and have notice of that?' Rennie replied 'I certainly thought so'.[2]

In answer to further questions, Rennie said that he had

been invited to attend meetings in Croydon and Brighton (the latter on 18 February 1835) so as to state the merits of the direct line; and that a resolution in favour of the direct line had been passed at that meeting in Brighton. Counsel's next questions related to Rennie's revisions to his plans towards the end of 1835, when the South Eastern company was still interested in coming to Brighton as well as to Dover. Rennie's answers were that he had had communication with the promoters of the South Eastern company and that he had reduced the steepest gradients from 1 in 180 to 1 in 264 at the expense of the tunnels being lengthened and some excavations being increased; and that he had been requested by the South Eastern company promoters to explore alternative routes from Oxted to Brighton. Rennie was questioned about the possibilities of communication to the east from the direct line, and said that from Merstham he conceived that the best line would be made to Dover and Tunbridge Wells, and that from farther on could be satisfactory lines to Lewes, Newhaven, and Hastings. He further thought that Newhaven was superior to Shoreham as a harbour, as well as being some 15 miles nearer to Dieppe than Shoreham was. Concerning communications to the west of a line along the centre of the country, Rennie said that Shoreham could be easily reached; and that 'by taking a branch higher up you could communicate with Horsham, and from thence to Portsmouth, and it has been long a very great desideratum to connect Portsmouth with London'.[3]

Rennie then gave evidence to the effect that in his opinion 'the circuitous line' did not present the same facilities as the direct one, and that the latter would be in the best interests of Brighton. The direct line passed through country in greater need of improvement than the Dorking route, and did not interfere with any properties of importance or private residences; Rennie added that on his route lime from the two great chalk ridges (the North and the South Downs) would be available to farmers for use as manure for the clay between the two ridges, which would improve the district concerned. Rennie also thought that there were no works of more than ordinary difficulty to execute on his route.

Mr. Pollock then turned to the reason why Sir John Rennie had changed his original proposal of starting his line from

Kennington, to the scheme then under review of starting at a junction with the London & Croydon Railway. Rennie replied that this alteration had, he understood, been made by the promoters to accommodate the feelings of the proprietors of houses and lands along the proposed route from Kennington as far as Croydon, where in any case his original scheme involved the line going within ½ mile of the Croydon Railway. Replying to subsequent questions, Rennie considered that the junction between the Croydon and Greenwich lines, situated on a viaduct with long views of trains approaching on the converging line, was an important point in reducing the possibility of collisions; the proposed junction of the Dorking route with the Southampton line was in a shallow cutting, effectively preventing drivers from seeing trains on the other route.[4] This part of Sir John Rennie's examination concluded by the latter stating that he had spare ground at London Bridge Station site (Greenwich line) for extensions, and that there would be no difficulty in widening the Greenwich viaduct if necessary.

Serjeant Merewether's cross examination initially concentrated on two main points — the reliance to be placed on Sir John Rennie's estimates and the factors that he had considered in planning to make use of the Greenwich and Croydon lines as part of his route.

Merewether began by asking Rennie to explain why the gradients that the latter had already given were at variance from his (Rennie's) book. The latter said that he did not understand several questions that had been put to him by Mr. Pollock, and, in consequence of that, the confusion arose; he said that he spoke to gradients which he had delivered in. The following dialogue ensued —

Were, or not, the gradients which you delivered in given from the book? — I misunderstood the question which Mr. Pollock put to me; otherwise I should have given a different answer.

I dare say it will occur to you that that is not an answer to my question, and therefore, I will repeat again, did or did not this correspond with the entries in the book? — I cannot give any other answer than I have given.

Then, I having asked you whether those answers which

91

you gave did or did not correspond with the book, your only answer is, that you misapprehended the question? — Yes.

As I am asking one question with reference to that book, will you allow me to ask you when that book was made? — That book has been in my use for some months past.

Not before some months past? — I can hardly answer to the date.

When you say some months, may I ask how many? — I cannot answer that question.

Three or four? — I cannot answer that question.

Two? — I cannot answer that question.

One? — I cannot answer that question.

Twelve? — I cannot answer that question.

Very good, then we will have that upon the notes. Sir John Rennie cannot give me an answer whether the book which now lies before him has been in his possession for 12 months. You have been asked particularly this morning (by Mr. Pollock, in examination) again with respect to the work which you executed at London Bridge; I think I understood you to say that your estimate for the bridge was exceeded by £30,000, but your estimate for the works for the approaches was so large, that the (bridge) committee had been enabled to complete many more works than were contemplated out of the excess of your estimate; is not that the answer you gave? — Yes.

Then both your estimate for the bridge and the approaches were inaccurate? — Certainly not.

One was exceeded, was it not; was not your estimate for the bridge exceeded? — If you consider the large sum of money which that bridge was estimated at, being nearly £600,000, and consider that only an excess £29,000 on that estimate took place that cannot be called, strictly speaking, very inaccurate.

I did not use the words very inaccurate; but, in point of fact, great or small, or what it may be, your estimate was exceeded by £30,000? – If it had been exceeded £1, it would have been very inaccurate, as far as that is concerned.

Perhaps, by one clear short answer, we can arrive at that which is the fact; it is a fact that your estimates were exceeded by £30,000 for the bridge? – You have got that yourself.

Will you allow me to ask you, do you represent to the Committee that that was the whole excess upon the bridge? – As near as I can recollect it was.

That we can ascertain hereafter with precision; you say that your valuation for the approaches exceeded so much what was required, that other considerable works were executed under your estimate; is that so? – I stated so.[5]

Asked what those extra works were, Rennie mentioned a street from London Bridge to the Bank, but said that certain other works had been left out, such as a street from the Monument to the Custom House.

Merewether then made play with the point that Rennie said that he had taken into account in his proposals the use of the London & Greenwich and London & Croydon companies' metals to reach Croydon from London. Merewether established that Rennie's proposed station at Kennington was being promoted up to the time of consideration by Parliament, and was laid down upon the deposited plan until he (Rennie) had given in the one which the Committee of the House had ordered him to deliver. Rennie explained that the station at Kennington had been positioned so that the line could have been extended 'to any part of the city that might hereafter be desirable'.[6] Rennie agreed that the terminus at Kennington was the only one which he had deposited in the House, and was the only one for which he had given a plan to the projectors at Brighton. Asked whether or not he intended that the Brighton trains should call intermediately on the Greenwich viaduct between London Bridge and the junction, Rennie replied 'Why not? there is a certain allowance that I have made for loss of time upon that'.

Serjeant Merewether continued to question Rennie on matters relating to the Greenwich line, and the following exchanges took place –

'Do you mean to stop on the Greenwich Railroad?—That is no business of mine.

I dare say not; but if you are to use the Greenwich Railroad, have you not taken the trouble of considering whether you will stop when you come upon the Greenwich Railroad before arriving at London Bridge?—I stated that I made allowance for sufficient time which I conceive may be lost in the junction between the Greenwich and the Croydon.

I am not asking now as to the time that will be consumed in the junction, but do you mean to stop with the passengers at any interval between the point of junction with the Greenwich Railroad and London Bridge?—That is no object of mine, certainly.

Have you considered it?—I say that it is no object of mine.

Have you thought of it at all?—I was considering in the stoppages with reference to between Brighton and London Bridge.

I am asking you, do you or do you not mean to set down passengers between the junction of the Greenwich Railway and London Bridge or not?—I refer you to my former answer.

My office is to cross-examine you; do you mean the answer that you gave, that you had not taken that into your consideration?—No, my calculation is between London and Brighton, making allowance for all the different stoppages that may take place between those places.

I am asking as to the disposition of the passengers; do you or do you not mean to set down passengers between the point of junction with the Greenwich Railroad and London Bridge?—That is no intention of mine'.[7]

After questioning the witness about his proposal to use London Bridge station, Merewether turned to the question of the need for widening the Greenwich viaduct to take the extra traffic inwards from the junction at Corbett's Lane.

'I want your direct answer, in an engineering point of

THE CHOICE OF ROUTE – DECISION

view, to this question, upon your credit and reputation as
an engineer, if the Dover traffic, and the Brighton traffic,
and the Croydon traffic, are to come upon the Greenwich
Railroad, is it in your judgment wide enough, or will it
be necessary to widen it? – If the Dover traffic, and the
Croydon traffic, and the Brighton traffic, come upon the
Greenwich Railway, it will be such a lucrative concern,
that it will be well worth while for the proprietors to widen
it'.[8]

The previous question was then read to the witness, and
opposing counsel continued –

'Upon reflection you will think that that is not an answer
to the question. I ask you, upon your credit and reputation
as an engineer, do you or do you not believe that the
Greenwich Railroad will be sufficient to receive the Dover
and Croydon and Brighton traffic besides its own? – That
will depend upon whether you state the present traffic or
the increased traffic.

The traffic which you contemplate? – I want to know the
present traffic or the increased?

The traffic which you contemplate upon your Road;
because I want to see whether the means which you contemplate are adequate to the end you have in view? – I
myself contemplate, for the Brighton traffic, it may do
very well. The Dover traffic I have not estimated.

You know, probably, that there is a Bill in Parliament,
which is in greater progress than this, for the South
Eastern Line, for Dover, joining the Croydon? – I have
heard so.

Will you let me know whether you do contemplate or not
that the Greenwich Railroad shall be increased in width? –
I state myself that, for the Brighton traffic, I consider it
will be sufficient; the Dover traffic I know nothing about;
and therefore I cannot give an answer to the question.

Can you give me no answer at all, because I want to frame
my questions accordingly, whether you do mean to have
the Greenwich enlarged, or mean to let it remain as it is at
present? – I state that for the present Brighton traffic I

consider the Greenwich Railroad is sufficient.

I saw by your evidence that you have contemplated that £200,000 might be necessary to increase the width of the Greenwich railroad? – I did say so, provided that the traffic should increase to a great extent.

What led you to make that calculation, that £200,000 would be necessary for that work? – That is supposing that the traffic between Brighton and London should be increased very materially, as I expect it will; and then, I think, it will be worth the while of the Greenwich Company to provide additional means for the increased traffic.'9

Rennie was then cross-questioned abou the possibilities of using vacant ground at London Bridge to the north of the site of the Greenwich company's station, to provide more accommodation, and suggested that the Greenwich company might take that site and leave their existing site for the Croydon and Brighton traffic (such an exchange was, of course, actually made a few years later, as will be recorded in due course). Rennie was then cross-questioned at length on certain aspects of the Croydon line, over which Brighton trains on his line would run. Some of the exchanges are of particular interest –

'Will you have the goodness to tell me at what curve you propose joining the Greenwich Railway by the Croydon? – I have not that plan with me; the engineer of the Croydon Railway will speak to that.

But I cannot be referred to other people for everything; I want to ask you, upon your character as an engineer, recommending the adoption of the line from Brighton to London, using the Croydon and the Greenwich, what opinion you proceed upon? – I have not the plan with me;

I wish I had it.

This is it? – (*the plan was handed to Sir John Rennie*).

You have a very large curve here; what is the extent of that? – I cannot give off-hand the radius of it.

Cannot you measure it? – I cannot.

I appeal to you that, being a great civil engineer, you might give me that? – But a great civil engineer must have assistance'.[10]

Opposing counsel then raised the question of the gradient from New Cross to Dartmouth Arms, which, he said, was laid down on the Parliamentary section as 1 in 80. Sir John Rennie made it clear that his proposal to use the London & Croydon Railway was based on a gradient of 1 in 110. Another interesting exchange then took place –

'Then we are to suppose the line going from the Greenwich up to the Croydon is to rise at 1 in 110? – You are.

Have you considered that that will increase the cuttings upon that line very much? – It will.

Have you calculated the extent of the cost of that? – That is the business of the engineer of that line.

Do you know, in point of fact, that that cost was not included in the estimate of that line when they were before Parliament? – I do not know what the estimate was.

Do you know that that was the case? – I have nothing to do with the engineer's estimate.

You must be able to tell me, because we are to consider whether that line is a practicable line, or not; your line depends upon the Croydon line; and if that line has been taken into Parliament with 1 in 80, and it is to be altered to 1 in 110, have you informed yourself of the means which they have for altering it? – I have no doubt that they have means for altering it'.[11]

A large number of questions on matters of some detail concerning the Croydon Railway were then put to Sir John Rennie, to many of which he replied that the engineer for that line (Mr. Gibbs) should be asked to answer them. After innumerable questions on details concerning the route which Rennie advocated south of Croydon, Mr. Serjeant Merewether asked about a meeting in the autumn of 1833 concerning his (Rennie's) proposals at that time. Counsel asked –

'And was it not on that occasion that it was resolved that you were the engineer for the purpose of the railway, upon terms and conditions to be thereafter agreed upon; and that Mr. Jessopp (pic), Mr. Stephenson, Mr. Giles, and Mr. Tierney Clarke, or such one or more of them as shall be deemed necessary by the engineers, to be consulted? – I believe there was a resolution to that effect.

That was communicated to you? – I do not think I have a copy of it; I believe I had it.

In your examination in chief, you stated that you would not agree to your plans being submitted to Mr. Stephenson? – Not as the sole arbitrator.

But when that resolution was entered into, was he not to be one of the consulting engineers to consider your plans? – I believe he was.

You have no doubt of that? – No.[12]

Further questioning by opposing counsel on Rennie's 1833 schemes was aimed to show that Rennie made various alterations to his plans and that these were not always ready by the required dates; and counsel went on to ask Rennie whether the proprietors had not complained about the constant changes of plan and of being kept in a state of uncertainty. Rennie's reply was that he did not recollect any specific complaints.

Mr. Serjeant Merewether then began a series of questions on Sir John Rennie's associations in 1833 with Robert Stephenson and with the promoters' committee. The grudging answers that Rennie was forced to make did not show him in a favourable light. Merewether led into the subject by asking the witness whether or not his plans were ready when wanted, and did not get a definite answer.

'Do you recollect when they were wanted for the purpose of Mr. Stephenson examining them when they were ready? – The finished plans were not ready certainly.

Will you have the goodness to state, whether at that time you did not state that (you) had not shown to Mr. Stephenson the plans that you meant to deposit? – I think I did say so.

Then you exhibited one plan to Mr. Stephenson and meant to deposit another? — No: to the best of my recollection, I stated to Mr. Stephenson that the finished plans were not ready, and therefore it was impossible for me to define what the plans would be.

That was the whole of the case? — Yes.

Did not Mr. Stephenson, when another plan was shown to him, remonstrate? — Not to my knowledge; I do not think I saw him after the plans were deposited.

Did you say, 'Do you think I am such a fool as to tell Mr. Stephenson what I am going to do?' — I cannot recollect those words.

That is a principle of conduct that must remain upon your mind? — The real fact was this, that I saw such indications on the part of the (promoters) Committee at that time, that whether the expenses would be paid or not, that I wished to take time before I delivered up the plan, but as far as regarded Mr. Stephenson, I did state to him that the section that he saw was not the finished section.

Did you state at that time that you were not such a fool as to show Mr. Stephenson your plans? — I cannot recollect.

You cannot deny it? — Really, I cannot recollect it.

Will you take upon yourself to say that you did not state so to Mr. Stephenson? — I cannot recollect.

Is that the best answer you can give? — Yes.

Was not a vote of censure proposed to the proprietors for your having so stated, and you having delivered one plan and deposited another? — I do not recollect a vote of censure at all; but I recollect perfectly well that the Committee themselves proposed to send a letter to the subscribers, giving up that concern, proposed to give Mr. Vizard (of Messrs. Vizard and Leman) a piece of plate and to pay Mr. Stephenson's expenses, but in regard to ourselves nothing whatever was said. That letter was altered, and I believe the only reason stated in that letter was, that the Committee themselves might have the power of adopting such improvements as were being made in rail-roads in order that they might make the best road.

That is the account of the transaction? — That is the account of the transaction.

I want to ask you most distinctly whether there was not one member of the Comittee who did propose a vote of censure upon you, whether you were not present at that time, and whether considerable altercation did not arise out of it; that is so plain a fact that you must be able to tell me, Aye or No, whether that existed? — A great deal of personality passed upon that occasion, in which I thought I was extremely ill-used; some members of the Committee had made observations, which appeared to me to be perfectly irrelevant. My Lord, (Lord George Lennox, the Chairman of the Parliamentary Committee) I am sorry to go into this discussion, it has nothing to do with the business; but I am quite satisfied, that the more that subject is investigated, the more it will be found that I am not to blame, but that I was the suffering party.

Then I will keep you to the discussion, and I will ask you, was not such a vote of censure proposed in your presence, and did not so much discussion take place upon it afterwards, that it is impossible for you to have forgotten it?

At this point Mr. Sydney Taylor stated that he considered that he might object, but that he would not, though he thought it very irregular.

Will you have the goodness to give me an answer to that directly, Aye or No. Did a member — and I will mention that gentleman's name if you wish it, — did not Mr. Jones himself, propose a vote of censure on you, for your having giving one plan, and withdrawn another; and from the difficulties which had arisen from your having misled them as to the plan? — Mr. Jones and I had a personal quarrel, and any observations arose entirely out of that personal quarrel.

Was not that personal quarrel with respect to his moving that resolution, because that is now brought to your recollection? – I do not recollect Mr. Jones moving that resolution; but I recollect that Mr. Jones and myself had a personal altercation upon several points, in which I thought that I was considerably ill-treated.

Did not that arise from his proposing at that meeting a censure upon you? – I think not; I think there were several other concurring causes.

Was that one? – I think not.

All the gentlemen present at that meeting are standing round me; will tell me whether there was such a vote of censure moved against you or not? – I really do not recollect the circumstance.

That is the best answer you can give me? – All I can state is, that Mr. Jones and myself had a personal quarrel upon several points.

You cannot tell me, Aye or No, whether such a Resolution was moved against you? – I do not recollect it.

Do you know, in point of fact, that your plans were submitted to Mr. Stephenson? – I was out of town at the time; I heard upon my return from the Continent that they had been submitted.

There having been a Sub-Committee, whose names I have mentioned to you, and which have been read to you, do you mean to say that they did not, with your consent, submit your plans to Mr. Stephenson? – Just tell me the period.

In the year 1833? – In the year 1833, certainly, I had a meeting with Mr. Stephenson once or twice, but then the finished plans were not put into Mr. Stephenson's hands, because they were not ready.

Now you have mentioned one interview you had with Mr. Stephenson; have you not again and again had interviews with Mr. Stephenson? – I stated that I had two to the best of my recollection; and I will not state that I did not have three with him; that was in 1833; but Mr. Stephenson did not then see the finished sections, or the finished plans.

Do not you remember Mr. Stephenson attending with you at your counting-house, and there representing to you, that the works that you proposed were of such a magnitude, that they would require more than double the time you calculated? – Mr. Stephenson came to my office, and we had a great deal of conversation upon the subject of our plans; but as the plans were not finished, I stated that it was quite impossible for Mr. Stephenson to form any opinion till the finished plans were put into his hands.

Was not that time December the 10th, 1833, when Mr. Stephenson came? – Very likely: I beg your pardon, I do not recollect that.

Were not your plans deposited in November preceding the date that I asked you? – They were, the 30th of November.

Will you allow me to ask you whether, since the time you have been speaking of, you have not applied to the Company to be the engineer? – I certainly stated, after the personal quarrel I had with several of the gentlemen, that I was willing to forget everything that had passed, and to try the Dorking line again for them if they wished it.

When was that? – That was, I think, some time in the spring of 1835 or 1834.

Having drawn your recollection to that last circumstance, let me put it again to you, will you venture to say that you had any ground of quarrel with Mr. Jones, except the fact of his proposal of that vote of censure? – I believe there were several grounds.

That you mean to represent? – Yes.

That there were several grounds besides that? – That there were several grounds.

Were you present afterwards at the meeting of the 12th of December 1834, Mr. Goldsmid in the chair, Mr. Kemp, Mr. Jones, Mr. Routh, Mr. Palmer, Mr. Faithful, Mr. Heaviside, and other directors of the concern? – When?

On the 12th of December 1834? – I think I was present

somewhere about that time.

That was the time that the subscription was entered into, there was a sub-Committee appointed, to consist of Mr. Goldsmid, Mr. Kemp, Mr. Routh, Mr. Jones, and Mr. Heaviside? – I cannot bear in mind.

Do not you recollect that a subscription was entered into by those gentlemen at the meeting? – I do not recollect.

Then your brother, Mr. George Rennie, attended the other meetings; but he is your partner, is he not? – In some cases he is; he carried on his own professional business perfectly independent of me as an engineer.

But with respect to his matter you were acting together? – We were in some cases.

Was it not altogether, as far as the connexion with the Brighton railroad was concerned, one in which you both took part? – we were certainly.' [13]

Sir John Rennie was then cross-examined by Mr. Maule on behalf of landowners on his route. Maule's approach was hostile, and he asked some searching questions, as follows:

'I understood you to have stated, that the only railways you have executed, were what you call temporary railways? [14] I have stated so.

By those temporary railways which you have executed, do you mean such railways as contractors are in the habit of creating, in order to convey materials and rubbish from one part to another? – I allude to railways which I have been in the habit of making for my own works.

That is not an answer to the question. Do you mean by such railways, the temporary railways or tram-roads which are constantly made, to convey rubbish or materials from one part to the other? – I do.

Which are laid down to last a few days or hours? – Years, sometimes.

But sometimes only days or hours? – Yes.

To be travelled by horses? – To be travelled by horses.

Not by locomotive engines? – No.

And to be travelled at the rate of two or three or four miles an hour? – Yes.

Then have you had any, the slightest, personal experience with any work of a railroad to be travelled upon by locomotive engines at a velocity of 20 or 30 miles an hour? – I certainly have not executed a railway of that description, but having paid attention to every part of that department, I conceive myself perfectly competent to do it.

I will not go through that great multitude of works that you were asked to by Mr. Pollock, but towards the end of them there was one which I have heard of lately, a pier at Whitehaven; was that one of your performances? – That is.

Did not that turn out a complete failure? – I say no; most distinctly no.

Has it not tumbled down into the sea? – It has not tumbled down into the sea.

Has it been removed? – I conceive that it has answered its purpose well.

Are you not aware that you are pretty nearly singular in that conception? – I am not.

Am I to understand that in your opinion, that it is a work of yours that has given satisfaction and answered its purpose? – I decline answering any further questions. I really must throw myself upon the Committee: there has been a personal set made upon me here. I am willing to give any information to the Committee upon this matter; but when I am run down with these things, I must seek the protection of the Committee.'[15]

Mr. Maule then asked Sir John if the latter's projected railway did not go over, in the town of Croydon, a portion of the land intended to be covered by the South Eastern Railway; Rennie replied that he could not answer that question, and only a little later made it clear that the plans for his own line, going to Kennington, would involve a variation if the line went to Croydon instead. Even so, Rennie did not know if the South Eastern had deposited their plans before he (Rennie) had deposited his.

Mr. Maule then asked various questions intended to make Rennie give technical answers. In some instances Rennie replied, and whilst in others he refused to be drawn, he undoubtedly continued to reveal his lack of knowledge of railway practice. Opposing counsel's hostile questions eventually roused Rennie to say that he could not allow counsel, or anybody else, to test his skill. He went on:

> 'I come here, Sir, to give every information I can with regard to this railway; but I cannot allow myself to be schooled in all these points which I am perfectly well acquainted with; but as a matter of personal feeling I cannot submit to it.'[16]

Mr. Maule continued to ask questions, many of them searching and some bordering on the hostile, and was succeeded by Mr. Bagshaw, cross-examining on behalf of Lord Abergavenny and other landowners. Sir John Rennie was then cross-examined by Mr. Wilcocks on behalf of Mr. Cundy, on the extent to which Rennie had taken profits from conveying chalk from along his route, into account.

Finally, Sir John was re-examined by Mr. Sidney Taylor, whose first question was:

> 'have you, on the consideration of any of the questions that have been put to you, been led to doubt as to the practicability of any part of your plan?'

Rennie's reply was simply 'Nonewhatever'.[17]

Taylor's main object was clearly, by careful questioning, to re-establish the personal credibility which his witness had lost under cross-examination. Rennie's answers to his questions were well reasoned, but there can have been no doubt that his reputation had suffered. At the end of Taylor's examination, he asked Rennie 'Do you not consider, that it would be a great accommodation to London, to have a termination at London Bridge, and another approaching Westminster?' Rennie replied 'It certainly would', and on being asked how best he would join his route to Stephenson's, Rennie replied 'I think ... I should go from Croydon to

Stephenson's line.'[18]

Later developments of course took in both these points.

Joseph Locke's examination started on Monday 25 April 1836. He had been summoned to give evidence as an independent assessor of the line proposed by Sir John Rennie, who had engaged him for the purpose, and his initial examination was undertaken by Mr. Harrison. After the usual preliminaries, Locke was asked a long series of questions on his (Locke's) opinions on Rennie's line and proposed methods of construction. He gave full support to Sir John's scheme, both in principle and in such details as the use of the near-vertical cutting sides in chalk, and he also considered that Rennie's estimates for the cost of tunnelling (£25 per yard) and earthworks (9½d per cubic yard) were very fair. On the question of the relative dangers of a junction on a viaduct, or otherwise where the drivers of converging trains could see one another clearly, and of one in a cutting, Joseph Locke said that there might be more danger in the latter case, but that with 'proper arrangements' (i.e. signals) the traffic might be carried without danger in either case.

Locke favoured the direct line because of the shorter distance, even allowing for the delays involved with assistant engines on the steep part of the Croydon line, and added that the advantage would be greater if the gradient of 1 in 110 could be improved (1 in 172 had been suggested). Concerning the matter of the increased traffic which the direct line would bring over the Greenwich viaduct, Mr. Locke considered that there would be no difficulty in widening the viaduct, and said:

'I think it would be much better to make the four lines rather than bring any new line into London.'[19]

Locke was cross-examined by Messrs. Wood, Bagshaw and Willcock, and various questions of a technical nature concerning the construction and working of the line were put to him. He was then further questioned by Mr. Harrison, and in one answer amplified his earlier statement to Mr. Harrison that he would prefer to use the Greenwich Railway to reach London rather than make an independent route even if it meant ultimately widening the Greenwich viaduct. In his further answer, Locke said that the reason for his

preference was that it would be cheaper to interfere a little
further with property along the Greenwich route, than to
make a new route altogether.[20]

Locke made his own position quite clear in answers to
certain questions put to him by the Committee of the House.
The first series of questions was:

'Have you looked over the country between London and
Brighton generally, or has your attention been exclusively
directed to Sir John Rennie's line? – I have not looked
over the country with any other view than to examine the
line of Sir John Rennie.

In looking over the line of Sir John Rennie, were you
directed to look at it with a view to speak of its merits or to
look at it comparatively, any better line in the country
through which it passed? – I could not afford the time to
look at it with any comparative object; I looked at the line
to see whether it was practicable.

Then whether a better line could be formed in any other
direction, or whether the line which Sir John Rennie has
taken to be the best, you say nothing but in reference to
Sir John Rennie's line? – Quite so, but I do not know
whether a better line could be obtained than this.'[21]

A little later, Locke's reply to a point on the affinity of
moisture and chalk, brought the following questions and
answers:

'You gave your answer, that we can scarcely consider you
an impartial witness? – I give no opinion upon any other
line of railway, except that of Sir John Rennie.

You have not calculated the difference of gradients upon
the two lines? – No; it has been stated to me that the
greatest inclination upon the other is one in 330; and that
the length is about six miles more; that is all that I know of
the other line.

Taking those data, and presuming them to be correct, that
the gradient in one case is one in 264, and in the other one
in 330, with an increase of distance of six miles, have you
made any calculation of the relative merits of the two

lines? – I have formed a decided opinion upon it, and I prefer one to the other.

Which have you preferred? – Sir John Rennie's, all other circumstances being the same.

You give that opinion as an engineer; upon two lines of railway being laid before you on paper, you would give that, without the circumstance having occurred of your being engaged by Sir John Rennie? – That would not affect my evidence at all.

You think not? – I think not.

You give that opinion as a civil engineer, that you would prefer a greater inclination with a smaller distance? – I would; but I should like to give that with this observation; that very much depends upon the object for the railway; if it be a passenger railway, I should say decidedly, that I would not go six miles further to save the difference in the gradients between one in 264 and one in 330, all other circumstances remaining the same.'[22]

After various questions on the operation of steep inclines, on the working of the Liverpool & Manchester Railway, and on the need for ventilation in tunnels, the Committee of the House asked Mr. Locke two questions concerning the general route:

'Will you be kind enough to abstract yourself from the character of being witness for Sir John Rennie, and state what you consider to be the defects of his line as they are laid before you? – I do not feel the slightest interest in Sir John Rennie's line, nor in any line whatever. If I were to take the defects upon his line, I should state that the inclinations were not so good as upon a level. I do not like tunnels and inclined planes, and fifty things which we cannot avoid. I like level gradients if I could get them, but at the same time I would not go round to any great extent to obtain them.

Even the advantage of a level line may be purchased too dearly? – Yes, it may. I am speaking of what I would have if I could get it. When I say that I do not like planes and tunnels, I mean that I would rather have a level line without tunnels if I could get it.'[23]

The Committee then questioned Mr. Locke on the advisability of using the Greenwich line into London Bridge, and sought clarification of Locke's view, already noted above, that such a course was preferable to having an independent line. Locke, in his replies, explained that, if London Bridge were to be the terminus, he would take the Greenwich line for a mile or two in order not only to save money but to save severance to private property; and he added that if the existing two roads of the Greenwich company could not carry the traffic, he would prefer to add two more rather than make an independent line. He said:

'My impression at present is, that the (Greenwich) line is adequate; but if you satisfy me that it is not, then I recommend two more lines of rail.'[24]

This part of his examination concluded as follows:

'Are you satisfied that any addition of the amount of traffic to an amount of traffic (already considered very large), would be productive of great inconvenience? – No; I think it may be productive of great advantage. I put it in this way; that before any new line is made in opposition to another, I think that the public and Parliament should be satisfied that one is not adequate to perform the work of both, because the public must pay the expense of this in the amount of extra tolls; if one line is adequate, the public may be carried cheaper than by having two lines.'[25]

The Committee then again turned to the relative merits of the rival schemes, and the following ensued:

'You have stated that you think that Sir John Rennie's line is the best line to Brighton, superior to Mr. Stephenson's? – No; I have stated that I have not seen any other line but that of Sir John Rennie's. I have examined that upon the points of which I have given evidence here; but I have answered the questions put hypothetically to me.

You stated that you considered it a better line than Mr. Stephenson's, did you not? – I stated, in answer to a question, giving me the length of the inclinations of the two lines which I would prefer; but I have not stated, because I do not know, all the circumstances to enable me to say which of the two is the best line.

Would you pledge yourself as an engineer, that Sir John Rennie's line is better than Mr. Stephenson's? — I would not answer that.

Or Mr. Cundy's or Mr. Gibbs'? — I cannot answer that question, because I am not in possession of facts to enable me to do it.

You stated that you prefer the line much, because of its being shorter than the other, you said six miles? — Yes, I prefer it very much in consequence of that.

Should you have the same preference for a shorter line if there was but only two minutes' difference in the time of arriving at Brighton? — Just the same.

Then it is not the time? — No, the expense of working it.

And you would prefer that to the shorter line with the inconvenience of joining two other railroads, and also tunnelling and assistant engines, and a curve of eight chains? — No, the Committee must allow me this explanation; I have not admitted, in the first place, that there is any inconvenience in the Greenwich line, for I do not believe it.

We will suppose that? — I cannot admit any answer to be coupled with that which I do not wish to admit; the question was asked me as to a line with an inclination of one in 264, and another of one in 330 (which I suppose was Mr. Stephenson's) which I preferred, and my answer was that I preferred the shorter one.

With those contingencies of going upon two different railroads? — O, certainly.

And with a tunnel? — O, certainly.

The curves? — The curves I suppose to be altered, I have always objected to curves; I have no objection to a tunnel.'[26]

110

Again the Committee asked Joseph Locke to confirm his professional independence, and also to amplify his statement about the relative working expenses of a longer and a shorter route:

'You have then no motive in giving your opinion adverse to your honest impression, whether it is in favour of the line (Rennie's) or against it? — No, I have none whatever.

You have spoken of the increased expense arising from the increased extent of the road, will not the expense also be greater to the traveller as the number of miles is greater? — Unquestionably.

Does your experience enable you to say what is the rate which passengers are charged by the mile on railroads? — Yes, the passengers upon the Liverpool and Manchester railroad are charged about two-pence a-mile.

If then it be true that one of those competing lines is longer than the other by six miles, and taking two-pence to be the average charge per mile to the traveller, will that impose upon him who goes by a longer line a shilling extra charge? — No doubt it would, if the tonnage rates and the Acts of Parliament were the same.'[27]

The Committee concluded their interrogation of Mr. Locke by questions on a number of subjects. The salient points were:

(a) That on the assumption that a preponderance of passengers on the Greenwich line were pleasure-seekers going to the country, it might be that the Greenwich traffic itself would diminish as lines (then under construction) such as the London & Birmingham, the London & Southampton and the Western Region, were opened and gave access to additional pleasure areas; and that passengers from Brighton might de-train at Croydon and continue to London by road. Locke agreed with both those points.

(b) Locke preferred London Bridge to Vauxhall as the London terminus if he were restricted to one only, but he would also like a west-end terminus if it were possible.

111

(c) On the Liverpool & Manchester Railway, Locke said that there were a number of branch lines joining the main line, each branch having up to twenty trains a day on it, joining or leaving the main line, without any practical inconvenience.

(d) Possible dangers from fog on the Greenwich line, adjacent to the Thames: Locke thought that an audible signal such as a bell might be used; the Committee suggested a gong.

and

(e) the effect on the travelling public of having tunnels on the line was thought by Locke to be likely to attract as many passengers from curiosity as it might deter from fear.

The taking of engineering evidence, dealt with above, was completed on Tuesday 26 April, but the arguments and debates continued for over a year, including, of course, in the House of Lords. The relevant factors were considerably clouded by questions of personalities and their actions and motives (real or imagined), as for example, allegations by Nicholas Cundy's supporters that Robert Stephenson had 'poached' Cundy's plans, and Rennie's attitude towards Robert Stephenson no doubt reflecting the fact that Robert Stephenson with his father had been authorized to undertake the detailed surveys for the London & Birmingham Railway after preliminary surveys of two alternative routes had been made by Rennie and by Francis Giles respectively. The absurdity of the Cundy party's attitude has already been shown by extracts from the Engineering Evidence before the Commons, whilst other extracts from that Evidence have made it clear that some members of the Brighton Railway committee had become disenchanted with Sir John Rennie.

Stripped of these complications, and also leaving aside the question of the site of the terminus in London, the choice requiring a decision was in essence a 'direct' route involving heavy engineering works, or a more circuitous route some six miles longer but with easier gradients and considerably lighter engineering works. Only the 'direct' route would serve Croydon. The easier route was a typical Stephenson line, and reflected the view of his father George and himself that the power of the locomotives should be employed to commercial gain by hauling heavy loads rather than being used to negotiate steep gradients. Rennie, as has been revealed, was not a 'railway' man, but his 'direct' route was strongly supported by Joseph Locke, who was a very successful champion of such routes, and who considered that the reduced mileage of a direct route gave commercial advantage over a longer route provided that the gradients could be surmounted in day-to-day operation. Locke had been one of George Stephenson's assistants, but had later established himself on his own, and before long attained a stature commensurate with Robert Stephenson, although not so well known to the public at large.

Although not discussed in the Commons during the taking of the Engineering Evidence in 1836, two other schemes were then still in being – Gibbs' and Palmer's (the South Eastern Railway). Throughout the ensuing year both these schemes were debated alongside those of Stephenson and Rennie, with interest waning among Cundy's supporters as it became clear that they could no longer present a credible scheme. Gradually opinion hardened in favour of Rennie's route for a direct line, and this trend was reported to Parliament on 13 May 1837. The Chairman of the Committee, Lord George Lennox, then moved that an Ordnance engineer be appointed to survey all four active routes and report back to the House; the proposal was approved and Captain Robert Alderson, R.E., was appointed on 2 June. Shortly afterwards the promoters of the four separate schemes joined forces to put forward an overall scheme, and this too was sent to Captain Alderson for his report.

Alderson reported on 27 June that Stephenson's scheme was the best from an engineering point of view. As, however, Rennie's scheme made use of the Greenwich and Croydon lines (the former already open as far as Deptford, and the latter under construction), and the Greenwich company had sufficient ground to enable the line to be widened if necessary, whilst London Bridge was the most suitable site for the London terminus, Alderson considered that the advantages of the direct line outweighed the necessity for heavy engineering works.

The overall 'agreed plan' of the four groups whose engineers were Rennie, Stephenson, Gibbs, and Palmer

113

respectively, was a more comprehensive scheme than any of the plans considered singly. It proposed in effect that Stephenson's Dorking route should be used from Wimbledon (off the London & Southampton Railway) to Brighton via Shoreham, but with a line on Rennie's route from Croydon (off the Croydon line) through Merstham to join the Dorking route at or near Capel. At Brighton, the terminus would be on the site selected by Rennie. New construction would have totalled nearly 70 miles, apart from using some 14 miles of other companies' lines to reach the two London termini of Nine Elms and London Bridge. Captain Alderson reported against this scheme on the grounds that, with no town on the route except Croydon having more than 5,000 inhabitants, and no manufactures or minerals, commercial return could only be looked for from London and Brighton themselves and this would be inadequate for the capital needed to construct the railway system.

Accordingly, Captain Alderson considered that the direct line would be the best for the interests of the company and would give the public all the accommodation required. He therefore repeated his opinion that the direct line should be adopted.

By this time the direct line itself had been modified. The junction with the London & Croydon Railway was to be south of Penge to eliminate the sharp curves of the original proposal at Croydon, and Merstham tunnel was shortened slightly. A considerable re-alignment was made from north of Balcombe tunnel for some 7½ miles, the line being taken farther to the east than before. This entailed lengthening Balcombe tunnel by some 350 yards, building a somewhat larger viaduct over the Ouse, and the construction of a deep cutting south of the viaduct, but enabled Cuckfield tunnel (1450 yards) to be abolished, and replaced by a short one south of Haywards Heath. Another modification farther south lengthened Clayton Tunnel by over 500 yards, and near Brighton a tunnel about ¼ mile long was needed as a result of a further re-alignment.

The Bill for the direct line received the Royal Assent, under 1 Vic. Cap.119, and covered not only the branch from Brighton to Shoreham which had always been included in Rennie's scheme, but also a branch eastwards from Brighton to Lewes and Newhaven. It also gave (clause 40) the company power to purchase the Croydon, Merstham & Godstone Railway whose route would in part be wholly obliterated, and also (clause 45) to divert the turnpike at Hooley (north of Merstham tunnel). It further required that the Brighton company should sell to the South Eastern company at cost price that portion of the Brighton company's line between Norwood and Redhill, as already explained in Chapter II.

(This requirement was later modified, as also explained in that chapter, to entail only the sale to the South Eastern company of the 6 miles from Coulsdon to Redhill. This will be dealt with in greater detail in due course).

NOTES

1. Minutes of Evidence taken before the Committee on the London and Brighton Railway Bills: Engineering Evidence. James & Luke G. Hansard & Sons Ltd., 174-175.
2. *Ibid.* 176.
3. *Ibid.* 181.
4. *Ibid.* 219-220.
5. *Ibid.* 226-227.
6. *Ibid.* 229.
7. *Ibid.* 230.
8. *Ibid.* 232.
9. *Ibid.* 233.
10. *Ibid.* 236-237.
11. *Ibid.* 237-238.
12. *Ibid.* 336-337.
13. *Ibid.* 339-343.
14. *Ibid.* 320, in answer to Mr. Serjeant Merewether in cross-examination.
15. *Ibid.* 346-347.
16. *Ibid.* 353.
17. *Ibid.* 368.
18. *Ibid.* 396.
19. *Ibid.* 402.
20. *Ibid.* 427.
21. *Ibid.* 435.
22. *Ibid.* 437-438.
23. *Ibid.* 444.
24. *Ibid.* 449.
25. *Ibid.* 449.
26. *Ibid.* 449-450.
27. *Ibid.* 451-452.

CHAPTER SEVEN

The London and Brighton Railway: Building the line

THE London & Brighton Company, as has been recorded, was the last of the four companies to be authorised to use London Bridge station. The first was the London & Greenwich (authorized on 17 May 1833), followed by the London & Croydon (12 June 1835) and the South Eastern (21 June 1836); the London & Brighton Act was dated 15 July 1837.

The London & Croydon Railway commenced about 1¾ miles south of London Bridge, as already stated, and the original plans for both the South Eastern and the London & Brighton Railways were to make end-on junctions with the London & Croydon at the latter's terminus at Croydon. The South Eastern's Act No. 2 of 3 July 1837 authorized their line to commence at Penge and to run parallel to, and on the east side of, the Brighton company's line (not yet authorized) for some 5 or 6 miles. It has already been explained that, when the Brighton company finally received their Act on 15 June 1837 the South Eastern were given the option of purchasing the Brighton company's line north of Redhill and of commencing their line to Dover at that point, rather than build their own line parallel with the Brighton line for several miles and then continue on a separate route through the North Downs. Although the South Eastern company did, in the end, take up the option in principle, their Act (2 and 3 Vic. Cap 79) repealed clause 135 of the Brighton's Act and instead gave the South Eastern power only to purchase the 6 miles north of Redhill. Since by this time the engineering works were in hand by the Brighton company (which in any case had to construct them); the building of the whole line south of the junction with the Croydon company will be dealt with as an entity.

The London & Brighton company's line started some 54 chains south of Jolly Sailor station on the London & Croydon Railway, about 12 chains north of where the latter crossed the little River Graveney (now no longer visible in the area), and commenced with a left-hand curve of about 1 mile radius (thus crossing the former canal near where the latter crossed the River Graveney). The line was on a rising gradient of about 1 in 220 (it is now at 1 in 215). The curvature then eased to over 1¼ mile radius, and then sharpened to 91 chains, through Croydon, the first station on the line and built on a rising gradient of 1 in 296. This station was to the east of the town. As far as this the line was virtually at ground level, but it now entered a cutting averaging 20-25 ft. deep, extending for about ¾ mile on a straight alignment and on a rising gradient of 1 in 263 (laid out at 20 ft. per mile, or 1 in 264, but later calculated more accurately as 1 in 263). The cutting was succeeded by an embankment some 3½ miles long, of varying height up to about 20-25 ft., initially continuing the straight alignment followed south of Croydon but later curving right at over 90 chains radius for about 1 mile and then, after a short length of left-hand curve of 300 chains radius, and a straight of about ½ mile, starting a left-hand curve about ¾ mile long and of 2¼-3¼ mile radius. The chalk began to appear a mile or two south of Croydon. Throughout this length the rise continued at 1 in 263, and shortly after the very easy compound left-hand curve commenced the second station was sited, placed on the north side of the underbridge over the road to Godstone up the Caterham Valley, and named accordingly Godstone Road. It was some 8 miles from the village it was intended to serve. It was not originally intended to have a station there, as will be explained later. Near the south end of the left-hand curve the embankment gave way to a short length of shallow cutting, followed by a low embankment for some ¼ mile until the formation became virtually at ground level. All the way from Croydon the line was situated to the east of the Brighton road and on the east side of the valley, so that cutting sides tended to be higher, and embankments lower, on that side than on the west side.

Beyond the end of the easy left-hand curve and along the low embankment the line continued straight for over a mile, a short way along which there was the first level crossing on the line, where, as will be recorded later, a small station called Stoats Nest was built subsequent to the line being opened to traffic. Near the end of this straight the Chipstead Valley turned right towards the south west and the railway then started its passage through the high ground of the North Downs. At first it was able to follow a short and some-what steeply rising valley, again hugging the east slope, but near the end of the mile-long straight there were left-hand and right-hand reverse curves each of 75 chains radius at the entrance to a cutting, which extended for all but 2 miles to the mouth of Merstham tunnel. This cutting was straight for about 1¾ miles, but then curved left initially at 190 chains and then at 90 chains, to the start of the tunnel. This cutting through the chalk of the North Downs, is one of the largest in the country, and is over 100 feet deep where the line enters the tunnel. The sides are very steeply sloping at about 4 to 1. The gradient continued at about 1 in 263 rising until shortly before the reverse curves, where the nominal figure of 1 in 264 was actually attained. The gradient eased off to 1 in 1024 about a ¼ mile before the north portal of the tunnel, and continued inside it for about ½ mile; this took the line to the summit, and was followed by a fall at 1 in 1181, steepening to 1 in 270 about 200 yards inside the south portal, at which gradient the fall continued for nearly 1¼ miles after emerging from the tunnel. The tunnel, as finally constructed, was 2013 yards long, and was straight. About ¼ mile after leaving Merstham tunnel the line emerged from cutting and entered a compound right-hand curve some ¾ mile long, starting at 120 chains but mostly at 79 chains, followed by a short straight and then about 500 yards of left hand curve (210 chains). By this point the chalk had given way to sand. The fall was no doubt intended to be uniform from just inside the south end of Merstham tunnel, but by later measurement it steepened very slightly to 1 in 265 while passing round the 210-chain curve. The site of the fourth station, Merstham, was just before the change of gradient. The provision of this station was the result of an Agreement between the London

& Brighton Railway and Rt. Hon. Frederick John, Lord Monson, made under the powers of the London & Brighton's Act, but it was not brought into use for nearly 5 months after the opening of the line, as will be recorded later. Lord Monson was the owner of Gatton Park, on the up side of the line. At the end of the 210-chain curve, there were over 1½ miles of straight, half way along which there was a reversal of gradient, the fall changing to a rise at 1 in 341. The fifth station (but only the third at opening) Red Hill and Reigate Road, was sited some ½ mile south of the commencement of the rise, some 20 miles 72 chains from London Bridge and nearly 12¼ miles from the start of the Brighton line proper. The station took its designation from the Red Hill gap in the hills, the sand being of a reddish tinge; it was intended to serve Reigate, an ancient market town once named Cherchfelle (Domesday book) but known as Reigata by 1170, about 1½ miles to the west. It was not the original intention to have a station there, as will be explained later. Red Hill itself had been called Redehelde in 1301. The earthworks were fairly light over this section.

South of Red Hill the line continued straight, as explained, for some ¾ mile, and then had a short 1-mile radius left-hand curve, a 600-yard straight, and nearly ½ mile of 60-chain left-hand curve succeeded at once by ¾ mile of 300-chain right-hand curve. After another ½ mile straight, and a further ½ mile left-hand curve of 400 chains radius, the line ran straight for nearly 7½ miles. The rise from just north of Red Hill became a fall at the 1-mile radius left-hand curve, and this continued for nearly 4 miles (i.e. over 1¼ miles along the straight) down the valley of the Mole; the gradient varied, but averaged about 1 in 250. Much of this length was on embankment ranging up to 30-35 feet high, the northern part passing over Earl(s) Wood Common (named after the Earl of Surrey) and hence being called Earlswood embankment. At the end of the fall the line had almost reached the level of the River Mole, and there was then a rise for some 6¼ miles, starting at about 1 in 880 and gradually steepening to conclude with 4 miles of 1 in 260. The top of this bank was half-way along a ½ mile length of 85-chain left-hand curve, which was part of the change of route to avoid Cuckfield tunnel — see end of Chapter VI.

The fourth station actually brought into use when the line was opened, named Horley*, was built about 600 yards south of the commencement of the rising gradient, about 25½ miles from London Bridge and about 16¾ miles south of the commencement of the London & Brighton Railway itself. Some 3½ miles beyond Horley was situated the next station, Three Bridges, rather more than halfway between which stations the line crossed the border between Surrey and Sussex and entered the latter county. Most of the line from Horley to the end of the long straight, some 2¼ miles south of Three Bridges, was practically at ground level, although there was an embankment on the north side of that station.

South of Three Bridges the soil changed, the sandy clay becoming an overburden to greensand and ironstone intermixed with beds of hard soil with occasional clay fissures. This area, known as the Sussex Weald and comprising Worth Forest on the east (or left-hand) side of the line, and Tilgate Forest on the west, had been a centre for the Sussex Iron trade, using charcoal for fuel to smelt the ironstone, and also for glass-making. It was, and still is, extremely well wooded. The ½ mile long 85-chain radius left-hand curve started on a short length of a low embankment and then entered a cutting which led to Balcombe tunnel, 1133 yards long and straight. As already stated, the summit of the rise from Horley was half-way around the curve to the north of Balcombe tunnel, where the line entered the cutting, some 25 chains before the tunnel mouth, and the route then fell for some 8½ miles, almost all at 1 in 264 (20 feet to the mile). On leaving Balcombe tunnel the line curved left for ½ mile at 80 chains radius, and then right for a slightly shorter distance at 75

---

*As originally planned, Horley would have been the third station on the line (the first and second being Croydon and Merstham respectively). Some 18 months before this section of the line was opened, however, it was decided to provide two further stations (at Godstone Road and Red Hill, as will be explained later) and this decision made Horley the fifth station. In the event Merstham was not brought into use until nearly 5 months after this section of the line was opened, so that Horley was actually the fourth station at opening.

chains radius. The cutting at the tunnel mouth was succeeded by an embankment. Almost at the start of the second curve was Balcombe, the next station, and this was followed by lengths of left-hand 86-chain curve (½ mile), straight (600 yards) and right-hand 100-chain curve (500 yards). Much of the line from Balcombe to this point was in cutting or embankment, up to about 40 ft. high on the west side. There followed the Ouse viaduct, 1475 ft. long.

South of the viaduct, the line had two right-hand curves each of about 100 chains radius, separated by almost a mile of straight. The embankment south of the viaduct was succeeded by a cutting, which commenced a short distance along the straight and ran on to a low embankment just after the line entered the second right-hand curve. The cutting was named after Copyhold Farm, on the left of the line. There was another farm with this same name near Redhill, but the name of that farm was not associated with any feature on the London & Brighton Railway. At the end of the second curve, already referred to, was Haywards Heath station, named after the adjacent town and the seventh on the line when the latter was opened, some 37 miles 55 chains from London Bridge and about 29 miles from the start of the London & Brighton Railway itself. From Haywards Heath southwards, the line was built almost straight for nearly 9 miles; the first curve was of 150 chains radius to the right, starting 2½ miles from Haywards Heath and extending just over ½ mile; a straight over 2½ miles long followed, and then there was ½ mile of 500-chain right-hand curve; finally there was a further 2½ miles straight broken by two very short left-hand curves of 80 and 110 chains radius respectively. The fall at 1 in 264 which started north of Balcombe tunnel continued without a break over the Ouse viaduct almost to Haywards Heath station, where it eased off slightly but continued to descend for 2½ miles until the 150-chain right-hand curve started. A rise for some 5¾ miles, mostly at 1 in 264, followed. Just south of Haywards Heath was a 250-yard straight tunnel, named after that town but sometimes incorrectly called Folly Hill tunnel. Haywards Heath tunnel was followed by Folly Hill cutting which ran out on to a long embankment which continued past the bottom of the descent and extended for some ½ mile up the succeeding rise. This embankment was mostly about 30 ft. high, and at the north end included a bridge over the Vale Stream. The southern part of this embankment ran to the east of St. John's Common.

Some 1¼ miles after the start of the rising gradient, the next station was built, named Burgess Hill after the adjacent village, whilst the succeeding one was over 2½ miles further on, and situated about the middle of the 500-chain right-hand curve; this station was named Hassocks Gate, after the toll gate on the turnpike road to Brighton to the west of the line. There were no major earthworks between the end of the embankment south of Haywards Heath and Burgess Hill, but from there south the line was to an increasing extent in cutting as it entered the chalk of the South Downs. About a mile south of Hassocks Gate there was the short 80-chain left-hand curve already noted, and after it the line then entered Clayton tunnel, 2266 yards long and straight. The rise at 1 in 264 continued through the tunnel, but at the south end it changed to a fall at the same gradient, the line rounding the short 110-chain left-hand curve already referred to, and then continued straight for some ½ mile. The tunnel was through the saddle connecting Wolstonbury Hill to the west of the alignment, with the western slopes of Ditchling Beacon, the highest point in the South Downs. The line of the tunnel was only very slightly to the east of the turnpike road south of Hassocks Gate, and the southern portal was at Pangdean just beyond where the western Brighton Road via Newtimber Gap joined the eastern one over Clayton Hill. South of the tunnel was the deep Clayton cutting, and beyond it a shallower cutting leading to another deep one, Brapool. The cutting was actually continuous from the portal of the tunnel to the south end of Brapool cutting, the line being taken on an 85-chain left-hand curve some ¾ mile long immediately to the west of the Brighton road. At the end of this curve there was about 30 chains of straight, followed by a similar length of 90-chain right-hand curve and a further 30 chains of straight, on which was situated Patcham tunnel, 488 yards long and straight.

Patcham tunnel was preceded and followed by short cuttings, themselves preceded and followed by embankments. South of the tunnel the alignment was almost all curved, starting with ½ mile of compound right-hand curve of 54/66 chains and followed immediately by ½ mile of 80 chains left-hand, thus forming a reverse curve. There was then ½ mile of straight, followed by a ½ mile compound left-hand curve of 100/30 chains. A very short straight was succeeded by reverse curves, left and right, of 47 and 30 chains radius respectively, to enter the station at Brighton. There was a further cutting south of the south embankment beyond Patcham tunnel, and the line was then taken along the eastern slope of a small hill so that there was a cutting side on the west and the occasional small embankment on the east. The terminus at Brighton was laid out on ground that was levelled for the purpose, the original cross-slope being downwards from west to east. The line terminated some 70 feet above the seashore, and about ½ mile from it. The falling gradient of 1 in 264 from the south end of Clayton tunnel continued to the start of the station yard, where the line was made level. Brighton station was 50 miles 46 chains from London Bridge, and was 41 miles 59 chains from the start of the London & Brighton Railway's line at (South) Norwood.

The lengths have already been given of the five tunnels on the line. All were of similar dimensions, 25 ft. maximum width by 25 ft. high to the crown of the arch, and all were brick-lined throughout. They were, of course, all built on slight gradients to facilitate drainage. Shafts were, as usual, sunk along the line of each tunnel to provide additional working faces and to facilitate removal of excavated material. Merstham tunnel was made by means of six shafts, giving, with the two ends, a total of fourteen working faces. At Balcombe tunnel there were five shafts and thus twelve working faces. Further south, Haywards Heath tunnel involved two shafts, Clayton tunnel eleven shafts and Patcham tunnel a single shaft. All shafts were left open, after completion of the tunnels, to facilitate ventilation. A castellated portal was built at the north entrance to Clayton tunnel, with a dwelling house between the two towers. This may have been built for the use of the man who had to look after the gas lighting in that tunnel — see the end of this chapter.

A large number of bridges was needed on the line, apart from the Ouse Viaduct. A typical overbridge just south of

123

Merstham tunnel is shown in Plate 5. Under-bridges were either brick arches or consisted of cast-iron girders on brick abutments; none presented any special features or difficulties. The Ouse Viaduct, for which David Mocatta was the architect, was 1475 feet long and the maximum height (towards the north end) was 96 ft; it consisted of 37 arches each of 30 ft. span, each pier containing a jack arch with a semi-circular soffit and invert to reduce the number of bricks needed as compared with a solid pier. The piers were tapered in elevation. At each end of each abutment there was an ornamental square open tower. The brickwork was faced with stone from Heddon quarries near Newcastle-upon-Tyne (Plate 6). All materials for the viaduct were brought by barge up the Ouse from Lewes. Overbridges were mostly brick arches of 30 ft. span. In all, 99 bridges had to be built between Croydon and Brighton. Bricks were as far as practicable made locally, to avoid unnecessarily long hauls over bad roads and ultimately, in some cases at occupation bridges, over farm tracks or fields.

Only two bridges need be referred to in any detail in this account. One of these was the first overbridge south of the junction forming the start of the Brighton company's line; it carried the public road from Croydon to Addiscombe and Beckenham across the line about ⅝ mile south of the junction and nearly ½ mile north of the Brighton company's Croydon station. The level of the public right-of-way, then, and now, called St. James' Road, leading into Addiscombe Road, had to be raised in order to cross the line. This bridge soon became known as Windmill Bridge, however, from an adjacent inn of that name, which had had to be resited to enable the railway to be built.

The second bridge to be noted in this history is situated about 6½ miles south of the junction with the Croydon company. This bridge had to be constructed over the line in order to serve a side road, in connection with the diversion of the Brighton turnpike. Previous to the building of the Brighton Railway, the turnpike had made a detour to the east south of Coulsdon, starting from a point on the present main road (A.23) about 200 yards south of the bridge which now carries the Quarry line over it immediately that line emerges from the former Cane Hill covered way; the original road, having gone near what was then called Hooley House and later Ashdown Park Hotel, rejoined the route of the present one about a mile farther south, and the track of the Croydon, Merstham & Godstone Railway kept close to the west side of the turnpike along this detour. About a third of the way along the original road, there was a side road to the right (or west). The need to obtain a nominally straight alignment for the London & Brighton Railway necessitated the purchase of the Croydon, Merstham & Godstone Railway as the latter's route had in part to be taken over and thus would have cut off the Croydon, Merstham & Godstone from its quarries at Merstham; this step was required under Section 40 of the Brighton company's Act, and the purchase was completed by the end of September 1838. The alignment of the Brighton company's route also entailed crossing the route of the turnpike twice, the respective levels at the north of the two positions being such that there would not have been sufficient clearance for trains to pass under a bridge. By straightening the turnpike and keeping it wholly to the west of the line required by the Brighton company's railway, difficulties of levels were overcome, but a bridge over the railway was necessary to maintain access from the diverted turnpike to the side road already mentioned. To-day it goes by the name of Woodplace Lane bridge, and is a straight-forward brick arch, square to the alignment of the railway.

There were five level crossings over public roads: at Stoats Nest, about a mile south of Godstone Road station; both north and south of Horley station; at Tinsley Green, 1 mile 53 chains north of Three Bridges; and south of Hassocks Gate station. The latter was soon replaced by an under-bridge. There were three crossings over private roads: Holmethorpe, north of Redhill; Copyhold, at the south end of Copyhold cutting; and Vale Road, about ½ mile south of Vale Pond bridge, and between there and Burgess Hill station. Footpath and occupation crossings were situated as follows: three footpaths between the south end of Earlswood embankment and Horley (Dene Farm, Pear Tree, and Denehurst respectively); four occupation crossings between Horley and Three Bridges (Oldlands, Forge, Summervere, and Park); three footpaths between Three Bridges and Balcombe Tunnel (Maiden Bower (later known as Humphrey

125

Farm), Balcombe Tunnel, and one other; a footpath crossing (Hour Glass) near Balcombe, and two others (Kemp's and Stone Hall) between Balcombe and the Ouse Viaduct; two occupation crossings beyond Vale Pond bridge (Farm, and Bodelands or Bedelands or Bedelwood); and two footpath crossings north of Burgess Hill. The occupation crossings had of course to be made where the line cut across the property of a single landowner and was more or less at ground level. Occupation bridges had naturally to be provided elsewhere.

The first station was at Croydon, which was laid out with four roads between the side platforms so that the latter were served by loops. A locomotive shed was also provided, as well as sidings and storage facilities, and the station had separate up and down booking offices. The station was planned for joint use with the South Eastern Railway, then under construction, and its general similarity of layout with the larger stations further south on the line to Brighton (see below) and on the South Eastern company's line, might be indicative of consultation between Rastrick and William Cubitt (the South Eastern's Engineer). Such layouts had already been used elsewhere by other companies, however, and the degree of commonality between the larger stations put up by the Brighton and South Eastern companies might have stemmed from such origins. The London & Brighton Railway survey of 1843 shows what appears to have been roofing extending over part of the length of each platform loop; this would have necessitated the use of columns between the loop and through roads on each side.

Godstone Road was only a two-platform station, but Merstham, Red Hill and Reigate Road, Horley, Three Bridges, Balcombe and Haywards Heath were provided with centre through roads and side platform loops as at Croydon. Burgess Hill (Plate 7) was only double-track with side platforms, but Hassocks Gate had four roads similar to Croydon. The Inspecting Officer, referring to Croydon, reported that 'not only here, but at almost all the stations on this line, the engineer had laid down four sets of rails, and built booking offices for both the up and down trains, so that the engines and carriages will not stop upon the main lines, nor the passengers have to cross the rails either in joining or leaving the carriages'.[1] This 'will tend much to the safety of the traveller, and is highly creditable to the Company'.[1] The 1843 survey shows that there was a short section of roofing over the middle of the down platform loop at Haywards Heath, presumably similar to the much larger roofs on both sides at Croydon, but at the other stations the platforms seem to have been uncovered.

Horley was laid out on a more extensive scale than the other intermediate stations south of Croydon, since it was decided that its position (almost half-way between London Bridge and Brighton) and its siting (with the line more or less at ground level on flat terrain, with water available from the River Mole), would be suitable for the erection of carriage sheds and workshops. Both the latter facilities were built on the up (or west) side of the line, whilst a goods yard was provided on the down (or east) side. Facilities were provided at Horley for horse and carriage traffic, in September 1841 — some two months after the station was opened and probably coincidentally with the opening of the line through to Brighton. The goods shed, on the down side, was however not completed until 28 November 1842.

Horley was built some 300 yards to the north of the present station, but was later rebuilt on its present site. Balcombe station was some distance north of the present station, and was later rebuilt on its present site. The present road underbridge immediately north of Haywards Heath station is somewhat nearer to London than the bridge which was at the north end of the station when the latter was opened, the station platforms being later extended northwards when the station was rebuilt.

No plan of Brighton at the time of opening has been found, but it is known that the station area was relatively extensive and was covered in part by a saw-tooth roof. There was a ticket platform beside the down road some 120 yards south of Montpelier bridge. The goods yard was to the east of the passenger station and some 30 feet below it due to the land sloping down to the east. Rail access was by an incline which started immediately east of the first bridge over the Shoreham line (i.e. New England Road), the track then descending in a cutting to reach a tunnel under the passenger station, from which it emerged to enter the goods yard area at the north-west corner of the latter. Reversals both at New England bridge and in the passenger station were therefore necessary for freight traffic between Brighton and stations to London. Although this connection to the goods yard was only used for a few years, part of the tunnel still exists. A photograph taken in 1970 by a member of a party being conducted around the area by the Author, is reproduced as Plate 8.

David Mocatta, who had been engaged as the Brighton company's architect, designed imposing buildings for Brighton (Plate 9), but prepared an overall plan for the buildings at intermediate stations. This plan was based upon the use of units or modules, and must have been one of the earliest instances on United Kingdom railways of the application of the principles of standardization in building design. Each station was given individual treatment regarding details: Hassocks Gate, for example, was finished in plain cottage style with Italianate touches (Plate 10), whereas Three Bridges included Italianate features.

Cottages for the accommodation of staff were erected at various places remote from villages, where water was available.

As previously explained, the Act for the construction of the London & Brighton Railway also covered the building of a branch line from Brighton to Shoreham and another from Brighton to Lewes and then on to Newhaven. Both of these lines were planned with an eye to the shipping traffic, as both towns, being at the mouths of rivers (the Adur and the Ouse respectively) had harbour facilities, which Brighton did not have. It was one of the arguments in favour of the Dorking route that the approach to Brighton would be through Shoreham, thus avoiding the necessity for a separate line to that place. Supporters of the 'direct' route to Brighton maintained that as Newhaven was closer than Shoreham to Dieppe on the French coast, the commercial return from a line to Newhaven would exceed that from one to Shoreham. The company received powers to construct lines to both ports, but in the event only that from Brighton to Shoreham was actually constructed by the London & Brighton Railway. The Newhaven line, which was built subsequently, will be described in a later chapter.

By comparison with the main line, the Shoreham branch,

which started at the entrance to Brighton station, was relatively easy to build, since it did not involve any heavy engineering works. Leaving Brighton by a 17-chain left-hand curve about ¼ mile long in the course of which it was joined by the branch from the goods yard, the line fell steadily at gradients ranging from 1 in 145 to 1 in 256 for a mile, having a straight stretch for some 30 chains after the curve at Brighton, and then again curving left at 150 chains radius for about ½ mile to bring the alignment round from the northerly direction on which the line started from Brighton, to a westerly direction. The line fell at 1 in 115 towards the end of this length. This section from Brighton had to be taken through the relatively high ground to the west-north-west of the terminus at Brighton, the land sloping down to the east over the area selected for the terminus (and thus necessitating the goods yard, east of the passenger station, being at a lower level than the latter, as already explained). With the line proceeding west it continued more or less straight and with a steady fall as it approached the coast at Shoreham. The gradient ranged from 1 in 222 to 1 in 330, with a few chains of 1 in 189 approaching Shoreham. The few curves, all relatively short, were over 180 chains radius except for a very short right-hand one of 80 chains about 5 miles after Brighton and approaching Shoreham. The line continued past Kingston, to serve the harbour, and finished at Shoreham. It was 5 miles 72 chains in length.

There was an overbridge (New England Road) followed by a 231-yard tunnel (Hove) shortly after leaving Brighton, and also various overbridges. Hove station* was situated a short distance west of the tunnel. There was one further overbridge, but there were nine under-bridges (Plates 11 and 12), all ten being brick arches except for one under-bridge with iron girders about ¾ mile west of Hove station. There were two level crossings over public roads: one on the east (or Brighton) side of Portslade,[2] the second station on the line; and the second approaching Shoreham. Also, there were four occupation crossings between Portslade and Southwick, the first being Brickfield and the second Gard-

*Later replaced.

ner's; the last two do not seem to have had specific names.

The stations were at Hove, Portslade, Southwick, Kingston, and Shoreham. None had any particular features of merit; fairly extensive siding accommodation was provided at Kingston, necessitating tracks, reached by wagon turntables, crossing the turnpike road on the level to reach the harbour. An extension beyond Shoreham was probably already in view as the west end of that station was not closed by buildings across the tracks.

The company having obtained its Act on 15 July 1837, commenced raising capital and setting up its organisation. It appointed John Urpeth Rastrick as its Resident Engineer,[3] with Messrs. E. I. Maude and T. H. Statham as Resident Engineers at Cuckfield for the Central District and Brighton respectively. There would probably have been a third Resident Engineer for the northern part of the line. It also established a Committee of Works which, because it usually met on Fridays, became known as the Friday Committee. This committee was chaired by Mr. John Harman, who was Chairman of the board of directors. Another director was Mr. J. L. Goldsmid, who owned an extensive area of property at Hove and through which the Shoreham branch would be taken; he attended the meetings of the committee dealing with matters between St. John's Common (south of Haywards Heath) and Brighton, and with the Shoreham branch, whenever points concerning his own property were to be discussed. It has been stated that constructional work actually commenced on 19 March 1838,[4] which was a Monday. Another account, which is probably correct, gives the date of commencement as 12 July 1838;[5] reports, quoted below, of the Committee meetings held in May certainly convey the impression that constructional work had not then started, and the first contract that the Author has discovered was not dated until 17 September 1838 (see Appendix to this chapter). It is thought that initial operations commenced north of Haywards Heath. At a meeting of the St. John's Common to Brighton and Shoreham Branch Division of the Friday Committee on 4 May 1838 it was resolved that:[6]

    (a) the Engineer (Rastrick) should prepare plans for obtaining such lands as might be required for the main line on the committee's district, and for the Shoreham branch;

(b) the Solicitors should take measures to obtain possession of the lands required for each of these lines;

and

(c) Captain Heaviside be authorized to arrange with the magistrates of Brighton as to the employment of police officers, and to make the necessary appointments.

Two Fridays later, on 18 May, Captain Heaviside reported to the Committee the satisfaction of the Brighton magistrates with the plan to appoint police when the works were commenced. It was also reported at that meeting of the Committee that two trial shafts were to be sunk at Burgess Hill to determine the nature of the soil, and that various matters concerned with the acquisition of property were proceeding. Accordingly Rastrick was authorized to advertise contracts for the works between Brighton and Shoreham, and to give orders for two engines to work the branch.

The following week the Committee met twice: on Friday 25 May to discuss compensation terms with Mr. Gorringe and his solicitor who owned wharf land at Kingston in the parish of Southwick; and on Saturday 26 May to reach an agreement with the Trustees of the Brighton and Cuckfield roads for diverting the turnpike over Clayton Hill to enable the tunnel to be constructed under the site of the existing road (through which the shafts had to be sunk). The next point which must be recorded was the agreement reached with Mr. Goldsmid on Friday 8 June 1838 that 'there shall be no manufactury allowed, nor coals deposited in the Depot to be made on his (Mr. Goldsmid's) property, so that Coals shall not pass down the road through his property (at Hove);' the Committee recommended to the Brighton company's board that they should accede to this agreement.[6]

In the meantime steps were being taken to acquire authorized property along the line of the route, including, in the parish of Croydon alone, some 124 dwellings, two ponds, the School of Industry, and the Windmill public house. The Croydon Merstham & Godstone company's property had also to be acquired, as required under Section 40 of the

Brighton company's Act. The Croydon Merstham & Godstone Railway asked £42,000 for their property, but the Brighton company considered this to be far too high. Eventually the matter went to arbitration, as a result of which the Croydon Merstham & Godstone company accepted the sum of £9,614. The purchase was completed by September 1838. These negotiations took place against the backcloth of discussions between the Brighton and South Eastern companies arising from the provisions of Section 135 of the Brighton company's Act, under which the latter company was liable to have to sell to the South Eastern company the line which they (the Brighton company) were authorized to build between Penge and Redhill. When this matter was finally concluded in 1839 by the provisions of South Eastern Railway Act No. 3, it only empowered the South Eastern company to purchase the southern part of the Brighton company's line from Penge to Redhill, but this part included that portion of the former Croydon Merstham & Godstone Railway's route south of Coulsdon which was actually incorporated in the London & Brighton's line.

Contracts were let during 1838 and 1839, details of those which the Author has been able to trace being given in the Appendix to this chapter. These all relate to the main line and the the Brighton station area, and show that at least nine different firms held contracts for this part of the work. All contracts listed covered maintenance of the work for 1 year after completion, and naturally laid down specific requirements for the works concerned, but Contract No. 13 in particular included provisions affecting the permanent way which must be referred to in this history:

Clause 74 stated that points and crossings were to be laid with sleepers on stone blocks;

Clause 71 required expansion gaps to be left between lengths of rail;

and Clause 70 called for wrought iron or wood keys, the rails to be inclined to suit wheel coning, and cant to be arranged as required by the engineer.

Clause 70 also stated that at that time (i.e. when the contract was signed, namely on 17 September 1838) the gauge of the railway had not been settled. The Author has not established when it was decided to adopt the standard gauge (originally 4ft. 9 in. was adopted on the Brighton line), but it was presumably some time before the London & Croydon company opened their line to traffic on 5 June 1839.

Contract No. 12 required stone to be taken from Tilgate Forest and Turner's Hill.

It would seem that formal contracts were not let for two, at any rate, of the sections north of Redhill, possibly because of the transfer of this part of the line to the South Eastern Railway.

There was a separate contract for the Shoreham branch, the contractors being Messrs. John Hale and George Wythes of Frimley.

Difficulties inevitably occurred during construction, Balcombe tunnel being one of the trouble spots due to water at the south end; this tunnel has always been very wet, sufficient water being contained above it to serve a well supplying the company's cottages built on top of the tunnel. Hence one normally kept one's head inside the cab of a steam locomotive when passing through this tunnel. The first mention of such problems seems to have been at a meeting of the Committee of Works on Wednesday 22 August 1838.[7] These constructional difficulties were overcome, however, and at a meeting of the Committee on Thursday 4 October it was reported that the works on both Balcombe and Clayton tunnels 'were progressing very fast and most satisfactorily', the works at Hassocks Gate were proceeding well, and that on the westward end of the Shoreham branch the contractor had already got temporary track in use for muck-shifting.[8]

Work at the northern end was not going so quickly, a major factor no doubt being the extremely heavy work involved in the construction of the enormous cutting north of Merstham Tunnel. Since chalk normally stood well, the cutting sides were to be steeply pitched in order to save costs by reducing the width of land needed at the top of the cutting, and also the amount of excavation. The steep pitch would have made it virtually impossible to have taken the excavated material to the top of the cutting sides by means of horse-runs, in the manner then common with clay or other soils. Moreover, the great depth of cutting accentuated the waste of effort which would have been involved if the chalk had been taken up to the top when it was actually needed at rail level to form embankments.

No record has been found by the Author of the method actually employed to make this cutting, or, for that matter, the other heavy chalk one south of Clayton Tunnel, but it may well have been similar to that later used in the construction of the chalk cuttings on either side of Falmer Tunnel on the line between Brighton and Lewes, and described in Chapter XII.

The Committee responsible for progress on the Croydon to Horley division instructed Mr. Rastrick on Monday 14 January 1839 to furnish the plans for the railway to cross the line of the Croydon Canal immediately south of the point of the junction with the London & Croydon Railway near Sellhurst Farm. These plans were needed so that the Committee could make suitable arrangements with the Croydon company (which of course now owned the canal) for possession.[9] A detailed description of the alignment of the Brighton line is given near the start of this chapter.

Shortly after leaving Brighton, the Shoreham branch passed through land owned by Mr. Kemp (whose name is remembered in Kemp Town on the east side of Brighton). It had originally been intended that there should be a tunnel at this point, but later it was decided to have a cutting here through the chalk.[10] As a result the straight tunnel under Mr. Goldsmid's property at Hove was only 231 yards long. Mr. Rastrick now recommended that the land in the fork between the London line and the Shoreham branch, just outside the terminus at Brighton, should be purchased as a tipping ground for the chalk from the cutting through Mr. Kemp's property. This land covered about 5 acres and was purchased and used as a tip accordingly. These decisions were ratified by a meeting of the committee on Wednesday 30 January 1839.[10] The resulting hill of chalk was thus man-made, and was not the remains of a larger hill through which the Main and Shoreham lines were cut, as has been stated elsewhere.[11]

The first permanent track on the main line was laid on Monday 4 February 1839 at Hassocks Gate, by Mr. Alfred Morris.[12] The committee meeting on Friday 5 April 1839 was adjourned until Saturday 6 April, when the members took note with satisfaction that the permanent way on the Shoreham branch had been laid for a distance of nearly 4 miles, and that Hove tunnel was well forward.[13]

It was no doubt now becoming clear that the Shoreham branch would be ready for opening at least a year before the main line to the junction with the London & Croydon company. Hence Rastrick suggested to the Committee on Friday 12 April 1839 that one line only be proceeded with on the Shoreham branch until the works were complete, thus postponing capital outlay unnecessary in the early stages of the company. The Committee agreed with this proposal.[14] Immediately after leaving Brighton for London, the Main line crossed over New England road, and a ceremony was arranged for Monday 27 May 1839 at which the first stone of the bridge would be laid. A lodge of Freemasons in Brighton assisted in the ceremony.[15]

Difficulties were developing at Kingston, where the Trustees of the Shoreham turnpike objected to the laying of rails across it to enable the railway to reach wharves at the harbour. Rastrick proposed that the rails on either side of the turnpike should be brought level with the surface of the latter, and that wagons should be drawn across the road surface and re-railed on the opposite side. The Committee met on Monday 6 July 1839 and agreed with Rastrick's suggestion.[16] This was not the end of the matter, however, as a final solution was only found in 1841 (see Chapter VIII).

It should now be recalled that the London & Croydon Railway had been formally opened on Saturday 1 June 1839 (Chapter IV), and that public traffic had commenced on the following Wednesday 5 June. As the way to London was now open once the Brighton company had completed their line, every effort was made to press ahead with the construction of the Brighton's lines. The following statistics have remained on record.[17]

Date	Men	Horses	Locomotives
July 1839	4,769	570	—
January 1840	4,370	695	5
July 1840	6,206	960	5

In the preceding chapter, reference is made to the reliance placed on the experience of the Liverpool & Manchester Railway, as being the first 'main line' railway to be opened. Experience in all railway matters was so limited that it was commonplace for one railway to take note of another company's practice when proposing to make some change in its own previous practice, or to institute something new. Thus it is recorded at the committee meeting on Friday 29 November 1839, that Mr. Rastrick was authorized at that meeting to build a booking office and waiting room for passengers at Hove on Mr. Goldsmid's land, the accommodation to be similar to that at Weybridge station on the London & Southampton Railway.[18]

The winter of 1839 — 1840 seems to have been very wet, as a result of which there was delay in making embankments — particularly that at Earlswood. A considerable amount of chalk from Merstham cutting was used as fill, but was so wet that it had to be put temporarily to spoil.[19] This was a factor in postponing the opening date of the first section of the main line, as will be recorded later, but the weather did not have so much effect on the easier works on the Shoreham branch, which was nearing completion in the early spring of 1840. It was, in fact, opened on Tuesday 12 May, apparently as a double line from the start. It no doubt facilitated building the southern part of the main line, at any rate, as material could be brought by sea to Shoreham and then taken by rail to Brighton.

In order to start earning revenue, now that the Croydon company had their line in use, consideration was given to opening the Brighton line between Croydon and the north end of Merstham tunnel, and providing a station there in the cutting below the Star inn at Hooley on the Brighton turnpike. The Committee of Works resolved on Friday 14 August 1840 that terminal facilities be built at that point, comprising a temporary roof to cover engines, carriages, etc., at Hooley Lane, steps from the cutting with covering, sheds for carriages, and a blacksmith's shop.[20] At Merstham, a short distance beyond the south end of Merstham tunnel, 'Turning plates' (i.e. turntables) and water tanks were to be provided, in readiness for opening a further length of line south of the tunnel.[20] Passengers would presumably have joined south-bound trains, and left north-bound ones, at a station further south which was to be built by agreement with Lord Monson, the owner of Gatton Park.

On the same date, the Committee also resolved that 'a small wooden building be erected at the junction of the Godstone Road for passengers', and that 'a small station be built at Red Hill'. It was clearly hoped that the former would provide some revenue as soon as the line could be opened from Croydon to Hooley, but the expectations cannot have been very high because, as already noted, the station would be some 8 miles from Godstone village. The station at Red Hill was intended to serve the ancient market town of Reigate. The Committee also decided that carriage sheds should be erected at Balcombe, and that engines and carriages be 'kept at Croydon, with an early train to London'.[20] Mr. Rastrick, who, as Resident Engineer, was responsible for the building of the railway, was asked to furnish plans as necessary and to proceed accordingly. Mr. David Mocatta had been engaged as the company's architect, and on Tuesday 1 September 1840 he accompanied Mr. Harman (the Chairman) and Mr. Rastrick to Croydon to set out the station there, and then proceeded to Redhill to mark the site for the station there.[21] In the event, the works at Hooley and immediately south of Merstham tunnel were not undertaken, and eventually the first section of the main line to be opened extended as far south as Haywards Heath (see later).

In the meantime there had been complaints about the draughtiness under the roof of Brighton station, and it was therefore decided on Saturday 26 September 1840 that the ends (of the saw-tooth roof) of that station should be closed in 'as a protection against the winter winds'.[22] No doubt the work was soon put in hand. Further north, there were difficulties where the Brighton turnpike was being diverted near Hooley House, troubles occurring in connection with road works, fences on the diversion, and the bridge (now called Woodplace Lane). The Trustees of the road made an inspection of the works on Monday 23 November, and were apparently very courteous and helpful.[23]

The winter of 1840–1841 brought bad weather, and the Committee became increasingly concerned about the slow progress, particularly of Messrs. Thornton's contracts (from St. John's Common, south of Haywards Heath, to Clayton tunnel). The position was noted at their meeting at the Old Ship Hotel at Brighton on Monday 8 March 1841,[24] and on Saturday, 17 April and Monday 19 April the Committee inspected the whole line. The position at that weekend was recorded as being as follows:

(1) Croydon station nearly completed;
(2) Still much earth to be removed from the cutting leading to Merstham tunnel;
(3) Earlswood embankment still slipping slightly;
(4) Coping being laid on Ouse viaduct, and structure ready for wheel timbers to be laid;
(5) Folly Hill cutting not finished, and temporary tunnel being opened out;
(6) Keymer Parish embankment south of the Vale Pond bridge still tending to slip slightly;
(7) Burgess Hill cutting not proceeding, and no work done since last inspection;
(8) Rails not yet laid, except in the tunnels;
(9) General — lack of stone to finish the Ouse viaduct, and lack of rails everywhere.[25]

Haywards Heath tunnel, immediately south of the station and north of Folly Hill cutting, was found to be very wet, and remained so until recent years.

Great efforts were made to supply stone and rails against (9) above, and also to complete the works at (1), (2) and (3), so that the line could be opened to Haywards Heath. The shortage of rails, at any rate, was in part due to the iron industry, although expanding, being unable to meet demands from all the railways then under construction. When the line was complete as far as Haywards Heath it was inspected by Lt. Col. Sir Frederick Smith, Inspector-General of Railways, and was opened thus far on Monday, 12 July 1841. Also, heavy pressure was put on Messrs. Thornton to complete their section without further delay. This was done quickly and enabled Rastrick to report to the Committee on Saturday 7 August [26] that the remainder of the line, from Haywards Heath to Brighton, might be opened by 14 September. The line was in fact eventually opened through to Brighton on Tuesday 21 September 1841, the Committee having held its final meeting on the Saturday before, in order to clear up details.[27] At London Bridge a small goods depot was constructed to the north of the Croydon station on land purchased by the Croydon company from the Greenwich company in 1836 (Chapter II) but not yet utilized. The cost of the line is stated to have been £2,634,059, or £57,262 per mile.[28]

The permanent way laid down on the London & Brighton Railway reflected the experience gained by the considerable number of important lines now open and carrying traffic. The London & Croydon Railway, it will be recalled, had used flat-bottom rail carried on longitudinal timbers, themselves resting on wood cross-sleepers, whereas the broad gauge Great Western had used a bridge-section rail carried on longitudinal timbers, themselves supported at intervals on vertical wood piles. Experience had shown, however, that the use of piles under longitudinal timbers was undesirable, and the Great Western decided to carry their road on longitudinal timbers only. Stone blocks had of course also been used by various companies (including the London & Greenwich). Other companies, however, were obtaining satisfactory results by using chairs carried on wood cross-sleepers without any longitudinal timbers, and this general mode of construction soon became accepted practice.

When the gauge was determined as the standard 4 ft. 8½ in. (originally 4 ft. 9 in. in the case of the Brighton company), probably early in 1839, the type of permanent way was also finally settled. It consisted of double-headed iron rails weighing 75 lb. per yard, carried in chairs mounted on timber cross-sleepers, except apparently in cuttings where the same track was itself carried on stone blocks. The section of the rail employed is shown in Figure 22, and shows that the bottom was larger than the top (or running surface). Special arrangements must have been made where the Brighton metals joined those of the Croydon company, but the Author has found no record of the matter.

Signalling seems to have been by means of pairs of round discs mounted one on either side of a vertical rod, which could itself be rotated in bearings through 90°. To stop a train, the two discs were presented full-face to the driver, who thus saw them side-by-side; when presented edge-on and thus nearly invisible, the signal signified 'proceed'. A lamp fastened to the rod, and thus rotated through 90° with it, was used for night working; presumably a red light was

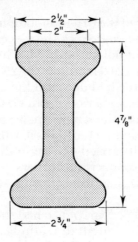

Figure 22. London & Brighton Railway Rail Section. (Bottom larger than top (or running surface)).

shown when the discs were turned full-face to an approaching train, and a white light when the signal was turned to 'proceed' (Figure 23). It is thought that the discs themselves were painted a red-orange colour.

Except that the Brighton company's signals were each provided with two discs, whereas those on the Croydon and

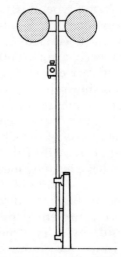

Figure 23. London & Brighton Railway Stop Signal.

Greenwich companies' lines had single discs, the basic principles and presentation of signals to drivers were the same. Working at the junction south of Jolly Sailor, where the Brighton joined the Croydon, was presumably regulated by drivers themselves keeping a good lookout, in addition to hand signals from the pointsman: there is no record of any route-indicating signals having been provided, such as were still in use at London Bridge and Corbett's Lane on the Greenwich line.

The three longest tunnels on the line, Merstham, Balcombe, and Clayton, were originally whitewashed and lit by gas, the jets being mounted on each side-wall. Small gasworks were established for this purpose. That for Merstham was situated on the down side of the line some ¾ miles south of the tunnel, at a position somewhat south of the present Merstham station. That for Balcombe was on the up side some ¼ mile south of the tunnel, just north of milepost 33. That for Clayton seems to have been on the down side, at Hassocks Gate, but this is not certain. It has been stated[29] that a small gas-works was built there by the railway company in 1849 to supply the lighting in Clayton tunnel, and was later taken over by a local company. Since the tunnel lighting had almost certainly been given up by 1849, a gas-works only constructed in that year must have been for some purpose other than lighting Clayton tunnel. What is more likely is that the site of the 1841 works was used in 1849 for a new works whose output was used for non-tunnel purposes.

The method of supplying coal to the Merstham and Balcombe gas-works is assumed to have been by carting it from the stations concerned, as sidings do not seem to have been provided at the works themselves. The assumed site of the gas-works at Hassocks Gate was, of course, adjacent to that station.

The other two tunnels on the main line (Haywards Heath and Patcham), and Hove tunnel on the Shoreham line, may also have been illuminated, but no records of this have been discovered by the Author, who considers that their relative shortness would not have justified their being lit.

The lighting of tunnels was presumably to lessen the fears of the public, then still quite unaccustomes to trains let alone travelling through tunnels in unlit stock, and it must have been of some help in maintaining the permanent way and the tunnel structures. Except in the vicinity of station or yard lamps, however, drivers could not (and still cannot) normally see the road in front of them at night in any case, so that passage of an unlit tunnel by day was to them little different from night-time travel. It must have been a virtually impossible task to have attempted to keep the tunnels clean enough for the whitewash to have been effective, even with coke-burning locomotives, whilst the passage of trains must have blown out gas jets from time to time. The Author has not found any evidence to show when the lighting was discontinued, but it was probably after a relatively short period.

It has also been stated[30] that some of the tunnels were lined with corrugated-iron sheeting to avoid water falling on open third-class carriages. If this is true, it presumably referred to the two wettest tunnels, Balcombe and Haywards Heath, and to the period when third-class accommodation was first provided on the main line (by 1843).

For convenience the dates of opening are repeated:

Brighton-Shoreham   Tuesday 12 May 1840.
Junction with London & Croydon Railway-Haywards Heath   Monday 12 July 1841.

Haywards Heath-Brighton   Tuesday 21 September 1841.

APPENDIX
LONDON & BRIGHTON RAILWAY
Contracts for Main Line
Particulars still exist of the following Contracts in date order:

NO.	DATE	WORK	VALUE	CONTRACTOR
13	17 September 1838	Burgess Hill-North end of Clayton Tunnel	£57,647	James & George Thornton of Walton.
6	26 September 1838	South of Earlswood Common to Horley	—	Thomas Earl of Woking, John Pearce of Weybridge. (John Gates of Hermitage and Thomas Brassey of Popham Lane giving sureties).
7	20 November 1838	Horley-North end of Balcombe Tunnel	—	David Harris and Thomas Gregory of Bristol, and William Henderson of Bath.
9	20 December 1838	South end of Balcombe Tunnel to North end of Ouse Viaduct	£41,500	John Hubbersty of Winchester.
11	3 January 1839	South end of Ouse Viaduct to Haywards Heath	£51,940	Samuel Briggs of Lindfield.
12	5 January 1839	Haywards Heath to Burgess Hill	£55,000	James & George Thornton of Walton.
10	21 January 1839	Ouse Viaduct and approaches	£38,500	Benjamin Baylis of Stratford-on-Avon.
16	6 April 1839	South end of Patcham Tunnel to north of New England road bridge at Brighton	£27,267 16s.	John Hale & George Wythes of Frimley.
18	6 April 1839	New England road bridge and east of Hove Tunnel to Brighton	£20,000	John Hale & George Wythes of Frimley.
17	6 April 1839	Auxiliary Works	£2,726 15s. 7d.	John Hale & George Wythes of Frimley, Francis Treadwell of Hartley Row, and John Treadwell of Littleborough.

The Author has been unable to trace the remaining contracts, but their scope may be deduced by re-arranging the above known contracts in geographical order so as to ascertain the gaps. The result is as follows:

NO.	WORKS	CONTRACTOR (WHERE KNOWN) AND REMARKS
(1)	Junction with Croydon company to Sanderstead Road	The bridge over Selsdon Road would probably have been the dividing point between Nos. 1 and 2.
(2)	Sanderstead Road to Coulsdon	Coulsdon was probably the dividing point between Nos. 1 and 2.
(3)	Coulsdon to North end of Merstham Tunnel	Penfold*†
(4)	(Merstham Tunnel)	Hoof*
(5)	South end of Merstham Tunnel to South end of Earlswood Common	(Treadwell (?))
6	South of Earlswood Common to Horley	Earl & Pearce.
7	Horley to North end of Balcombe Tunnel	Harris, Gregory & Henderson.
(8)	(Balcombe Tunnel)	—
9	South end of Balcombe Tunnel to North end of Ouse Viaduct	Hubbersty.
10	Ouse Viaduct and approaches	Baylis
11	South end of Ouse Viaduct to Haywards Heath	Briggs.
12	Haywards Heath to Burgess Hill	Thornton & Thornton.
13	Burgess Hill to North end of Clayton Tunnel	Thornton & Thornton.
(14)	(Clayton Tunnel)	—
(15)	(South end of Clayton Tunnel to) (south end of Patcham Tunnel)	—
16	South end of Patcham Tunnel to north end of New England Road bridge	Hale & Wythes.
17	Auxiliary Works	Hale & Wythes and Treadwell & Treadwell.
18	Brighton Station area	Hale & Wythes.

*Formal contracts not let.
†The Contractors name has also been given as Green (see Charles E. C. Townsend, *Further Notes on Early Railways in Surrey*, Newcomen Society, 1950, 3).

NOTES

1. Sekon, C. A. 'The Evolution of a Popular Railway', quoting the Inspecting Officer's report. *Railway & Travel Monthly.* 3 (1911), 183.
2. The station was resited to the east of the level crossing in 1881.
3. Rastrick had had a distinguished career, having held partnerships in locomotive building firms and having been one of the judges at the Rainhill trials on the Liverpool & Manchester Railway in 1829, as well as having been engineer to a number of railways.
4. *Centenary of the Opening of the Shoreham Branch and Brighton Station.* Southern Railway, 1940, 11. (Author's Note: This pamphlet contains many errors in its statements).
5. *Surrey Life,* 4 (May) 1975), 36. This gives numerous quotations from *The Illustrated London News,* without identifying the actual Issue(s) of that periodical in which the original statements were made. (Author's Note: The I.L.N. statements probably appeared in 1844).
6. Original Minutes held by Public Records Office at 66 Porchester Road, London, W.2.,* local reference LBR 1/26.
7. *Ibid.,* LBR 1/25.
8. *Ibid.,* LBR 1/26.
9. *Ibid.,* LBR 1/24.
10. *Ibid.,* LBR 1/26.
11. Morris, O. J., and Lacey, E. R. 'The Railway at Brighton — in 1859 and 1934'. *Southern Railway Magazine.* 1934, 337.
12. Dendy Marshall, C. F. *A History of the Southern Railway.* Southern Railway Company, 1936, 267. Also 2nd Edition, revised by Kidner, R. W., Ian Allan, 1963, Vol. 1, 201.
13. Original Minutes held by Public Records Office at 66 Porchester Road, London, W.2.,* local reference LBR 1/26.
14. *Ibid.,* LBR 1/23.
15. *Ibid.,* LBR 1/26.
16. *Ibid.,* LBR 1/26.
17. Dendy Marshall, C. F. *A History of the Southern Railway.* Southern Railway Company 1936, 266.
Also 2nd Edition, revised by Kidner, R. W., Ian Allan, 1963. Vol. 1, 201.
18. Original Minutes held by Public Records Office at 66 Porchester Road, London, W.2.,* under local reference LBR 1/26.
19. *Ibid.,* LBR 1/24 (entry for Wednesday 5 February 1840).
20. *Ibid.,* LBR 1/23.
21. *Ibid.,* LBR 1/23.
22. *Ibid.,* LBR 1/26.

*Correct at date of going to press.

NOTES — *continued*
23. *Ibid.*, LBR 1/24.
24. *Ibid.*, LBR 1/26.
25. *Ibid.*, LBR 1/26.
26. *Ibid.*, LBR 1/26.
27. *Ibid.*, LBR 1/26.
28. *Surrey Life.* 4 (May 1975), 36. This quotes from *The Illustrated London News,* probably in 1844.
29. Southern Railway Magazine XII (1934), 375-376.
30. Sekon, G. A. 'The Evolution of a Popular Railway', *Railway & Travel Monthly,* 3 (1911), 183.

CHAPTER EIGHT

The first years
of the Croydon
and Brighton Companies

A S THE first length of the main line of the London &
Brighton Railway, from Norwood to Haywards Heath,
was not opened until 12 July 1841, whereas the London &
Croydon Railway had been opened on 5 June 1839, the
Croydon company had some two years experience of operating and of working over the Greenwich company, before the
Brighton company's trains started to run over the metals of
both these railways. It is therefore now necessary to devote
some space to the methods of operating concerned and to the
provisions being made for handling the traffic of the
Brighton company, and, later, that of the South Eastern
company.

The Greenwich company's line was virtually level, and so
was the first part of the Croydon company's line from
Corbett's Lane to New Cross. Between New Cross and
Dartmouth Arms there was a rise mostly at 1 in 100, whilst
from Dartmouth Arms to Croydon the line was again practically level. The steep rise from New Cross to Dartmouth
was unavoidable as the line had to climb the northern slope
of the arc of hills south of London, as explained in
Chapter I, and it was early decided to employ assistant
locomotives over this length. This policy was no doubt one
factor leading to the decision that the locomotive department should be situated at New Cross, at the foot of the bank,
or 'inclined plane' as it was called.

Down passenger trains started from London Bridge and
stopped at all stations. Hence there was no difficulty in
putting an additional engine on the train at New Cross if
this were necessary, and subsequently taking it off at

Dartmouth Arms. As will be recorded later, however, the light weight of passenger trains (taring under 20 tons!) could hardly have given much trouble up the bank in the ordinary way. Down freight trains would have been another matter, but as they commenced their journeys at New Cross, as already explained, they could readily be assisted from the start. No positive evidence has been found by the Author as to whether the extra locomotive was attached in front as a pilot engine, or assisted in the rear as a banker, but the probability is that for freight trains the practice was to bank. This method reduced the risk of breakaways due to weak couplings, as well as enabling the banker to drop off at Dartmouth Arms without stopping the train. The latter method was certainly employed in later years, and persisted when necessary up to the end of steam traction, and it seems reasonable to assume that it was used from the start. No record has been found of the method of returning assisting engines to New Cross, but it is not impossible that they may have been worked back as pilots to up freight trains when necessary, rather than light, to provide additional brake power down the bank. In 1845 the only crossover between the down and up lines at Dartmouth Arms was at the country (Croydon) end of the station, and there is no evidence of any crossover at the London end at an earlier period. Hence if returning engines were placed in front of up trains, the latter would have had to have been stopped for the purpose before entering Dartmouth Arms station. Engines off down trains could be stood by in the down sidings south of the station, to await a path for a working back to New Cross.

A regular hourly interval service of passenger trains was operated from the opening day, starting from each end at 20 minutes past the hour and, as already stated, calling at all stations. The first up and down trains left Croydon and London Bridge respectively at 08 20, and the last at 21 20. There were no trains in either direction at 12 20 or 13 20. This service ran on Mondays to Saturdays inclusive, and there was a similar one on Sundays, which however did not start until 09 20 and in which 'church interval' was observed by omitting the 11 20 and 12 20 services from each end. An interval service had been instituted from the start on the London & Greenwich line, and the Croydon's service no doubt took into account the desirability of regular timings when running over the Greenwich. As the Greenwich services themselves were at 15-minute intervals, it follows that there must have been some relatively short headways in each direction above Corbett's Lane, thus illustrating the need for the route-indicating signal at the junction.

The trains of the two companies were distinguished by different head signals. By day, the conductor of each Croydon train rode on the leading vehicle and held out, on the right-hand side, a red ball at the end of a rod; by night, engines of Croydon trains carried 'a double white light'. Greenwich trains were not marked in any way, and their engines carried no head light at all at night. (Presumably no operating or engineering staff were expected to be on the permanent way of that company at night). A red tail light was carried at night by all trains of both companies, but there seems to be no record of any tail signals by day.

With the exception of the route-indicating signals at Corbett's Lane and London Bridge, which of course had to be treated as stop signals by the trains of one company if they showed that the road was set for the trains of the other company, all movements were made largely 'on sight'. Concerning the route-indicating signals, it will be appreciated that display of a white signal signified that the road was made for Greenwich traffic (which could thus proceed) whilst Croydon traffic had to stop; but that when a red signal was displayed it signified that the road was made for Croydon traffic, which could thus proceed, Greenwich traffic then having to stop. That is, for Greenwich trains, white meant proceed and red meant stop, whereas for Croydon trains red meant proceed and white meant stop. This must have been one of the very few instances where a red signal actually signified 'proceed' (but continue to run 'on sight', of course) in the early days of railways.

The London & Croydon originally provided only first and second class accommodation, the trains being usually formed of two first-class carriages and two seconds, each vehicle weighing less than 5 tons so that a normal train weighed under 20 tons empty.

When the London & Greenwich received their Act in 1833, it was essentially for the *building* of the railway, for the use of which passengers would have to pay a toll. This was of course a principle that dated back to turnpike roads with their toll gates, and was followed with the earlier 'railways' such as the Surrey Iron Railway (on which operators had to pay a toll). The London & Greenwich position was therefore that, because it provided the trains itself and operated them, the fares charged should be compounded of two factors — a toll, and a charge for locomotive power and carriages. It fixed the toll element of the fare at 3d per passenger, and adjusted the charges element from time to time to bring in the maximum profit for the time being. The Act authorized a maximum toll fare of 1s.6d if the Greenwich company provided the locomotives and carriages, but empowered the company to demand a maximum toll of 9d from anyone providing his own locomotives and stock.

The financial policy of the Greenwich was that the fares should be related to the cost of constructing the railway, on the not illogical argument that the expensive viaduct had been needed because the line served areas which included a large and growing population. However, the Greenwich had always had competition from road transport and river craft, and soon found that they could only charge what the traffic would bear.

As the traffic was entirely short-haul, operation was relatively costly. This resulted in a low return on capital, which, moreover, had had to be greatly increased over the original estimate in order to cover a heavy overspend on the viaduct. Capital had also been sunk in the purchase of property which later was not needed. All this naturally made the Greenwich board particularly watchful of the financial position of their Company.

The London & Croydon had also had to spend far more than their original estimate, and were therefore initially no doubt relieved that they did not have to service out of revenue a separate and costly independent approach to London. The Croydon could, moreover, look forward to income arising from tolls which would be paid to it by the Brighton and South Eastern companies as soon as those companies commenced operations over the Croydon. The Greenwich, on the other hand, had no way of augmenting its revenue other than by increased income from extra tolls from traffic off the Croydon, or by extending its line. It never did the latter.

The first toll agreement between the two companies was signed on 30 December 1835, just over 6 months after the Croydon received its Act, and provided that the Croydon should pay the Greenwich 3d for each of their passengers travelling between Corbett's Lane and London Bridge. This agreement was made before any part of the Greenwich company's line had been opened. This rate of 3d per passenger was therefore the same as the Greenwich company's notional toll element of their own fares. It became operative when the Croydon commenced its public service on 5 June 1839. It should be noted that this rate of 3d per passenger was only one-third of what the Greenwich company could ostensibly demand under their Act, as the Croydon company were of course using their own locomotives and stock over the Greenwich company's metals. The Croydon had not spent so much in building its line as the Greenwich had in building its, and in addition the Croydon's board did not have the same financial policy of relating fares to cost of construction, as had been adopted by the Greenwich, but instead charged on a stage basis, with three fare stages from London Bridge (at New Cross, at Dartmouth Arms, and at Penge respectively).

When the London & Croydon Railways was opened, it ran through practically open country once it left New Cross until it reached Croydon, and there can have been little ordinary traffic to and from the intermediate stations. However, there were good views between Dartmouth Arms and Croydon, and it seems that very soon after the opening the company was extolling the beauties of the route and the opportunities for anglers in those parts of the canal which were still filled with water. In fact, the company set out from the start to attract traffic, and to encourage people to live in Croydon when their places of business were in London. It was thus very early in the field in trying to build up a regular traffic and hence to establish support from what would now be called commuters. As an inducement to people to live in Croydon, it charged the same fares from London to Penge and all stations beyond (1s 9d first class, and 1s 3d second class). However, the inclusion of the Greenwich company's toll of 3d meant that the Croydon company only received 1s. from a second-class traveller from London to Croydon. The population of Croydon in 1839 was probably about 15,000; it had risen to 16,712 in 1841.

The two companies did not work together harmoniously regarding the use of the Greenwich's line from Corbett's Lane and London Bridge. The Greenwich company reported that on 18 June and again on 28 June 1839 (i.e. in the first month of operation of the Croydon trains), two of the latter company's trains had no tail lights showing and that as a result there were narrow escapes from rear-end collisions, involving following Greenwich trains; the Croydon company's replies were to the effect that the road was in such a bad state that the lamps must have been shaken out. On 25 July a Croydon locomotive was derailed outside London Bridge.

In October the Croydon company revised its timetable without any consultation with the London & Greenwich, and unfortunately caused a clash of timings. The fact that the former company's head office was at Croydon whilst the Greenwich company had its head office at London Bridge, at a time when there was no electric telegraph in use by either company, may have been a factor in this nonsense, but there must have been poor staff work by the Croydon company, which had to withdraw its revised timings.

Just before the Croydon opened its line, the Select Committee on Railway Communications had examined various witnesses in order to gather evidence on the usage of London Bridge station and the viaduct, and, as recorded in Chapter II, eventually reported that the trains of the four companies (Greenwich, Croydon, Brighton and South Eastern) should not be allowed to run on the Greenwich line above Corbett's Lane until some arrangement had been made to eliminate danger. In the meantime Croydon fair had been held, and the London & Croydon had run a greatly augmented service to cope with the traffic on the second day, during which it conveyed over 11,000 passengers; the maximum frequency was a train every 10 minutes, so that between Corbett's Lane and London Bridge there were in all ten trains each way per hour at the peak period, including the Greenwich company's own 15 minute interval service.

Corbett's Lane junction must have been busy!

Although all this traffic had been handled safely, it was clear to both companies that if the conclusions of the Select Committee were ignored, statutory action might be taken. As both the Greenwich and the Croydon companies were looking to the Brighton and to the South Eastern companies, when they started to run trains, to enhance the earlier companies' revenues substantially by tolls, both the Greenwich and the Croydon concerns realised that the viaduct would have to be widened above Corbett's Lane as the only really practicable solution to the problem. Suggestions made by witnesses before the Select Committee included two by Benjamin Cubitt on behalf of the South Eastern Railway (then still in the early stages of construction) for new lines off the Croydon to a terminus at the Elephant & Castle; one of these would have started at Dartmouth Arms and run via Nunhead and Peckham; and the other farther out, from near Jolly Sailor to run via Herne Hill. These schemes are referred to in more detail in the next chapter.

The Greenwich company first suggested to the Croydon company that it would be possible to lay a third line on the existing viaduct if the Croydon company were prepared to limit the width of its rolling stock to that of the Greenwich — namely 6 ft; such a suggestion would of course have had to have had agreement to a similar limitation by the Brighton and the South Eastern companies, and in any case, if adopted, would obviously merely have postponed taking the inevitable decision to widen the viaduct.

The London & Greenwich then tried again. It proposed that it should make available to the Croydon company (or to the other three companies jointly) on a perpetual lease the land needed to enable the viaduct to be widened, provided that the lessees did the widening (at the lessees' expense) and that the relevant toll to the Greenwich company should be an additional 1½d. To this the London & Croydon made two counter-proposals; one was based on the Greenwich company's proposal, but with the extra toll at 1d; the other was that the Croydon should buy the land and should widen the viaduct, but pay no toll at all to the Greenwich company.

Throughout the discussions the Brighton company supported the Croydon. The South Eastern company, however, took the view that relations with the Greenwich should be severed and that one of the lines to the Elephant & Castle which had been suggested by Benjamin Cubitt on their behalf, when giving evidence to the Select Committee in the late Spring of 1839, should be built. The South Eastern Railway's suggestion was received coldly by the London & Croydon, since the building of any such line would inevitably have resulted in the Croydon company's expectations of tolls for running over its line, not being realised because of the reduced distance to be run over its line. The Croydon cannot therefore be blamed for refusing to put up any capital for a scheme which would cut the Croydon's own throat, but the absence of the Croydon's financial support for a line to the Elephant & Castle caused the South Eastern — itself finding difficulty in raising all the money needed to construct its own authorized line — to drop the proposal.

As neither the Croydon nor the Greenwich company would accept any of the proposals of the other, both took steps late in 1839 to obtain Acts to widen the viaduct, and to reconstruct the stations at London Bridge. The Greenwich, moreover, sought permission to increase the existing toll to 6d to help to pay for the work if they received their Act for the widening.

Before Parliament considered the two rival Bills, two events occurred which had important consequences. The first of these was that the Select Committee was disturbed by the state of affairs that had come about between the Greenwich, Croydon, South Eastern and Brighton companies regarding the means by which the Committee's recommendations for conducting their traffic would be implemented. The Select Committee had already, before the arguments concerned had taken place, advised Parliament that there should be some form of governmental control of railways; early in 1840 the Committee reported that no agreement had yet been reached on the dispute between the four companies on the best way to proceed, and hence it reiterated its firm recommendation for governmental oversight.

The second event was a double rear-end collision outside London Bridge station in fog, on 30 January 1840. An up Greenwich train had stopped as usual, to be tow-roped into the terminus, and while stationary was run into by an up

Croydon train as the latter was itself preparing to stop for tow-roping, two vehicles of the stationary Greenwich train being derailed and jack-knifed; soon afterwards, an up Greenwich special ran into the Croydon train, whose rear vehicle was naturally some way from the position where all up trains stopped for tow-roping to be done, this second collision causing the derailment and jack-knifing of two vehicles in the third (Greenwich) train. Slight injuries, only, were caused to a few persons in the two Greenwich trains, but the Select Committee took the opportunity to stress to Parliament that the risks of accident to which it had earlier alluded, were very real.

The Parliamentary Committee appointed to review the rival Croydon and Greenwich Bills for the widening of the viaduct did not first meet until after the report on the collision at London Bridge had been published, and so was in a position to appreciate the support which the Select Committee had recently received for its fears. Lt. Colonel Landmann, on behalf of the Greenwich company, said that enough land had been purchased to enable the viaduct to be widened, and that it had been erected along the centre-line of that land. However, he maintained that the Select Committee's opinion that the present arrangements were unsatisfactory, and that before the Brighton and South Eastern trains started to run some arrangement should be made for eliminating the danger, had been seized upon by the Croydon company in order to embarrass the Greenwich company. Charles Austin, the Croydon company's counsel, suggested that the Greenwich company had been empowered by Parliament to acquire land on either side of the viaduct so that the latter might be widened when necessary, and said that if that company tried to exact a toll of 9d (to which it considered that it was entitled), its own fares would have to be raised to such an extent that no one would travel in its trains.

Parliament finally decided to pass the Greenwich company's Bill, and the Act (3 & 4 Vic. cap. 127) was dated 7 August 1840. Both companies' Bills for work at London Bridge station were passed on that same date. Essential details of both of these station Acts have been included in Chapter II.

The Greenwich company's widening Act made two very

important stipulations: the first, that the widening was to be on the south side of the existing viaduct and was to provide two extra roads for the exclusive use of the Croydon, Brighton and South Eastern companies; and the second, that the Greenwich company was to be compensated for being barred from using the two new roads by the Croydon company paying an additional toll (Section 14). The Act went into detail on the use to be made of the four lines ultimately to be provided by the Greenwich company, Section 15 stipulating that no traffic from or to Greenwich, or eastwards of the junction at Corbett's Lane, was to pass over the two additional lines, and no traffic to or from the Croydon line was to pass over the two existing lines, except for access to and from the stations at London Bridge.[1] This Act was thus of extreme importance, its provisions dictating all future plans for the area for many years.

The Act required the work to be finished in two years, with a penalty of £50 per day to be paid to the London & Croydon Railway (for division between itself and the London & Brighton and the South Eastern Railways) for exceeding that time. The Act also laid down that any unoccupied arches were to be fenced. It additionally contained the provisions — no doubt inserted in response to demands — that no locomotives were to be used between 11.00 a.m. and 1.00 p.m. on Sundays, Good Friday, or Christmas Day. The Greenwich company was authorized to raise £200,000 for the new works.

The new toll for traffic to and from the Croydon line was fixed at 4½d. per passenger, to become effective when the two new roads were finished and hence when the Croydon's traffic (including, later, that of the Brighton and South Eastern companies) commenced to use them.

The London & Greenwich Railway lost no time in preparing specifications and in calling for tenders for the widening works, of which the cheapest was accepted. Work actually started in January 1841, the southern 'boulevard' being closed so that the widening could occupy the site and the northern 'boulevard' being appropriated for the contractors' use. The first stone was laid on 17 March 1841 by Lt. Col. Landmann. Three days later, on 20 March, an inspection train containing the Brighton company's directors, left London Bridge to enable that company's board to see progress towards completion of the works on that line below the junction with the London & Croydon Railway at Norwood, thus underlining the urgency of the Greenwich company's widening works. The widened viaduct was to be asphalted from the start. A Greenwich company's train was derailed on 28 May 1841, soon after the widening works started, due to the train running over some heavy timber on the line where part of the parapet wall had been removed in connection with the work.[2] Croydon traffic was delayed as a result.

Whilst the forthcoming use of the two roads on the south side of the widened viaduct (i.e. the two new ones) for traffic to and from the Croydon line, and the use of the two on the north side (i.e. the original ones) for Greenwich traffic, was undoubtedly right, it at once brought to the forefront an awkward situation at London Bridge, where the siting of the two stations was the opposite to that of the forthcoming arrangement of the approach roads. With hindsight, it is easy to criticize the Croydon company for acquiring, in 1836, the land for their station from that held by the Greenwich company, without being sufficiently far-sighted to realize that the fact that that land was on the 'wrong' side of the Greenwich company's station would later be objectionable. Few could probably foresee the increase in traffic which was to occur in a short time, and it would have been difficult to have justified to the shareholders (none of whom probably understood the least thing about practical railway working) that it would be advisable for the Croydon company to acquire additional land to the south of the Greenwich company's station at a price that would undoubtedly have been higher than that needed to purchase surplus Greenwich land on the north side of that company's station. St. Thomas' Hospital owned the land to the south, and powers would have had to have been obtained for the purpose of purchase of any property.

Various suggestions seem to have been made in the next two or three years (i.e. up to 1839) that the two companies should exchange stations. There was, however, no pressing need for such action as long as the viaduct only carried two roads. Moreover, the relationships between the Croydon and the Greenwich were not conducive to such a matter proceeding to the point of serious discussion.

The positions of the two stations at London Bridge having become established, and more accommodation clearly being needed in the near future, it was presumably the continued lack of understanding between the Greenwich and the Croydon companies that caused each to go separately to Parliament for powers of enlargement. The Greenwich company might be said to have shown some logic in seeking powers to build an enlargement on the south side of their existing station, in the parish of St. Olave's, for the accommodation of the Croydon, Brighton and South Eastern companies, although the Croydon's existing station was, of course, to the north of the Greenwich's existing station. The Croydon company might be said to have been faced with 'Hobson's Choice' in seeking powers to build an enlargement to their station, already clearly on the 'wrong' side of the approach lines. Both the Greenwich and Croydon companies obtained their Acts, as already recorded, on 7 August 1840, and it was not until the next year that plans were drawn up on behalf of all the companies under which the rebuilding and enlargement would result in the Greenwich accommodation being to the north of that of the other three companies.

In the meantime, the Croydon, Brighton, and South Eastern companies had set up a joint committee for the twin purposes of co-ordinating their cases against the Greenwich company's Bill, and for watching the progress through Parliament of their own Bills. This committee first met at Brown's Hotel on 20 March 1840, under the title of the Brighton, Croydon and Dover Joint Station Committee, with John Harman, the Brighton company's chairman, in the Chair.

The Brighton was represented by Messrs. Donald McClean and John Shewell, the Croydon by Messrs. Frederick Roberts and Benjamin Barnes, and the South Eastern by Messrs. Joseph Baxendale and William Wilson. Others present were Messrs. William Burchell and George Sutton, the solicitors to the Croydon and Brighton companies; Mr. Bennett representing Mr. J. P. Fearon, solicitor to the South Eastern company; and Mr. Robert S. Young, Secretary to the Croydon company. The following Minutes are recorded:[3]

> The chief object of the meeting as stated by Mr. Burchell was to determine whether it would be advisable to seek by a motion in Parliament to refer the Croydon Bill in Committee to any other List than the West Kent, or to move that the Members to be added by the House should consist of Members of the Select Committee on Railways or any others officially named.
>
> Resolved that it appears advisable to this Meeting that the Bill should be referred to the West Kent list and that it would not be expedient to make any motion for the addition of Members, but that the Dover and Brighton Members be requested to claim their privilege of sitting on the Committee.

From the foregoing it seems that the Croydon may have had in mind the possibility of influencing Parliament, but that wiser counsels had prevailed.

A second meeting was held on 3 April, chaired by Mr. W. A. Wilkinson (Croydon company), with Messrs. Harman and Shewell (Brighton) and Messrs. Frederick Roberts and Barnes (Croydon). After dealing with the joint funding of the activities of the committee, the latter asked for advice on the station layout and on the buildings to be given to them by Messrs. John Rastrick (the Brighton Engineer), William Cubitt (the South Eastern Engineer) and Henry Roberts (the Croydon Architect): Rastrick and Roberts were asked 'to arrange if possible some plan for buildings, etc., which may meet the view of the Governors of St. Thomas' Hospital as regards ventilation and absence of noise'.[3] This of course related to the new joint station.

Henry Roberts prepared a preliminary plan during the summer of 1840, showing how the land at London Bridge was to be allotted among the four companies, but his proposals were subsequently amended. At the sixth meeting of the Committee, on 30 September 1840, Messrs. Cubitt and Rastrick were appointed joint Engineers, and Roberts was appointed Architect, to carry out the works at London Bridge station. At the next meeting but one, on 3 December 1840, it was reported that—

'£111,500 be considered the cost of the Croydon Co's property at London Bridge, so ⅓ of this should be paid by the Brighton and S.E. Cos'.[3]

Eventually final plans were prepared, which included designs by Rastrick and Landmann as well as by Henry Roberts and George Smith (Architect to the Greenwich company), but this was not until early in 1841, and the plans were not approved until June of that year to enable the Greenwich company eventually to erect their new station to the north of their existing one. On 24 June 1841 the Joint Committee took over the existing Croydon station so as to be ready for the opening of the first section of the line to Brighton (which event occurred on 12 July); at the same time extensions of the arches on which the stations were built, were being made towards the south.

General rebuilding went on for nearly 2 years, until the spring of 1843, but it is now necessary to revert to 1840 to deal with important events concerning the Brighton company.

As soon as the Brighton-Shoreham line was opened on 12 May 1840, the passenger traffic started to build up satisfactorily in all three classes. It was reported at a meeting of the Committee of Works ('the Friday Committee') on Wednesday 8 July 1840 that upwards of 300,000 passengers had already been carried, with no complaints except from persons who had been 'dis-apointed (sic) in procuring places in the trains'.[4] People were, however, obviously unaccustomed to railways, and the Minutes of the meeting go on to record that 'The Committee regret to report, that the cases of Accidents on the Line have increased to a fearful degree. There have been admitted to the County Hospital upwards of 240 patients, of which there were eleven urgent cases last week'.[4] It may be inferred that these accidents were largely, if not entirely, to members of the public, no doubt due to various types of foolhardiness — such as walking or standing on the permanent way, or boarding or leaving carriages without care (possibly when the vehicles were in motion).

The committee appreciated that a growing number of personal injuries would be bad publicity for the company, and therefore suggested that 'it might be well to appropriate

1 CROYDON CANAL
Remaining section, as preserved in Betts Park, Anerley, looking south on
14 June 1973   (Author)

2 LONDON & CROYDON RAILWAY
Former offices, as used as Station House at West Croydon, L B S C Rly
                                    (Author's collection)

3 CORBETT'S LANE JUNCTION
Looking south in 1839, with Croydon lines curving to right
(Author's collection)

4 CORBETT'S LANE JUNCTION
Looking south on 14 June 1967, from a similar position to that in Plate 3
(Author)

5 ROCKSHAW ROAD BRIDGE, MERSTHAM
Looking north towards Merstham Tunnel   (Author's collection)

6 OUSE VIADUCT
Looking south-east towards Haywards Heath   (Author's collection)

7 BURGESS HILL STATION
Looking north, showing wayside nature of platforms
(National Railway Museum)

8 BRIGHTON STATION
Old tunnel under passenger station formerly providing rail access to
Goods Yard from Shoreham line, as used as rifle range, on 18 April 1970
(G. H. Platt)

9 BRIGHTON STATION
David Mocatta's buildings for passenger station
(National Railway Museum)

10 HASSOCKS GATE STATION
David Mocatta's buildings in 1945 (station long since renamed Hassocks)
(National Railway Museum)

11 KINGSTON BRIDGE, SHOREHAM
Looking south in 1840   (National Railway Museum)

12 KINGSTON BRIDGE, SHOREHAM
Looking south in 1945   (National Railway Museum)

13 STOAT'S NEST STATION
Building in 1842   (National Railway Museum)

14 ARUN BRIDGE
Looking south, with train travelling towards Brighton
                                   (National Railway Museum)

15 FALMER TUNNEL
Looking east towards Lewes in 1846 (Author's collection)

The First Railway Station Horsham. 1848.

16 ORIGINAL HORSHAM STATION
Looking north-west in 1848 (Author's collection)

the receipts from the Traffic of the Shoreham Branch for one day for the benefit of the Hospital; it would be a popular measure and might induce many people to give it (the company or the hospital?) their support.[4] The proposal was adopted, but it was decided on 28 September 1840 that 'County Hospital Benefit Day' should be postponed to 'the first fine day, as 28 September was exceedingly un-favourable.'[4]

Despite the satisfactory traffic figures, two administrative matters were brought to the attention of the committee. The first of these was that at Hove there was no work for the clerk to do; he was therefore paid off in July. The second matter was that delays were reported on 28 September to be occurring at intermediate stations due to guards of trains having to issue tickets and to collect money and give change. It was therefore resolved that 'the persons stationed at each of the intermediate stations should be furnished with Books of Tickets (the name of the Station to be inserted on the Ticket), take the money from the passengers, and the Guard collect the Tickets as he puts the passengers into the carriages.' The committee further resolved that 'the persons entrusted with these Books of Tickets to pay the money by each of them every day to Mr. Dean.'[4]

Some three weeks earlier, Messrs. Heaviside and Robinson had complained to the committee at their meeting on 5 September at the Old Ship at Brighton, about the working of the Shoreham branch, and had asked for written regulations to be prepared which should be strictly enforced.[4]

Locomotive and rolling stock defects began to appear. As early as 5 September 1840 (barely 4 months after the public opening of the Shoreham line), it was reported to the committee that an engine was giving trouble, it being unsafe to use it because spokes in the wheels were loose.

Mr. Harman (chairman of the committee and also chairman of the company) agreed to write a private note to Sir John Rennie, who had supplied the engine, telling him that the subject would be brought before the directors of the company at their next meeting.[4]

At the following meeting of the committee, on 28 September 1840, it was reported that some of the carriages supplied by Mr. Wright had defective wheels. The committee decided that the wheels should be replaced by new ones at Mr. Wright's expense.[4]

Although the Committee of Works had approved on 6 July 1839 Rastrick's suggestion for taking wagons across the Shoreham turnpike at Kingston (see Chapter VII), the proposals had not been accepted by the Trustees of the turnpike, and in consequence freight traffic had not commenced when the line was publicly opened in 1840. It had of course been originally planned that there should be a level crossing over the turnpike, but the Trustees had objected to laying rails across the road. Rastrick's proposed solution was that the rails should be brought level with the turnpike on either side and that wagons should be drawn across and re-railed on the opposite side, but this, as already explained, was also turned down by the Trustees. A condition of stalemate then seems to have set in for over 12 months, but the railway company clearly had to find a solution in order that freight traffic might be started in earnest to bring in revenue.

Local efforts to solve the problem were also apparently made, as it was reported at a meeting of the Committee of Works on 24 November 1840 (six months after passenger traffic had commenced on the line) that stone blocks had been placed across the turnpike and that the solicitors of the Trustees had written to the company to desire that they be taken up. The committee resolved that the legal position should be investigated. This examination must have supported the company, as it was reported to the committee on Monday 26 July 1841 that rails had been laid across the road and that a bridge was about to be built.[4]

No date for the regular commencement of freight traffic has been found, but the facts given above suggest that it would have been a short time before the 26 July 1841.

The question of taking road coaches by rail on the branch engaged the attention of the Committee of Works at their meeting at the Old Ship at Brighton on Monday 8 March 1841. The bad state of the roads had apparently concerned the coach proprietors, and as a result the committee decided that two wagons should be altered to carriage trucks by Mr. T. H. Statham (Resident Engineer at Brighton), whilst 'temporary stages for loading be erected at both Brighton and Shoreham'. The committee also ordered that the vehicles and loading facilities should be ready by 15 March (i.e. one week after their meeting).[4]

It has already been recorded that the Brighton line from the junction with the Croydon company was opened as far as Haywards Heath on 12 July 1841, and through to Brighton on 21 September 1841, these dates having been later than originally envisaged due to earthworks not having stabilized properly. It was clearly necessary to have the line open as soon as possible in order that revenue could be earned, but experience soon showed that it would have been wise to have allowed a further period of consolidation before commencing regular traffic.

When the line was opened to Haywards Heath a service of four trains each way was provided on weekdays, leaving London Bridge at 09 30, 11 30, 13 30, and 17 30, and leaving Haywards Heath at 09 00, 11 00, 14 30, and 17 30. A standard schedule of 2 hours was established, trains being booked to call at Red Hill, Horley and Three Bridges but making conditional stops at all other stations (and also at Stoats Nest and Merstham where stations had not yet been opened) when necessary to 'take up' or 'put down' passengers. A coach connection between Haywards Heath and Brighton was given for each train, arriving at Brighton 2 hours after reaching Haywards Heath and leaving Brighton 2 hours before departure from Haywards Heath. The overall timing between London Bridge and Brighton was thus 4 hours. The use of standard timings will be noted. On Sundays there were two down trains and two up, with an additional short to and from Horley only; there was also a train from Croydon to London Bridge at 08 30 and one from London Bridge to Croydon at 22 30. Above Croydon, the Brighton company's trains called only at New Cross.

Previous-day booking was required for through conveyance to Brighton, to cover the coach portion of the journey, some dozen hostelries in London being named as agents for this purpose if intending passengers found it inconvenient to book at London Bridge the day before starting their journeys. Bradshaw makes no mention of prior bookings from Brighton in the coach service to Haywards Heath, but it is assumed that certain Brighton hotels (for example, The Old Ship) were given a franchise in order that matters could be regu-

163

lated. The coach services needed 300 horses.[5]

A policy of fairly high fares was adopted, no doubt to bring in maximum revenue in return for the heavy capital cost of building the line and on the assumption that large numbers of passengers would use the line — an estimate that was soon proved right. Typical single fares were: London Bridge to Haywards Heath, 10s (1st class) and 7s 6d (2nd class); London Bridge to Brighton (coach from Haywards Heath), 15s and 11s; and Brighton (coach to Haywards Heath) to Croydon, 13s and 9s 6d. Fares to and from Brighton would have reflected the coach proprietors' profits, because after the line was opened throughout the first- and second-class fares to and from London were reduced from 15s to 14s 6d and from 11s to 9s 6d respectively. All London fares of course included an element of toll to the Croydon and Greenwich companies.

The down services at the opening to Brighton were as follows:

London	09 45	10 45	13 45	14 45	15 45	16 45
Bridge	All Stations	1st class Stations only	All Stations	All Stations	1st class Stations only	Fast to Brighton
Brighton	12 15	12 45	16 15	17 15	17 45	18 30

The First class stations were Croydon, Redhill (Reigate), Three Bridges, and Haywards Heath, and the trains concerned conveyed first-class passengers only. The 'All Stations' trains conveyed first- and second-class passengers. The 16 45 London Bridge would have been first-class only, and had no public stop on the way to Brighton; a stop for water would have been necessary, however, and this is recorded as having been at Redhill.[6]

The up service was of a similar type.

By February 1842 the daily services to and from Brighton had been retimed, down trains leaving London Bridge at 09 00, 10 45, 13 45, and 15 45, whilst the up ones left Brighton at 08 00, 10 45, 13 45, and 15 45. The two Sunday trains had also been retimed. Part, at any rate, of the revisions were probably to take account of the desire of the public to travel in daylight whenever possible.

Records of average train formations do not seem to have survived, but only first and second class vehicles were conveyed initially, although, as already recorded, third class had been provided on the Shoreham line from the start.

Slips and falls of earth or chalk occurred from time to time, and a slip in Copyhold cutting may well have caused an irregularity in the road which resulted in the derailment of a double-headed down train on 2 October 1841. Although the derailment was attributed by some to the running of a 2-2-0 locomotive as pilot to a 2-2-2, the Board of Trade was not so sure. The Author considers that this, at worst, may only have been a contributory factor; had it really been the main, if not the sole, cause, the train would surely have left the unconsolidated road before getting as far as Copyhold.

Nearer London, a serious fall occurred in the clay cutting north of Dartmouth Arms, on the Croydon company's line, on 2 November 1841. This stopped all traffic of both the Croydon and the Brighton companies, the roads not being reopened for 17 days. It was the forerunner of a number of other slips between New Cross and Dartmouth Arms during the winter of 1841-42, following which the Croydon decided to flatten the cutting slopes at a cost of some £30,000.

At this stage, it is appropriate to refer to the preparation in 1840 by Mr. C. H. Gregory, in his then capacity as Resident Engineer to the London & Croydon Railway, of a series of regulations for the first appointment of an engineman. These were adopted by the directors of that company and were published in a rare paper entitled 'Practical Rules for the Management of a Locomotive Engine', published in 1841.[7] The regulations concerned are of sufficient interest to justify their reproduction as an Appendix to this chapter.

Three events concerning the Brighton company remain to be recorded for the year 1841. The first was that Merstham station was opened on Wednesday 1 December 1841, under the Agreement made with Lord Monson, the owner of Gatton Park. It had centre through roads and side platform loops, but had a life of less than two years, as will be explained in due course. The site of the station was marked later by Thornton's siding, on the up side of the line, of which the earliest trace seems to be inclusion on the 1877 edition of the Ordnance sheet. B.R. (Southern Region) opinion, however, is that this siding would not have been built on the site of an already-abandoned station, and hence that it may well have been constructed at the same time as the station. The name of the station has been erroneously quoted as Gatton.[8]

The second event to be noted was the decision to build a wayside station at the level crossing at Stoats Nest, nearly a mile south of Godstone Road station and intended to serve Epsom racecourse, several miles to the west. No date has been found for the first use of this station, but it would presumably have been for the Spring meeting in 1842; it can hardly have produced much revenue in view of its distance from the racecourse it was intended to serve (Plate 13). Trains had made conditional stops at Stoats Nest since the line was opened, as already recorded.

On the Croydon line, the traffic at Penge, always light, apparently fell to below an economic figure, and the station was closed in 1841.

Another event in 1841 was the erection at New Cross of the first semaphore railway signal. This was put up by Mr. Charles Hutton Gregory, Resident Engineer to the Croydon company — who was not, however, contrary to what has hitherto been accepted, the actual inventor of railway signals of this type. The latter honour goes to Mr. Rastrick, who proposed the idea to Gregory (see Volume II of this account).

In the meantime, work on the widened viaduct between London Bridge and Corbett's Lane was proceeding rapidly, and early in 1842 construction was nearly finished, enabling the Greenwich company's directors to inspect it in March of that year. The arches were asphalted from the start, as already recorded. The permanent way for the two new roads was laid on longitudinal timbers as this was apparently considered to be the most suitable form of construction for the fast trains of the Brighton and the South Eastern companies (the latter was expected to be opened soon after the viaduct widening was completed). Until the widening was brought into use, the traffic of the Greenwich, Croydon, and Brighton companies had perforce all to use the original two roads. There was certainly congestion at London Bridge, but no accidents had taken place at Corbett's Lane junction although many thousands of trains must have passed over the junction since it was brought into use in 1839. In fact, the trains of all these companies on occasion used the 'north' line of the original pair, as a single road, without mishap, during the later stages of the widening works.[9] The roads were laid on the widened viaduct by 19 April 1842, and the widening was brought into use on 10 May 1842. The increased toll of 4½d per passenger had to be paid to the Greenwich company from that date, all the Croydon and Brighton companies' traffic then using the two new roads.

The scene was thus set for the opening of the first portion of the South Eastern Railway. This will be dealt with in the next chapter. In the meantime, Rastrick had recommended that the double-disc signals (see Chapter VII) used on the London & Brighton should be replaced with semaphores of the pattern already used on the London & Croydon (see later).

APPENDIX
LONDON & CROYDON RAILWAY
Regulations for the First Appointment of an Engineman

Framed by the then Mr. C. H. Gregory, in his capacity as the Company's Resident Engineer, and adopted by the Directors in 1840.*

1. The candidate must not be under twenty-one years of age, and must produce a certificate of a sound constitution and steady habits.

2. He must be able to read and write, and, if possible, understand the rudimental principles of mechanics.

3. It will be a great recommendation if he has served his time to any mechanical art, especially as a Fitter of Locomotive Engines; and, if possible, he should produce testimonials stating his qualifications as such.

4. If the candidate has been a Fitter or a stationary Engine-man, he must, for several months at least, have been a Stoker on a Locomotive Engine, under the direction of a steady and competent Engine-man; and before his appointment, he should produce a testimonial from the Superintendent of Locomotives, or at least from the Engine-man under whom he has served, stating full confidence in his acquaintance with the construction of an Engine and the principles of its management.

5. If the candidate has not been a Fitter or a stationary Engine-man, he must have served as a Stoker for at least two years, and produce the testimonials named in the preceding rules.

6. If required by the Board of Directors, for greater security, the candidate must undergo an examination from their Engineer, Superintendent of Locomotives, or other competent person, as to his knowledge of an Engine and its management, and the general result of this examination must be committed to paper, signed by the examiner, and presented to the Board.

7. The Engineer or Superintendent of Locomotives of the Railway to which the candidate is desirous of being appointed, shall sign a certificate stating that he has conversed with him, has seen him drive, and has confidence in his steadiness and ability.

8. Before being allowed to take the entire charge of an Engine and train, the candidate must drive for several days under the direction of an experienced Engine-man, who must be on his Engine, and certify to his ability.

9. All certificates and testimonials must be deposited with the Secretary of the Company, who will restore them to the owner on his leaving their service.

*Published at end of Mr. Gregory's paper entitled 'Practical Rules for the Management of a Locomotive Engine'. John Weale, London, 1841.

This paper was itself based on Mr. Gregory's earlier paper read in abstract before the Institution of Civil Engineers on 16 February 1841.

NOTES

1. Banister, F. D. Engineer of the London Brighton & South Coast Railway, Official Report entitled 'Historical Notes' and relating to relations with the London & Greenwich and South Eastern Railways 1888.
2. Thomas, R. H. G. *London's First Railway: the London & Greenwich*. Batsford, 1972, 119-120.
3. Original Minutes held by Public Records Office at 66, Porchester Road, London, W.2.,* local reference LBR 1/28.
4. *Ibid*, LBR 1/26.
5. *Southern Railway Magazine*, XI (1933), 58.
6. *Ibid*, XIX (1941), 148.
7. John Weale, London, 1841.
8. *The Railway Magazine*, 86 (1940), 553.
9. Thomas, R. H. G. *London's First Railway: the London & Greenwich*. Batsford, 1972. 121-122.

*Correct at date of going to press.

CHAPTER NINE

The opening of the South Eastern Railway and its effects, 1842-1844

THE RELATIONS between the Brighton and the South Eastern companies regarding the area of Red Hill and northwards, were of very great importance to both companies. As already recorded in Chapter II, the length of line between Norwood and Red Hill was the subject of a number of Acts and Agreements, the essential factor being that the South Eastern company had received its Act before the London & Brighton had received its. Hence it was decided that the South Eastern was to be the owner, originally of the whole length between Norwood and Red Hill but later of the southern portion, only, between what is now Coulsdon and Redhill. The practical effect of the South Eastern's ownership south of Coulsdon was, of course, that that company's trains passed over the metals of three other railways before they reached their own line at Coulsdon — namely, the London & Greenwich from London Bridge to Corbett's Lane; the London & Croydon from Corbett's Lane to Norwood; and the London & Brighton from Norwood to Coulsdon. The Brighton company's position was even worse, as their trains had to travel over lines in four different ownerships before finally entering their own line at Red Hill, namely, the Greenwich to Corbett's Lane; the Croydon from Corbett's Lane to Norwood; their own line from Norwood to Coulsdon; and the South Eastern from Coulsdon to Red Hill.

The Brighton not only got the worst of the bargain from the operating point of view, but in practice it may well have incurred a larger capital expenditure, despite the provision that it had to build the whole of the 12 miles of line from Norwood and Red Hill and then to sell the southern half of

170

it — the most expensive to construct, containing the very heavy works of Merstham tunnel and cuttings — at half the cost of the whole length. The South Eastern ultimately paid £340,000 for their share, this figure including an element of interest on the debt. The whole 12 miles must therefore have cost the Brighton company well over £600,000; no trace has been found of a breakdown of the latter sum. The account with the South Eastern Railway was not settled until 1844, as the Brighton was until then apparently unable to supply details of the costs. The South Eastern Railway assumed control of the 6-mile length concerned on 19 July 1844; the London & Brighton company had, of course, operated it until that date, although the S E Rly considered it theirs.

From the junction at Red Hill, the South Eastern company's route lay roughly east-south-east by east for the 66½ miles on to Dover, the change of direction from the near north-and-south alignment of the line to Brighton being by means of a left-hand curve of about ½ mile radius (it is now 41 chains) nearly a mile long. The first part of the curve was on a rising gradient of some 15½ ft. per mile (it is now at 1 in 341), after which there were very gentle undulations for over 4 miles before the line started to descend to the Medway valley. The only large work was a tunnel of 1326 yards at Bletchingley, the western end of which was nearly 4 miles from the junction at Red Hill. There were about 100 bridges on this 19½ mile stretch to Tunbridge (then so spelt), and a second, very short, tunnel. Bletchingley tunnel was unusual in that the bricks for it were actually made at the top of each working shaft, rather than being brought in from elsewhere.[1]

The South Eastern's Engineer was William Cubitt, who had been concerned with the building of the London & Croydon Railway. He must have been involved in the latter when he took up his appointment with the South Eastern. Perhaps because of his experience in the construction of the London & Croydon, he himself undertook the building of the South Eastern line except for certain works. Construction started in 1840, and by the autumn of 1841, when the London & Brighton had opened their line throughout, the first section of the South Eastern was well forward. At Red Hill, a station was to be provided just beyond the junction, and was to be called Reigate. It should not be confused with

171

Redhill and Reigate station on the Brighton line. No reference is made to stations beyond Reigate, or works beyond Tunbridge, as being outside the scope of this account.

The permanent way on the South Eastern Railway was formed of double-headed iron rails weighing 71 lb. per yard, laid in cast-iron chairs with ash keys; transverse wooden sleepers of triangular cross-section, arranged with the apex downwards, were used. Although the rails were double-headed, it was not apparently the intention to turn them, when worn.

Signalling seems to have been done with semaphores from the opening of the line, no doubt because Cubitt would have known of them from Gregory when the latter installed them on the Croydon line.

The first section to be built by the South Eastern Railway, from Red Hill to Tunbridge (then so spelt) was opened on 26 May 1842, just over 8 months after the Brighton had opened their line throughout, and 16 days after the widening above Corbett's Lane was brought into use. The South Eastern was opened on to Headcorn 3 months later, on 31 August, and to Ashford on 1st December 1842. A service of five trains each way per day was provided, and a policy of relatively low fares in three classes was adopted, no doubt with the idea of creating traffic from an area which might not otherwise have attracted many travellers. Hence by the end of 1842 there was a considerable traffic flow, from three companies, along the original pair of Croydon lines above Norwood, and over the two new lines on the 'south' side of the viaduct above Corbett's Lane; and all this traffic had to cross the Greenwich company's traffic on the level outside London Bridge. The widening Act stipulated (clause 15) that no traffic to and from New Cross was to use the northern (i.e. the original) pair of lines on the viaduct, and that no traffic to and from Greenwich was to use the southern (i.e. the new) pair of lines. The former then became known as the Greenwich lines, and the latter as the Croydon lines. Despite this limitation, a connection between the Up Croydon and the Up Greenwich was laid in during July 1842, no doubt to facilitate the working.[2] The agreement of 25 April 1839 between the South Eastern and the Brighton companies provided that each company should run over the other company's section as between Norwood and Red Hill, without payment of toll (see Chapter II). The South Eastern reached Folkestone on 28 June 1843 and Dover on 7 February 1844 (public opening).

While the South Eastern company was building and opening its line, the question of the tolls charged by the Greenwich company (3d per passenger) had become a matter of major importance to the Croydon company, as already recorded in Chapter VIII. As early as the Autumn of 1840, the Croydon had suggested to the Greenwich that various changes should be made, but the Greenwich, not surprisingly, would not agree — it could hardly be expected to reduce its revenue per passenger when it already had a very large capital to service, without any real guarantee that the numbers of passengers coming off the Croydon line would increase substantially. In consequence, in the Summer of 1841 the Croydon company tried to force the issue by inducing passengers to travel by bus between New Cross and London Bridge, thereby depriving the Greenwich company of all tolls. As even this step did not cause the Greenwich board to weaken, the Croydon did not continue with their new policy for long. Matters finally came to a head in May 1842 with the opening of the widened viaduct and the consequential increase in the toll to the Greenwich company from 3d per passenger to 4½d — a 50% increase.

The effect on the traffic of the Croydon company to this new, higher, toll was very marked, and the latter railway went so far as to propose at one of its Company meetings that it should cease to work its line and instead should rely solely for its revenue on the tolls paid to it by the South Eastern and the London & Brighton. The London & Croydon's shareholders agreed to this suggestion, and in December 1842 the Croydon then asked the Brighton, the South Eastern, and the Greenwich companies to work its (the Croydon's) traffic. The other companies refused, however, and the Croydon then decided to advertise the fact that it would discontinue to run its trains from 25 March 1843. Board of Trade diplomacy caused the London & Croydon not to proceed with its decision to suspend its traffic, until all the circumstances had been investigated. The Board of Trade's review satisfied them of the need for the toll to be reconsidered, but, despite the personal intervention of Mr. Gladstone (then Vice-president of the Board of Trade), the Greenwich directors could not see their way to making any change.

In the meantime the Croydon and the South Eastern companies had been adopting their own methods of bringing pressure to bear on the Greenwich company. The Croydon charged a higher fare for the portion of the journey between London Bridge and New Cross, than between New Cross and Croydon, with the object of inducing its passengers not to travel by train above New Cross; whilst the South Eastern adopted something in the way of strong-arm tactics by refusing to convey third-class passengers north of New Cross, the trains running between London Bridge and New Cross with the third-class vehicles empty. The Greenwich remained obdurate, and it is only fair to say that, looked at from its point of view, it could not afford to accept the loss of revenue which would follow any reduction in the toll, without any certainty of a considerable increase of traffic; whilst elimination of the toll could not be contemplated. As long as the companies serving the south and south-east had to use the London & Greenwich as their sole means of access to London, the Greenwich was undoubtedly in a very strong position, but the Greenwich company must surely have realised that its monopoly would not continue indefinitely in view of the undoubted need for its whole toll policy to be reconsidered on account of the very heavy pressures which could justifiably be brought to bear on itself. It was this apparent refusal to accept the need for a new look at matters, that was the basic reason for the ever-widening gulf between the Greenwich and the other three companies, and the writing was soon on the wall.

From what has already been recorded (Chapter VIII and earlier in the present Chapter) it will be seen that the South Eastern was in the forefront of the opposition to the Greenwich, and considered that the best way of overcoming the impasse would be to break the monopoly of the Greenwich company by building an entirely new line to an independent terminus in London. The South Eastern's earlier proposals that the new line should start at either Dartmouth Arms or at Jolly Sailor had been cold-shouldered by the Croydon company, whose own tolls from the South Eastern and the Brighton traffic would have undoubtedly fallen drastically on account of the reduced mileage of Croydon metals that would have been used by the other two companies' trains. Hence the South Eastern eventually suggested that the solution to the 'Greenwich question' would be for a new line to start as close as possible to Corbett's Lane, and to run to an independent terminus. This was a masterly suggestion, because on the one hand it gained the full support of the Croydon company who would not lose any of its (the Croydon's) entitlement to tolls (and of the Brighton company, which normally supported the Croydon); and on the other hand it greatly shortened the length of the new line, with resultant reduction in capital needed to build it. This will be dealt with fully in the next chapter.

In the meantime relations with the Greenwich company continued to be 'coldly correct'. At the meeting of the Joint Committee (now being called the Joint Board) on 3 August 1842, a letter from the Greenwich company was read which advised the Joint Board that on Sunday evenings the Greenwich traffic would be run over the 'North line of the new works, the Greenwich north line of rails being closed for the purpose of Asphalting'.[3] A temporary running connection must therefore have been laid in at Corbett's Lane to enable down Greenwich trains to cross to their own line; presumably up Greenwich traffic ran normally, on the up Greenwich ('south') line of the original viaduct, although the down traffic working contravened Section 15 of the Greenwich company's 1840 Act.

Apart from difficulties with the Greenwich company, the Joint Board had to deal with troubles caused by its own members. For example, at its meeting on 16 November 1842, it was reported that great delay had occurred on 4 November 'by goods trucks arriving at 5.30 p.m. on a Brighton passenger train'.[3] The man in charge of the station at which the freight vehicles were attached may well have never been to London and seen the working at what must already have been a peak period, but he was no doubt a much wiser (and possibly chastened) man as a result of the action taken by the Brighton board, who are recorded as having decided at the meeting on 16 November that they would 'issue orders for this not to be done in future.'

Up to 1842, the tolls which the Croydon company received from the Brighton and South Eastern companies, for each passenger conveyed over the Croydon's line between Norwood and New Cross, had been compounded of two elements: a fixed sum of 1/-; and an additional sum calculated on a proportion of the fare actually paid by the passenger, and based on the relative proportions of the mileage of the journey over the Croydon and over the other company's metals. This second element notionally increased as the length of the journey on the 'foreign' company itself increased, but was directly regulated by the fares policy of the 'foreign' company — the lower the fare, the lower the sum which came to the Croydon company for a given length of travel over the foreign line. Tunbridge (then so spelt) for example was 38 miles from New Cross whereas Hassocks Gate was 40½ miles, but the fares were roughly in the ratio of 1 : 1.6 respectively. Hence, initially, a greater return was had by the Croydon for each passenger carried to or from a station on the Brighton company, as compared with the sum that it would receive from the South Eastern for a comparable distance on that line. When the South Eastern reached Ashford, however, passengers to and from there paid a similar amount to the Croydon as passengers to and from Brighton; and when the South Eastern reached Folkestone in 1843, and Dover in 1844, the long-distance traffic on that line would have become lucrative to the Croydon company than that from the Brighton line, provided that the numbers of passengers carried were similar.

However, a new agreement was made late in 1842 between the South Eastern and the Croydon company which modified the above principles and resulted in a toll directly associated with fares and distance; and a similar one was made in 1843 between the Brighton and the Croydon companies, which resulted in the tolls from the Brighton company normally exceeding those received from tolls from the South Eastern company. The South Eastern company benefited as it henceforth retained a greater proportion of the fares received from its passengers; the Brighton company benefited as it now became the larger contributor to the Croydon and so could have a larger say in its affairs.[4]

The plans for the new station at London Bridge were completed in time for the contract for its erection to be let to Messrs. Grimsdale & Co. in March 1842, and over the next few months the Joint Committee bought most of the remaining Greenwich land, whilst the Greenwich company decided to buy the existing Croydon station to save the expense of rebuilding it. On 5 October 1842, a letter from the Greenwich board was read to a meeting of the Joint Board which stated that it (the Greenwich company) was willing to exchange substructures at London Bridge and to pay an annual rent of £175 to the Joint Board 'as an equivalent for the difference in value between the substructures of the Greenwich and Croydon companies; any liabilities to which the Greenwich company were subject in regard to appropriating any of the Arches of their Station so proposed to be exchanged, for thoroughfares or otherwise, to be borne by the Joint Station Committee.'[3] A fortnight afterwards, on 19 October, it was resolved by the Joint Board that the offer made by the Greenwich company in respect of the exchange of substructures, and read at the meeting on 5 October, be accepted subject to searches for liabilities.[3]

Matters were now proceeding steadily. At the Joint Board's meeting on 16 November Messrs. Stevens & Sons' tender of £643-8-11 for gas fittings for the new station, 'being the lowest, was accepted'; whilst at its meeting on 30 November it was reported that the Governors of St. Thomas' Hospital had accepted special compensation of 500 guineas because the Joint Station buildings in Joiner Street had been erected by the Joint Station committee so as to be nearer to the hospital than was warranted by the plan and agreement.[3] On 7 December it was agreed by the Joint Board that 'the exchange of Greenwich property south of the present carriage sheds be approved subject to the Brighton, Croydon, and Dover boards';[3] whilst on 14 December the secretary to the Joint Board reported that he had received letters from the Croydon and Dover boards confirming the Joint Board's resolution.[3] Presumably the Brighton board later also acquiesced, as matters went ahead although the formal agreement for the exchange of properties was not made until early in 1845.

It must now be recalled that, from south to north, the

existing site at London Bridge was apportioned as follows: on the south side, the original Greenwich station; then the original Croydon station (later also used by the Brighton and South Eastern companies); and on the north side a site in Croydon ownership but used by the Brighton company, partly for limited freight traffic. The plan was, in essence, that the Greenwich company would take over the Croydon's area (both their station and the Brighton's goods depot); whilst the original Greenwich station, together with the extensions authorized in 1840 under the Greenwich company's Act for providing accommodation for the other three companies in the Parish of St. Olave's, would go to those three companies. It was therefore, in essence, the *sites* of the Greenwich and Croydon stations which were mutually transferred rather than the stations themselves (as has often been erroneously stated); the existing Croydon station did become the Greenwich station, although modifications were made to it (see later), but everything else was new, and the new joint station was much larger than the former Greenwich station (which had occupied a part, only, of the site of the new joint station).

Clearance of land to the south of the existing stations, and the erection of arches, started in 1842, and continued steadily, work on the new joint station itself being well forward by the end of that year. However, further difficulties arose with the Greenwich company. These were, as usual, associated with the question of the toll to the Greenwich company, as background to a proposal to handle more freight at London Bridge. At its meeting on 4 January 1843, the Joint Board decided that, 'provided that the Greenwich Co. would consent to the principle of a proportionate Toll like that paid to the Croydon by the South Eastern Company, they (the Joint Board) would endeavour at any sacrifice to obtain additional space at London Bridge as would enable the several Companies to carry on their respective Goods Traffic there, although they still considered that such trade could only be carried on at London Bridge to a limited extent, with considerable difficulty, and at a great outlay of capital.'[3] The secretary was directed to write accordingly to the Greenwich Railway board, requesting the matter be reviewed. It appears that no change was made to the existing terms, and the result was no doubt made known to the Board of Trade investigating the whole question of the tolls, as already recorded.

The Board of Trade's conclusions from their review, and the rising pressure already recorded that some solution had to be found to the toll problem, seem to have hardened the attitude of the London & Greenwich board towards the Joint Board and to have caused them to adopt an unhelpful manner during the alterations to the station.

The traffic of all four companies had obviously to be handled throughout the period of the alterations, important stage-works therefore being involved. The first of these was the commissioning of sufficient of the new joint station that the existing Croydon station (also used by the Brighton and South Eastern companies) could be vacated. The second stage was for the Greenwich to move into the existing Croydon station (which, it will be recalled, they had already purchased) and so to vacate the temporary station which had been erected on the remainder of their existing site — some part of which had already been given up to facilitate the erection of the new joint station. The third stage was for the remainder of the former Greenwich station to be demolished and the site taken into the joint station. Stage 1 was therefore chiefly on the new arches to the south of the general site, whilst stages 2 and 3 mainly involved work on the site of the two original stations.

The platforms and track in the new joint station were sufficiently complete for the traffic of the three companies to be transferred there at the end of 1843, thereby enabling the original Croydon station to be vacated and handed over to the Greenwich company as stage 2. The Greenwich board held matters up, however, until March 1844 on the grounds that certain alterations had to be made to the old Croydon station before their company could use it — despite the fact that the Greenwich company had decided to purchase the station, as already explained, to save itself the cost of demolition and rebuilding. Even when it had moved into the former Croydon station, the Greenwich did not finally vacate the remaining part of its original site until November 1844, whilst the agreement for the exchange of properties was not finalised until the spring of 1845.

The layout of the new joint station consisted of six roads

between two side platforms, there also being a very narrow platform between the two roads on each side so that the outermost road on each side had a platform on either side of it. All six roads were cross-connected by two rows of turntables, one near the stops and the other near the country end of the platforms; an additional row of turntables connected the first four roads, only, from the north side, which was used for departures. Each narrow platform was, of course, interrupted by the turntable lines, and, in the case of that on the arrival side, did not extend towards the stops farther than the inntermost row of turntables. End-loading and side-loading docks were provided at the inner end of the station, and others at the outer (east) end to the south of the arrival platform. Additionally the three roads of the former temporary Greenwich terminus were included under a separate roof. A carriage shed was built well to the south of the arrival platform, itself flanked by a covered road for cabs and carriages; this carriage shed, and the loading docks on this side of the station (already referred to) were reached by a series of turntables, in accordance with usual practice at the time. An engine turntable was provided on its arrival side, to the east of a goods warehouse which in turn was east of the up-side loading docks. This goods warehouse appears to have been used only by the South Eastern and Croydon companies, presumably for perishable traffic, as the Brighton company still retained the use of their small goods depot north of the former Croydon station, itself now in Greenwich hands.

The passenger platforms of the joint station were covered by a two-span iron roof supported on cast-iron columns, the centre row of which was between the third and fourth roads from the north (departure) side. These two roads therefore had a slightly increased '6 ft.' space to leave room for the columns. A single-span roof beyond the departure platform covered the three roads of the former 'temporary' Greenwich station, which thereafter became known as the 'new shed'. The booking office, down and up parcels offices, waiting rooms, etc., were in the main block of buildings arranged across the inner end of the passenger platforms, with the three companies' board rooms above. Offices for each of the three companies, and the Joint Station offices, were arranged in a separate building to the south of the booking-office block, and behind the stops of the carriage shed. All were in the Italian style. A campanile, 71 feet high above rail level, was included at the south end of the main block, and contained a four-faced clock. The buildings were by Messrs. Roberts and Smith, architects for the Croydon and the Greenwich respectively. The architect for the campanile was Thomas Turner. The Greenwich company should also have had accommodation in the main block of buildings, but in the event their part of the block was not built and instead a temporary single-storey building was erected to contain their booking office, etc., behind the stops of their station (the former Croydon station).

Events which occurred in 1843/1844 and which will be recounted in the next chapter, caused work on the building at London Bridge to be stopped, and it was never completed despite the publication of prints depicting the station as finished. The new joint station was opened (unfinished) to the public in July 1844.

Whilst regular passengers no doubt knew their way about the combined stations, even during the rebuilding operations, other persons must have found it bewildering in an age when train travel was still, to the majority, a great novelty and involved much of the unknown. A paragraph from *Punch* in 1843 is worth quoting.[5]

Mr. Punch left his office one evening last week, and proceeded by omnibus to the terminus of the Dover Railway, determined upon travelling by the new and fashionable route *via* Folkestone. The process of taking your ticket is here exceedingly diverting, and forms the first amusement which the tourist encounters. For it is only by dint of running in and out of half a dozen doors, and interrogating as many policemen, that a vague idea is at last formed of where he ought finally to apply. This accomplished, and the money paid, he is sure to get upon *some* railroad; but whether the one upon which he intends to travel, is only found out on arriving at the end of the line. Travellers for Brighton are usually set down at Deptford, and the best way of ensuring a deliverance at Dover is to take a ticket for Greenwich. For near the terminus, the lines of rail cross and recross, and interweave in such a mysterious manner, that it only remains a wonder how the engine eventually gets anywhere at all, beyond through the walls of the line and down into St. Olave's schools.

The Author has been unable to find a diagram of London Bridge actually dated 1844/45, and so the particulars already given has been taken from a plan showing certain proposed alterations, and dated 26 May 1847. It is thought that the lay-out itself had not been altered when this plan was prepared, and that the proposed alterations so dated may well have been shown on a plan prepared about 1845.

It is now necessary to revert to 1842, in which year, in his capacity of Engineer-in-Chief to the London and Brighton Railway (to which position he was appointed after the Brighton line was built), John Urpeth Rastrick sent a report on 29 August to the chairman and directors of that company.[6] This report dealt with three separate subjects, as follows: locomotives on order for the company; signals; and the construction of the line and on permanent way on the Croydon line. Those portions of his report dealing with locomotives and signals will be noticed in Volume II of this account, but attention must now be given to the third section of his report.

Concerning the construction of the line and the permanent way on the London & Croydon Railway, Mr. Rastrick stated that on Saturday morning 20 August 1842 he went to New Cross to see Mr. C. H. Gregory (then Resident Engineer to the London & Croydon Railway), and while waiting for Mr. Gregory he examined the line in the vicinity of New Cross. This part of his interesting report is reproduced in the Appendix to this chapter. His prophecy of falls in the cuttings south of New Cross, in addition to those that had already occurred, was soon to be proved correct, and in fact such falls have continued occasionally up to the present day.

Mr. Rastick concluded his report as follows:

I am further of opinion that the Brighton will never be complete till we have a line direct from our own line at Croydon to the West End of the Metropolis but more of this at another opportunity. The following works must be done as the Stations cannot be used:

A road to Horley Station;

A road to Balcombe Station;
Coal Shed at the lower station at Brighton to be covered
in;
And Cranes for the different Warehouses on the line.
But I understand that the money I had received out of the
amounts of my Estimate in January last has been differently
appropriated, and that these works have been ordered to
be suspended.

Mr. Rastrick's view in 1842 that there should be a line from
the Croydon area to the west end of London is of great
interest, although it was not for well over a decade that the
first route in that general direction was opened, and over
18 years before Victoria was reached. His reference to Horley
and Balcombe presumably meant that wheeled vehicles could
not reach them, as they had of course been opened to traffic on
12 July 1841 when the line had been brought into use as far as
Haywards Heath. The 'lower station' at Brighton referred
to the goods station, to the east of, and at a lower level than,
the passenger station — see Chapter VII.
A number of other events must now be chronicled. The
first of these was that Spa Road station, which had been the
original temporary London terminus of the Greenwich line
from 8 February 1836 until London Bridge was brought into
use on 1 December 1836, and which had been closed at the
end of 1838, was reopened in September 1842. While it was
closed the Croydon's and later the Brighton's trains had run
past it, but the opening of the widened viaduct on 10 May
1842 meant that the Croydon, Brighton, and South Eastern
trains thereafter never passed it directly unless running over
the 1842 connection (see earlier in this Chapter); the rebuilt
station only served the two northern lines (the original
Greenwich lines) on the viaduct, and hence the reopening
had no real bearing on the Croydon, Brighton, and South
Eastern companies.
The next matter of importance to be recorded here was
that asphalting of the original Greenwich viaduct was completed in the summer of 1843. After then, there is no record
of any use of the two 'Croydon' lines (on the widened part of
the viaduct) by Greenwich trains.
The third event meriting attention was that the South

Eastern Railway, who of course owned the line from Coulsdon to Red Hill, closed Merstham station (opposite Gatton Park) on 1 October 1843, at which passengers had been accustomed to change when travelling between the South Eastern east of Red Hill and the Brighton south of Red Hill. Such passengers had now to change stations at Red Hill (Reigate) where both companies' stations were on the country side of the junction. The South Eastern wished, not unreasonably, to have an interchange station immediately on the London side of the junction, and apparently adopted a somewhat strong-arm method of achieving their purpose, which had been opposed by the Brighton company. The fact that the agreement for the first station at Merstham was made between Lord Monson and the London & Brighton company, whereas the line and station were subsequently transferred to the South Eastern company, seems unlikely to have been a factor in the closure of the station. Whatever considerations lay behind the South Eastern's action, they duly opened a new station at Red Hill under the name of Reigate, on Monday 15 April 1844, and closed their own station a short way round the curve towards Tonbridge on the same day. The Brighton also closed their Reigate station on the same day, so that thereafter there was only the one station there, immediately north of the junction. Finally, the South Eastern opened a new station at Merstham over ¾ mile farther north than the earlier one, and thus nearer the village, on 4 October 1844.

Another matter of importance was that the South Eastern Railway purchased Folkestone Harbour in 1843, and in 1844 laid a branch line to it, initially for goods traffic only. Folkestone Harbour had been built in 1809 by Thomas Telford, but had not been a commercial success. A shipping connection with Boulogne was established in connection with the South Eastern railway, which thus entered the continental business.

An important improvement made by the Croydon company was the elimination of the level crossing at the north end of Dartmouth Arms station. This crossing must have been the source of considerable delay to road traffic, apart from its being a nuisance on a line carrying the traffic of three companies. The road coming down the hill from the west (now London Road), was diverted to the left and then taken to the right under the Croydon line, to join its former alignment to the east of the railway. The work was completed during the winter of 1843-44, and was reported at the half-yearly general meeting of the London & Croydon company on Thursday, 7 March 1844.[7]

Finally, at that half-yearly general meeting, the Chairmen of the Croydon drew attention to the heavy expenses that had been incurred due to slips occurring in the cuttings, and went on to point out that earth piled on the tops of cutting sides as an economy measure in the latter period of constructing the Croydon line, had been a major source of trouble in causing slips.[8]

It will be recalled that, before any line to the south or south-east was authorized, the South Eastern company were interested to reach Brighton as well as Dover. It was therefore not entirely surprising that on 29 November 1843 the South Eastern company offered to lease the Brighton company, a firm proposal to pay the London & Brighton company £100,000 per year for the lease for 21 years being made by the South Eastern Railway on 11 January 1844. This matter was reported at the half-yearly general meeting of the London & Brighton company held at London Bridge on Wednesday 7 February 1844, with the statement that the Brighton directors had declined the South Eastern's proposal; the meeting later gave unanimous approval to the directors' action.[9] The South Eastern also considered attempting to gain some form of control over the Croydon, but this, too, came to nothing.

By 1843 third class vehicles had been introduced on the main line to Brighton (they had always been available on the Shoreham branch), being run on trains conveying also first-class and second-class stock. Additionally, certain trains were formed of first-class stock only and stopped only at principal stations (which became known as 'first-class' stations); two compartments in these trains were allocated to servants in attendance on their employers. Hence there were four levels of fares: first class by first-class trains; and first, second, and third class by ordinary trains. In the summer of 1843 the single fares between London and Brighton were 14s. 6d. first class by first-class train, and 14s., 10s., and 7s. for

185

first, second, and third class respectively.

In August 1843 the Brighton company reduced some of its fares, the new ones to Brighton being 8s. second and 5s. third. This resulted in greatly increased traffic, the additional revenue more than offsetting the extra working expenses. The latter for the half-year ended 31 December 1843 were, in fact, given as only £30,075-7-0, whilst the receipts were £119,660-4-1, a most impressive operating ratio.[9] At this period day return tickets between London and Brighton cost 20s. and 14s. first and second class respectively. Additionally, season tickets were announced in Bradshaw at rates of £14 for one month, £24 for two months, and £100 for a year; presumably these rates were for first-class travel. Weekly traffic figures for the London-Brighton line in 1843 were: passengers, 11,317; receipts, £3,073. Presumably these were average figures.[10]

At the half-yearly meeting referred to above, the view was expressed that an improved service of steamers should be established between Shoreham, Brighton, and France, to encourage traffic. Also, consideration was given to supporting new lines from Shoreham to Chichester and from Brighton to Hastings, both promoted independently.[11]

Reverting to 1842, the unusual step was taken by the Croydon and the South Eastern companies of working and maintaining their locomotives and rolling stock in common, to effect economies. The establishment of the pool under a joint committee was announced in a report issued by the South Eastern Railway dated 31 May 1842. At the end of 1843, repair of London & Brighton locomotives and stock ceased to be carried out at Croydon and Horley, and was concentrated at Brighton; and on 1 March 1844 the Brighton company's locomotives and stock were brought into the pool.

The Illustrated London News for 17 February 1844 referred to meetings having been held by hackney-carriage proprietors to raise objections in Parliament: to the arrangements made by some railway companies in connection with certain of the hackney-carriage proprietors. In brief, the railways concerned had made arrangements for certain privileged cabs to enter their termini to take up fares, thereby of course militating against other cab proprietors. The Author is not aware of any arrangements of such a nature at

London Bridge, at any rate at this time.

As a result of observing the semaphore signals on the Croydon line, Rastrick recommended in his report dated 29 August 1842 that this type of signal should be adopted by the Brighton company in replacement of the latter's double-disc signals. This change was started soon after the date of Rastrick's report, but a new pattern of double-disc signal was later introduced as a distant signal, so as to distinguish it clearly from a normal stop signal (see Chapter XVI). This matter will be dealt with in greater detail later in Volume II of this book, but in the meantime it is worth recording that the Brighton company included a quantity of signal discs in a collection of surplus material auctioned on Tuesday 18 April 1844.[12]

The Government had already recognised the usefulness and importance of railways, and made arrangements with a number of companies for the conveyance of army personnel and horses under special regulations effective from 1 January 1844. These arrangements were made with the London and Brighton and with the South Eastern companies, as well as with many others not associated with the south and south-east of England, but the Croydon company was not involved — no doubt because of its local character.[13]

The Regulations of Railways Act of 1844 (there were earlier Acts on this subject, in 1840 and 1842) gave the Government authority to purchase a railway, subject to various conditions. It might therefore be said that the seeds of ultimate Nationalisation were sown in that year.

The first excursion tickets to Brighton were issued on Easter Monday, Tuesday, and Wednesday, 8-10 April 1844, the return journey being at single fare (then 12s. first class, 8s. second class and 5s. third class). Passengers were limited to what were advertised as Mixed Trains (i.e. all three classes), and special trains were not scheduled. Tickets were avilable by the 08 30, 12 00, 15 00 and 18 30 down trains, and by the 07 00, 10 00, 13 45 and 18 30 up trains. A notice to this effect was published on 29 March.[14] The South Eastern made similar arrangements; the South Western was apparently the pioneer in arranging cheap return tickets, on an earlier occasion.

It has been stated that the first excursion train to Brighton, run on the Easter Monday, left London Bridge with 45 vehicles worked by four engines, another engine and six more vehicles being put on at New Cross, with a further similar strengthening at Croydon.[15]

The Illustrated London News for Saturday 13 April (i.e. at the end of that Easter week) stated that the train was formed of 35 carriages and was worked by four locomotives, and arrived at Brighton at 12 20 instead of its usual time of 11 00 (thus revealing that the train concerned represented the 08 30 London Bridge). This journal went on to say that upwards of 7,500 passengers travelled between Brighton and London on the Easter Monday.

The Author has been unable to find any authority for these statements, but Herepath on Saturday 13 April 1844 (i.e. on the same day as the Illustrated London News) stated that the first down train to Brighton "contained thirty-eight carriages, and was propelled by four engines".[16] What really matters, however, was the resulting traffic, and this is recorded as follows:[16]

London & Brighton Railway:	number of passengers	5468
	Extra receipts	£1943
	(over previous week)	
South Eastern Railway:	Extra receipts	£700
	(over previous week)	nearly
	(Easter Monday only)	

On 1 March 1843 a train ran into a flock of sheep at Horley.

One other matter requires to be noted. North of Redhill the road was being used by two companies (the Brighton and the South Eastern) for some 12 miles. From thence (i.e. south of Jolly Sailor) to Corbett's Lane Junction the Croydon company's trains also used the road (which that company of course owned between those places). Some method of ascertaining to which company an oncoming train belonged was therefore found to be necessary, particularly after the Locomotive Pool was completed by the inclusion of the Brighton company's engines into the common stock on 1 March 1844.

Hence locomotive headcodes were introduced, at first primarily to identify express trains from the rest.

APPENDIX
EXTRACT FROM REPORT
BY
MR. J. W. RASTRICK
On his Inspection of the State of the Deep Cutting at New Cross and Forest Hill* on 20 August 1842.

The means that Mr. Gregory is taking of Cutting away the sides and making the slopes flatter will certainly be one means of arresting the Soil from running down into the Cutting but I have great doubts whether even the greatest Slope that can be given to the sides in the deep Cutting (although the plan will no doubt answer better where the Cutting is shallower) will effectively prevent the Soil from running over the Rails in very wet weather.

I observed that even notwithstanding the very long term of fine dry weather that the Soil breaks off and presses the masses forward in a most extraordinary degree and if the greatest perseverance and constant attention had not been used to clear away the material as it fell down, the Road would have been stopped occasionally during the Summer. I likewise observed on walking along on the sides of the Cutting where at present nothing has occurred to give any appearance of Slips being likely to happen that there are wide deep Cracks for most part all along the top Edge of the Cutting into which I could put my Stick down to a depth of three feet and this dry weather continuing will increase the evil by extending and enlarging these cracks and occasionally fresh ones and when the wet weather commences (and I am apprehensive that it will be of some continuance when it once sets in October) all these Cracks will be filled with wet and a great portion of the wet will sink further down into and saturate the Soil and then very considerable Slips may be expected to take place and I will venture to state that Slips will take place where there is not the least Symptoms at present.

Between the deep Cutting at New Cross and Forest Hill the Soil from the original Cutting has been placed very near the Top Edge of the Cutting.

I observed that Gullets had been cut in a great variety of places which I learned from Mr. Gregory had been done to obtain the Cross Sections and that the Soil and Spoil was all to be sloped off to the level of the bottom of the Gullets. This is all very proper and very judicious and I hope they will be able to get the whole removed before the wet Season sets in, as there is I believe nearly 15 or 20000 Cubic Yards to remove they must use extraordinary means to get this work done in time.

*The station at this point was called Dartmouth Arms until 3 July 1845.

There are other stations on this line that I apprehend some serious Slips will occur: the first is a Cutting just on the South side of Sydenham Station and another on the South side of Anerley Station. The material here is equally as treacherous as the Soil at New Cross and at Forest Hill and different results cannot be expected.

On the whole I consider that these Cuttings will have to be maintained at a very heavy expense to the Croydon Company and I very much fear that we may have the Brighton Traffic seriously interrupted during the Winter.

I have occasionally noticed the state of the Rails and the Timbers on which they are laid and my firm conviction is that they will at a much earlier period than is anticipated have to be entirely removed and replaced by others of a more substantial quality and different construction.

Having had the opportunity of viewing the Croydon Railway and these being my sentiments upon the state and condition thereof I have thought it my duty as Engineer in Chief to the Brighton Railway Company to communicate to the Directors these few Remarks, that they may be taken into serious considerations and when any interruptions take place they may be prepared to apply such means as to occasion the least inconvenience to the Public.

I am further of opinion that the Brighton Railway will never be complete till we have a line from our own line at Croydon to the West End of the Metropolis but more of this at another opportunity.

The following Works must be done as the Stations cannot be used:

A Road to Horley Station.

A Road to Balcombe Station,

Coal Shed at the lower Station at Brighton to be covered in,

And Cranes for the different Warehouses on the line.

But I understand that the money I had received out of the amount of my Estimate in January last has been differently appropriated and that these Works have been ordered to be suspended.

I am

Gentlemen

Your most Obt Sert

John U. Rastrick.

10 Angel Court
Throgmorton Street
LONDON

NOTES

1. Simms, F. W. *An Account of Brickmaking at Bletchingley Tunnel*. Excerpt Min. Proc. Inst. C.E., 25 April 1843.
2. Thomas, R. H. G. *London's First Railway: the London & Greenwich*. Batsford, 1972, 122-123.
3. Original Minutes held by Public Records Office at 66 Porchester Road, London W.2.,* local reference LBR 1/29.
4. *Herepath's Railway and Commercial Journal, VI* (13 January 1844), 41-42.
5. Punch's Continental Tour, *Punch*, 5 (1843-44), 157.
6. Original Minutes held by Public Records Office at 66 Porchester Road, London, W.2.,* local reference LBR 3/12.
7. Herepath, VI (9 March 1844), 265.
8. *Ibid.,* 271.
9. *Ibid.,* (10 February 1844), 133-140.
10. *Surrey Life,* 4 (May 1975), 36.
This quotes from *The Illustrated London News*, without identifying the actual issue of that periodical in which the original statements were made (Author's Note: the Illustrated London News statements probably appeared in 1844).
11. Herepath (10 February 1844), 133 and 138.
12. *Ibid.,* (6 April 1844), 396.
13. *Ibid.,* (6 January 1844), 15.
14. *Ibid.,* (6 April 1844), 391.
15. Dendy Marshall, C.F. *A History of the Southern Railway.* Southern Railway, 1936, 270-271. Also 2nd Edition, revised by Kidner, R .W., Ian Allan, 1963, Vol. 1, 203.
16. Herepath, VI (13 April 1833), 391.

*Correct at date of going to press.

CHAPTER TEN

The
Bricklayers Arms
Branch

EXTENSIVE reference has already been made to the effect of the tolls legally exacted by the Greenwich company for every passenger brought along its metals by the Croydon, Brighton, and South Eastern companies; and to the various proposals and (in some cases) trials of strength by the Croydon and South Eastern companies to affect a change. The Brighton company gave moral support to the Croydon, but little more. This was because the Brighton board was friendly towards the Greenwich board, and often included a Greenwich director. It must also be recalled that both the Brighton and the South Eastern companies, although running mutually toll-free over the length from Red Hill to Norwood (of which one-half was owned by each of those companies), had themselves to pay tolls to the Croydon company for running over the latter's line from Norwood to Corbett's Lane. Because the two larger companies were dependant on the Croydon, in order to reach London, they supported the Croydon's efforts in attempting to get an agreed change in the toll paid to the Greenwich; and because the Croydon was itself getting into financial difficulties, each of the larger companies sought means of guarding against any possibility of the Croydon being no longer in a position to afford them access to London.

The constant bickering, and the financial state of both the Croydon and the Greenwich companies, led to suggestions in 1842 that the Brighton and the South Eastern should themselves lease the two smaller companies. Nothing came of this idea at the time, but later a further suggestion was made that the South Eastern should lease the Croydon, and

towards the end of 1843 the South Eastern made a firm proposal to lease the Brighton, as already noted. Both the
Croydon and the Brighton turned down a lease by the S E Rly,
for different reasons: the Croydon was then considering an
extension of the line from Croydon to Epsom which it felt
would bring in much traffic and revenue to itself; whilst
the Brighton thought that the terms actually proposed by
the South Eastern were inadequate. In addition, the Brighton
did not want the Croydon to fall into South Eastern hands,
as this would strengthen the latter at the expense of the
Brighton. Viewed in the above light, it will be clear why the
only really practical solution — namely the building of a new
line turning off from the Croydon line just south of Corbett's
Lane, and running to an independent station in London,
thus avoiding the Greenwich altogether — was finally
decided upon by the Croydon and South Eastern companies.

Two other factors each had a bearing on this policy
decision. One of these was the desire to take passengers to
and from a station more convenient to the evergrowing
western part of London, with stations such as Euston and
Paddington giving a considerable traffic potential. The
other factor was the need to provide adequate facilities for
freight traffic, including livestock, nearer to London than
those then at New Cross, supplemented by the small depot
at London Bridge used by the Brighton company. A decision
was therefore taken by the South Eastern and the Croydon
companies to seek authority to build a line to a station
beside the Old Kent Road, from which it might later be
extended still nearer to London. The Brighton company
apparently had no part in this decision.

The London & Greenwich company naturally opposed
the new line with all means at its disposal, as, if built, it
would enable the other companies to divert all their trains
on to it and so avoid the payment of tolls to the Greenwich
company — a situation which that company could not afford
to face. However, despite all opposition the proposition went
ahead, in the shape of a line starting some 36 chains south of
Corbett's Lane and finishing at a station on the north-east
side of the Old Kent Road close to the Bricklayers Arms
hostelry, after which the station was named. Passengers and
their luggage were to be taken by road between Bricklayers

Arms station and 'the west end'. The line itself soon also acquired the title of the Bricklayers Arms branch. The Act (6 & 7 Vic. cap. 62) received the Royal Assent on 4 July 1843. Section 19 stipulated that the South Eastern was to bear two-thirds of the cost of the line, and the Croydon one-third: and by Section 20 the South Eastern was also given the option of buying out the Croydon's share.

The terminus of the line at Bricklayers Arms was at ground level, and a site of 26 acres had been acquired[1] to give adequate space for both passenger and goods stations. Entrance was from the Old Kent Road. The line ran beside this on its north-east side, curving gradually to the left mostly at about a mile radius for some 60 chains until it entered a straight approximately 35 chains long, after which it curved right at about 60 chains radius for some 40 chains to form a junction with the Croydon company's line 36 chains south of Corbett's Lane. The gradients were level or negligible over the initial curve, after which the line rose at about 1 in 200 to the junction with the Croydon line. There was an overbridge just clear of the throat of the yard, which carried Upper Grange Road (now Dunton Road) across the line and which was generally called Greyhound bridge, and a level crossing some 10 chains farther on, where the initial left-hand curve finished and the straight began. This crossing was known as Mercer's. The line next crossed over a lane known as Hyson Road, and then over Corbett's Lane by an underbridge later called Victory bridge, after the adjacent inn. At this point the right-hand curve commenced which ended at the junction with the Croydon.

An embankment started soon after Mercer's crossing and continued for a short distance beyond Victory bridge. There being no excavation on the line, the spoil for this embankment came from the down side of the cutting south of New Cross, where land was owned by the Croydon company in the space between the railway and the alignment of the former canal. Beyond the south end of the embankment there was a timber viaduct leading up to the Croydon line, this form of construction being cheaper to build than the making of an embankment for which suitable spoil would have had to have been brought from a considerable distance. Details of this viaduct are given in Figure 24. It is of interest

194

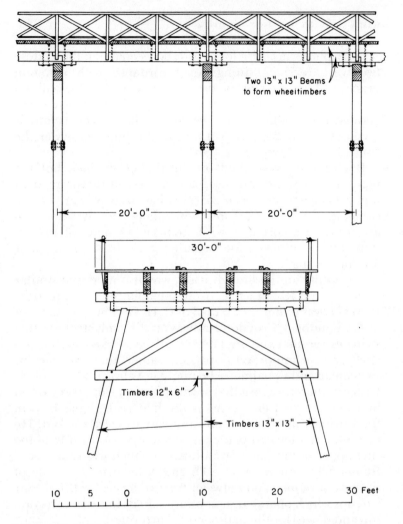

Figure 24. Bricklayers Arms Branch: Timber Viaduct approaching Bricklayers Arms Junction.

to note the lack of any form of bracing between successive uprights.

No particular difficulties seem to have occurred in building the line, but the station roof at Bricklayers Arms collapsed on 11 April 1844 while under construction. One man was killed and nine injured.[2] The contractors for the Bricklayers Arms branch were Messrs. Grissel & Peto, and the

195

work only took a few months.

Bricklayers Arms station had the usual arrival and de-parture platforms, with four roads between them: the middle two were carriage sidings in accordance with common practice. The exterior of the station was due to William Tite, and was the subject of a drawing which grossly exag-gerated the height of the facade. A plan of the layout is given in Figure 25. The working of the line was under the control of Mr. George.[3]

Bridge rails were used on the timber viaduct, but the types of chairs and rails used for the rest of the permanent way are shown in Figure 26. This has been prepared from contemporary drawings, but with plans and elevations re-arranged in accordance with modern methods of projec-tion. The positions of the fastening holes in the joint chair are interesting.

Signalling on the branch itself, was also no doubt similar to normal S E Rly practice, using semaphores. The junction, however, was under the control of C. H. Gregory as Engineer of the London & Croydon Railway, and he felt strongly that switches (points) and signals should be worked in conson-ance at this important junction, rather than by various switchman and signalmen who might not always be in unison. Gregory therefore installed at this junction what is regarded by railway signal engineers as the first real 'signal box' in the world, from which points and signals were worked. He provided an elevated platform on the up (south) side of the line opposite the junction points, on which was mounted a framework containing, at each end, a lever to work one of the sets of points, and between the two levers he fitted four stirrups which operated semaphore signals for each direction (up and down) for the main and branch lines.

The semaphores, which were mounted in pairs on two posts above the signalman's platform, were so arranged that, as seen by drivers approaching from New Cross, the left-hand arm on the left-hand post applied to movements on to the Bricklayers Arms branch, and the arm to the right of it but on the same post, applied to movements off the branch. Similarly, the left-hand and right-hand arms on the right-hand post applied to movements to and from Corbett's Lane respectively. Gregory also introduced the first elements of

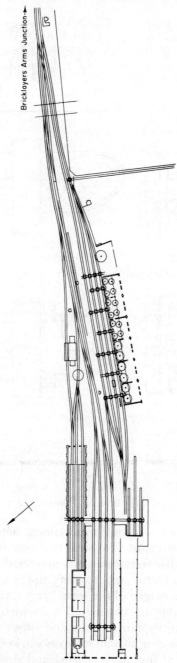

Figure 25. Bricklayers Arms Station: Layout in 1844.

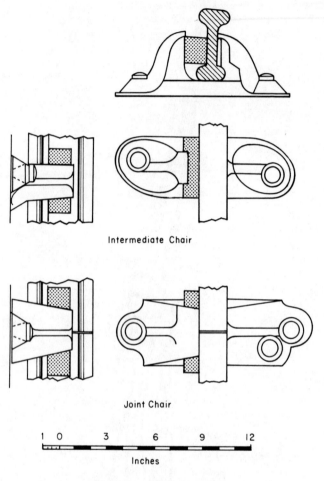

Figure 26. Bricklayers Arms Branch: Types of Chairs.

interlocking, but without mechanism between the point
levers and the stirrups to insure their consonance.

A shelter for the signalmen was provided on the platform,
and the use of a framework to carry the point levers and the
stirrups was the origin of the term 'frame', thereafter used to
describe the apparatus in a signal box which contains a set of
levers operating signals, points, and other functions.

The semaphore signals themselves worked to two positions
only — horizontal for 'on' and inclined downwards for 'off',

and did not move to the vertical position then used in connection with time-interval working. The fact that the 'off' position corresponded to the 'caution' position under time-interval working, was in accordance with the then practice of requiring all movements through junctions to be made carefully. Red and green lights, only, were used at night, green being then the usual colour for 'caution.'

During fog, men with Cowper's detonating fog signals were employed, a driver having to stop as soon as his engine exploded such a signal. He then gave the appropriate route code on his engine whistle, and listened for a mechanically-worked bell which the signalman at the junction operated under a code of rings when everything was in order for the driver to proceed.

This installation is always stated to have been brought into use in 1843 (and so before the official opening of the Bricklayers Arms branch on 1 May 1844). No doubt useful experience of operating this signalling system was obtained in the intervening period, particularly in connection with the working of engineer's trains to and from the branch while the latter was under construction. A similar installation was put in soon afterwards at Brighton (or Croydon) junction south of Jolly Sailor (soon to be renamed Norwood) — see Chapter XV.

During construction of the line the Croydon company made a further attempt to solve the 'Greenwich Problem' by what would nowadays be called a take-over bid, emphasizing to the Greenwich directors that unless they agreed to discuss the Croydon's proposals for toll revisions the Greenwich company would suffer a 'fearful diminution of their sources of revenue.' The Croydon company also referred to their proposals for atmospheric working (which is dealt with separately in Chapter XIV). The Greenwich board, however, would not agree to toll discussions with the Croydon board, and the overall positions remained unchanged for all practical purposes until the Bricklayers Arms branch was opened.

As soon as the line to Bricklayers Arms was brought into use, the London & Croydon Railway diverted many of its trains on to the branch and the South Eastern company followed a policy of putting all its traffic on to the branch.

The Croydon's service was hourly from Bricklayers Arms at 08 05 to 12 05 and from 13 20 to 21 20 (with the 11 05 and 12 05 omitted on Sundays), with a similar pattern from Croydon. Fares were advertised as follows:

Bricklayers Arms to:		New Cross	Dartmouth Arms and Sydenham	Anerley, Jolly Sailor, and Croydon
Singles:	First	Not advertised originally, but later shown as same as Day Returns (below)	1s.	1s. 3d.
	Second		9d.	1s.
	Third		6d.	9d.
Day Returns:	First	8d.	Not advertised	2s.
	Second	6d.		1s. 6d.
	Third	4d.		1s.

*Advertised to Anerley only.

Connecting omnibus services at scheduled times were advertised from four points in the West End and the City, the fares being 6d. to and from the West End and 3d. to and from the City.

The foregoing fares represented substantial reductions over and above the elimination of the Greenwich company's fixed toll element of the previous fares to and from London Bridge, as shown below:

Fares to Croydon	From B. Arms	From L. Bridge
First	1s. 3d.	2s. 3d.
Second	1s.	1s. 9d.
Third	9d.	—

The reduced fares greatly stimulated traffic. Statistics, covering in 1844 both London termini, and in 1843 London Bridge only, and including Brighton and South Eastern companies' passengers carried over the Croydon, were:

	First Week		Second Week	
	1844	1843	1844	1843
Passengers	10,815	4,049½	11,478	4,630½
Receipts	£449 16s 11d	£252 1s 10d	£458 19s 11d	£282 17s 3d

Some of the extra traffic naturally came as a result of extensions to the South Eastern's line during the year, but most of the greatly improved traffic was undoubtedly due to the lower fares. At about the same time a start was made on enclosing the second-class stock, and in roofing the thirds.

Although, therefore, the Croydon's position was better than before the Bricklayers Arms branch was built, the respective costs per mile of the four companies must not be overlooked, since the large capital involved had, in both the small companies, to be serviced from low mileages:

		Figures for 1844		
Company	Miles Open	Capital and Loan: £	Cost per mile: £	Typical Week's Total Receipts: £
Greenwich	3¾	nearly 1,000,000	264,228	770- 6- 0
Croydon	10½	811,000	80,400	412-12-11
Brighton	46	2,518,000	57,262	3,667-15- 5
South Eastern	78	2,765,000	36,835	4,069-13- 4

After the branch was opened, the tolls received by the London & Greenwich company were limited to those from the Brighton company (which continued to run all its trains to London Bridge) and to those arising from the reduced service of Croydon trains into London Bridge. This position had naturally been fully foreseen by the Greenwich company and resulted in the half-yearly general meeting on 29 January 1844 being of such a nature as to cause Herapath to state that 'We do not remember ever to have witnessed a more stormy and vexatiously protracted meeting than that of this Company, held on Tuesday last.'[4] The company's report[5] was inevitably concerned with the question of the toll, including the Croydon company's proposal that the flat rate of 4½d should be changed to a sliding scale of 4d first-class, 3d second class, and 2d third class—a proposal with various strings which the Greenwich Board had rejected.

The Author has analysed the accounts of the Greenwich company as presented to this meeting, which were shown in such a way that it is difficult to extract the true operating costs from certain maintenance costs.

The Author's assessment is that the result of various economies had borne fruit and that the half-year ended 31 December 1843 the operating revenue had been £19,664 exclusive of tolls which were £6,460, the operating cost having been about £5,500. This in itself was good, but of

201

course the servicing of the company's relatively very large capital of some £942,000, together with some £84,000 owing in various quarters, meant that nearly all the profits were required for interest on bonus and preference shares, and on temporary loans, leaving nothing for the ordinary shareholders. If the revenue from tolls were markedly reduced, either by the diversion of traffic to Bricklayers Arms or by a reduction in the level of tolls, the company's position would clearly be greatly worsened.

The Greenwich proprietors were naturally angry because no dividend was paid on the ordinary shares, and even the preference shareholders did not receive their full amount of 5%. It was proposed that the dividends should be made up from the company's general funds (as George Hudson apparently did with certain lines under his control!), but advice from counsel was to the effect that the directors were not authorised to do this. Hence it at last became clear to everyone concerned, that the Greenwich could not continue indefinitely in the way it had done hitherto. In the meantime, a further exchange of letters between the Croydon and Greenwich secretaries, on behalf of their respective boards, had taken place in April 1844, the correspondence, of considerable importance, being printed in Herapath.[6]

As a result, the London & Greenwich board suggested to the South Eastern either that the shares of the two companies should be amalgamated, or that the South Eastern should take over the Greenwich on a perpetual lease, the Greenwich favouring a lease. On 23 May 1844 the Brighton company offered the Greenwich the opportunity for amalgamation, purchase, or lease—possibly having heard of the action of the Greenwich board, since there were fairly close relations between the Brighton and Greenwich boards. The South Eastern were in no hurry to discuss details with the Greenwich, and the latter then tried to force the pace by investigating the possibility of extending the line into Kent (as had from the start been a dream of the company); and at the same time telling the Brighton that as negotiations with the South Eastern had broken down, the Greenwich could begin discussions with the Brighton. The South Eastern's reply to the Greenwich company's action in investigating the possibility of a line to North Kent, was themselves to carry out a similar review, their proposed line (for which they had invited the Croydon's support) starting from Bricklayers Arms.

In the meantime the Croydon finally reached an agreement with the Greenwich on a sliding toll in proportion to the total length of journey, in the course of a larger agreement, involving the construction of one further road above Corbett's Lane in connection with the intended 'atmospheric' working on the Croydon line; this aspect is dealt with in detail later in this history. The toll agreement enabled the Croydon company to reduce their fares to and from London Bridge to the same level as those to and from Bricklayers Arms, this step taking place on 25 July 1844 and being reported in Herapath for 27 July.[7] William Cubitt was responsible for the proposals accepted by the Greenwich board.

The effect on the traffic flow was immediate, the bulk of the passengers transferring back to London Bridge and comparatively few still continuing to use Bricklayers Arms. Moreover, although the average toll to the Greenwich company was now 1¼d, the big increase in traffic (which had trebled due to the lower fare structure) gave an increased return to that company. The gross receipts to the Croydon also increased slightly.

The agreement with the Greenwich which the Croydon had at last achieved did not, however, bring peace to the former company, and discussions on leasing the Greenwich continued. Eventually terms were agreed between the Greenwich and the South Eastern for the former to be leased to the latter after midnight 31 December 1844, the South Eastern taking charge on and from 1 January 1845. The agreement included an annual rent to the Greenwich of £45,000 for the viaduct and adjacent land; and for locomotives, rolling stock, and stores be taken over on a separate valuation. Matters were legalized by an Agreement dated 11 February 1845, and were finally covered by an Act which received the Royal Assent on 21 July 1845. The Greenwich company continued to exist until 3 January 1923, but its activities were concerned solely with receiving the annual rent from the South Eastern company and distributing it as a dividend to the shareholders.

Hence, as from 1 January 1845, the Croydon and Brighton

companies paid tolls to the South Eastern for the use of the line between London Bridge and Corbett's Lane.

The construction of the Bricklayers Arms line caused work on the rebuilding of London Bridge station to be suspended, as explained in Chapter IX, and that station was never completed to the designs shown in the published accounts.

It must now be recorded that the locomotive and rolling stock pool which had been set up in 1842 by the South Eastern and Croydon companies, and which the Brighton company had joined in 1844 (see Chapter VIII), was not proving as advantageous as had been expected. Moreover, the South Eastern had failed to reach agreement with the Croydon that they should lease the latter company's locomotives, a step that they had hoped to achieve after reaching their agreement to lease the Greenwich company.

Hence the South Eastern decided late in 1844 to withdraw from the Joint Locomotive Committee which administered the pool, and to establish its own independent locomotive shed and repair shops. The most convenient location for these was considered to be at Bricklayers Arms, and hence the South Eastern informed the Croydon that it had decided to exercise its option to buy the Croydon company's share in the line in order to obtain possession of a suitable site. The latter was on the north-east or down side of the line, beside the station. The S E Rly locomotive depot at Bricklayers Arms seems to have been brought into use in the Spring of 1845.

NOTES

1. A curious story in the 'Kentish Mercury' of 12 May 1944 apparently implied that a portion of the site had been obtained irregularly; the owner, Henry Fuller, is stated to have gone to Ireland in 1834 and never returned, while his son went to America and left the land vacant.

2. Herapath's Railway and Commercial Journal VI (13 April 1844), 423.

3. *Ibid.* (4 May 1844), 517.

4. *Ibid.* (3 February 1844), 113.

5. *Ibid.* (3 February 1844), 101.

6. *Ibid.* (4 May 1844), 507-508.

7. *Ibid* (27 July 1844), 888. The new fares were put into operation on 25 July.

CHAPTER ELEVEN

The Shoreham and Chichester Line

R AILWAY communication with Portsmouth had been the subject of various proposals for horse traction (see Chapter I), but such schemes never came to fruition. There were two basic reasons for this: lack of public support, and defence.

No railway scheme could hope to progress unless it had firm promises of adequate finance, and such promises were generally lacking—certainly for a horse-era scheme for a route to Portsmouth. However, even if there had been sufficient support for such a line, it would probably not have been allowed to enter Portsmouth itself, on account of military considerations. Apart from being the major naval port, it was also an important army centre, most of the defence facilities being sited on Portsea island. The waterway along the north side of that island, and separating it from the mainland, was a natural moat against attack from the north, but in Napoleonic times additional fortifications were erected on Portsdown Hill, farther north, with their guns sited so as to command the landward approaches to Portsmouth. At the same time, incidentally, a series of circular forts was built in Spithead to give added protection against attack from the sea. On the west side of the entrance to the harbour stood Gosport, also fortified. Because a proposal for a railway in any form on to Portsea island would have had to pass the various fortifications, it is likely that the naval and army authorities would have opposed it sufficiently strongly on defence grounds that it would not have been authorized.

After the battle of Waterloo in 1815, and the resulting

disappearance of Napoleon from the European scene, a considerable period elapsed before defence questions assumed a peace-time perspective. By this time steam-operated railways, having proved thoroughly practicable following the opening of the Liverpool and Manchester Railway in 1830, were being built or projected in various directions, and conditions had become such that a railway to Portsmouth could be seriously considered.

The first railway approach to Portsmouth did not come direct, but from the west. The London & Southampton Railway, authorized in 1834 but not opened throughout until 11 May 1840, promoted a line from Bishopstoke to Gosport to serve the Portsmouth area, and received the Act for this line in 1839 (2 & 3 Vic cap. 28); the terminus was outside the fortifications at Gosport. That Act also authorized the London & Southampton Railway to change its title to the London & South Western Railway. The Gosport line was originally opened on Monday 29 November 1841, but was temporarily closed again four days later because of the Engineer's doubts on the stability of Fareham tunnel; it was brought back into use on Monday 7 February 1842.

A line westwards along the coast from Brighton had been an essential part of the London & Brighton's scheme, and that company was authorized on 15 July 1837 to build a branch from Brighton to Shoreham as well as its main line to Brighton. It is likely that extension of the Shoreham line towards Portsmouth, although not originally covered by the Act, would have been kept firmly in mind in any case, but authorization of the line to Gosport while the Brighton-Shoreham line was being built would naturally have under-lined the desirability of an extension from Shoreham so as to obtain a share of the traffic from and to the Portsmouth area. In the light of the foregoing, Shoreham station was built in a form suitable for extending the line westwards, as already recorded, and so never had station buildings behind the stops of the platform roads.

Supporters of a line westwards from Shoreham, originally proposed to run only to Worthing, later formed an inde-pendent company which issued a prospectus early in 1844 for a line as far as Chichester, an ancient Cathedral city and a centre for the agricultural district of West Sussex. It had been occupied by the Romans. The company, under the title of the Brighton & Chichester Railway Company, had a provisional committee including Captain Kelly, R N, the deputy Chairman of the London & Brighton Railway: Mr. Crowley, a director of the Brighton company; and nine other gentlemen all resident in the district. The Engineer was Rastrick. The proposed capital was £300,000 to be raised by 6,000 £50 shares, this being based on the estimated cost to build the way and works for a double line but to lay only a single line. It was calculated that the revenue, chiefly from passenger traffic, would be 'upwards of £40,000 a year' and the operating costs would be £16,000 a year, the balance of £24,000 a year giving a return of 8% on the total capital. On this basis, the prospectus went on to say that the London & Brighton directors had agreed, subject to confirmation by their proprietors, to lease the Brighton & Chichester · for 10 years from its completion at a rent of £12,000 per annum (giving 4% on the capital) together with half the net profits — the other half being retained by the Brighton company. The prospectus added that if the Chichester proprietors preferred to retain control of their line, the Brighton company 'will find the working power on terms to be agreed on'. The prospectus, published in Herapath for 27 January 1844,[1] asked for application for shares to be made on or before 6 February 1844, and said that the necessary notices had been given and the plans and sections deposited in Parliament, and that it was intended to apply for the Act during the current session.

The Brighton proprietors approved the proposals on 7 February, and progress was then rapid, because arrangements were completed in time for the Act to be dated 4 July 1844 (7 & 8 Vic cap. 67), the latter empowering the London & Brighton company to purchase the Brighton & Chichester company or an interest therein (Section 324). The Brighton & Chichester company was, in the event, one of those forming the London Brighton & South Coast Railway in 1846 (see Chapter XVI). The company had to recompense the Duke of Norfolk for the presumed loss of tolls from the nearby road bridge, and also purchased a wooden bridge some little way up-river from which it (the company) henceforth drew tolls.

The line commenced at Shoreham with a short rise of 1 in 80 to gain enough height to cross over two roads, before starting a fall 1¼ mile long. Just before the start of the steep rise, the line entered a 70-chain left-hand curve which commenced at the west end of the existing platforms at Shoreham (they have since been extended to the west a short way around that curve), this continuing for nearly ½ mile to the east end of the bridge over the estuary of the Adur. The summit of the bank was on this curve, and the fall that succeeded it for 1¼ mile included the estuary bridge, the gradient over which was 1 in 291 falling towards Chichester. The alignment was straight for 4 miles after the 70-chain left-hand curve, along which straight the falling gradient changed to a rise 1 mile long, first at 1 in 440 and then at 1 in 330. The first station, Lancing, was situated near the end of this rise. The rise was succeeded by some 65 chains of falling gradient, starting at 1 in 527 and later steepening to 1 in 425, after which there was a further 3 miles of generally rising gradient, ranging from 1 in 354 to 1 in 880. Nearly half-way along this rise the 4-mile straight ended in a 90-chain right-hand curve some 15 chains long, on which Worthing station was situated.

Beyond Worthing there was 1½ mile of virtual straight which was followed by a 140-chain right-hand curve some 15 chains long, at the west end of which the 3-mile rise ended in a short level before the line fell for about 1¾ mile, mostly on easy gradients but with about ½ mile at 1 in 471/338 near the bottom of the bank. About 50 chains down this bank, was situated the third station, Goring, beyond which the alignment was still generally straight but involved a short left-hand curve and later a short right-hand curve, of 80 and 150 chains radius respectively. It has been suggested that there was a proposal to have a station at Tarring Crossing, some 1¾ miles on the Worthing side of Goring, possibly instead of the latter, but positive evidence is lacking. The end of the 150-chain curve was near the end of the falling length, and the following straight, nearly ¾ mile long, was rising (mostly at 1 in 347). The end of this rise coincided with the end of the almost-straight alignment from Shoreham, as the route now involved a number of curves (80 chains radius or over) joined by lengths of straight for the next 4 miles. This

4-mile length started with 2 miles of fall (except for a short rise near the foot of the bank), a considerable part of it at 1 in 328; and there followed 1 mile rising at 1 in 660. Angmering, the fourth station, was situated about ¾ mile down the 2-mile fall, and the fifth, Littlehampton, was built at the end of the 1 in 660 rise. The station was about 2 miles north of the town of Littlehampton; its remains still exist.

There was then a further mile with a falling tendency and an easy right-hand curve to take the line down to the bridge over the river Arun. After the bridge, there was a left-hand curve nearly ½ mile long at 80 chains radius, after which the line was for practical purposes straight for nearly 8¾ miles to Chichester. There were constant changes of gradient, up and down, along this length, the steepest being a rise, going towards Chichester, at 1 in 228 for over 1 mile. The sixth station, Arundel (now Ford), some 2 miles south of the town (whose name has been suggested as a corruption of the French word Hirondelle, the name of Bevis' legendary horse), was placed part-way around the 80-chain curve west of the Arun bridge; the seventh, Yapton, was built about 1¼ mile farther on, a short way up the rise of 1 in 228. There was then a distance of about 2½ miles before the eighth station was reached, at Bognor (later Woodgate) and another 3¼ miles on to Drayton situated on a rise of 1 in 528. Chichester station was just under 2 miles beyond Drayton, and was approached down a falling gradient of 1 in 330 on a right-hand 80-chain curve.

The land is generally flat along this part of the Sussex coast, and construction costs for the railway were kept low by having the minimum in the way of earthworks, the line being built as far as possible at or near ground level and hence involving a large number of changes of gradient. For the same reason there were only a small number of bridges over roads on the length between Shoreham and Angmering, where the route was relatively close to the sea, but there was a considerable number of underbridges beyond Arundel where the route was some way inland. Virtually all bridges were brick arches. The ground level nature of much of the route, however, involved large numbers of level crossings.

Immediately west of Shoreham station there was a public road crossing now known as Buckingham Road, whilst beyond the 14-span bridge over the Adur (officially known as Shoreham Viaduct), there were three occupation crossings before reaching North Road crossing at the east end of Lancing station (now officially known as Lancing Crossing). There were two occupation crossings and two other crossings (Ladydell and Chesswood) approaching Worthing, Broadwater Road crossing (later replaced by an overbridge) and South Farm Road crossing west of that station, and three more (Tarring, Elm Grove, and Limbrick) before Goring. After Goring, there was a public road crossing (Goring Road) immediately west of the station, followed in quick succession by an occupation crossing, Ferring crossing, five more occupation crossings (the second one known as Nash's), Roundstone crossing, one other occupation crossing, and one other crossing before Angmering. Angmering Road crossing was immediately west of that station, and there then followed two occupation crossings, Brook Lane private road crossing (sometimes known as Bee Brook), three more occupation crossings, Norway Lane crossing, and Toddington crossing before reaching Littlehampton station. Arundel Road crossing was immediately west of Littlehampton station, and there were two occupation crossings on towards the Arun bridge.

Beyond that bridge there was a crossing east of Arundel station, and over the company's road to Arundel (as the company had had to make this road, wheeled vehicles had to pay tolls); another at Yapton; and a third at Lake Lane; as well as three occupation crossings, followed by seventeen crossings of different types on to Drayton (including two public roads, Woodgate and Drayton, and two others, Woodhorn and Oving Lane). Beyond Drayton there were a number of others including four over public roads (Portfield, Whyke Road, Basin Road, and Dell Quay). Stations seem to have had the usual two platforms with small yard, there also being a small engine shed on the south side at Littlehampton, just west of the station.

The two main engineering works on the line were Shoreham Viaduct and Arun Bridge. The former was a girder bridge. The Arun Bridge had to be constructed so as to provide free access for shipping to and from Arundel, and an opening 60 ft. wide had to be provided. This was done by arranging for a substructure to be built extending from the east bank of the river half-way across, on which there were wheelways. To the east of this substructure, a further sub-structure was constructed at right-hand angles to the line of the bridge and south of it, and also provided with wheel-ways. The bridge itself consisted of two moveable units, the main span 144 ft. long with an east approach unit 63 ft. long. The east approach unit was mounted on wheels arranged at right angles to its axis, the wheels running on the wheel-ways of the east substructure. The east approach span could therefore be moved sideways to the south along its sub-structure, and when so moved left a gap to the east of the main span which was nearly half the length of the latter. Hence, when the east approach span was moved sideways, the main span (also provided with wheels) could be run back by almost half its total length, thereby providing a clear opening parallel to the west bank of the river (Plate 14). The design of the bridge met the requirements of the Lords of the Admiralty.

To re-open the bridge to rail traffic, the main span was first returned to its normal position (in which the west end of the span was carried on an abutment on the west side of the river), and the east approach span was then moved sideways into place to complete the road. The spans were moved by hand-operated winches.

Construction was in timber, strengthened by iron, and the main span, which weighed 70 tons, included a framework 35 ft. high over the track from which diagonal tie-rods were taken down to the main frame of the moveable portion. The bridge was designed by Rastrick, for a single line only, perhaps because it was considered impracticable for such a design to carry the weight of two trains simultaneously, or even one train off centre. The width of the moveable por-tions was 12 ft. It will be remembered that the rest of the way and works were constructed for a double line, although initially only one road was provided (except, obviously, passing loops at certain stations).

The construction of the line was let to Messrs. Hale and Wythes separately, who, in partnership, had built the line from Brighton to Shoreham. The two men had apparently now set up independently, George Wythes for this contract operating from Patcham and John Hale from Emsworth. Wythes was awarded the contract for the length from Shoreham to Lyminster (Littlehampton station), a distance of 12 miles, 23 chains, 40 links, at a price of £67,500 including maintenance for one year after completion. Hale was awarded the length from Lyminster to Chichester, 10½ miles, the price being £62,000 including maintenance for one year after completion, but the construction of the drawbridge was let to Mr. John Eede Butt of Littlehampton. Some of the stations were built by Robert Bushby.

There do not seem to have been any particular troubles in building the line, and the work appears to have gone smoothly. The railway was opened for traffic in three stages:

Shoreham — Worthing..................................24 November 1845
Worthing — Littlehampton (Lyminster)...........16 March 1846
Littlehampton (Lyminster) — Chichester...............8 June 1846

Construction of the line to Chichester had hardly commenced when circumstances became propitious, at last, for a railway to enter Portsmouth, and matters were then pushed forward so that an Act for the extension was obtained on 8 August 1845. This line is dealt with in a later chapter of this book, but the extension is noted here because it meant that Chichester station would not be a terminus.

The permanent way consisted of 80-lb. bridge rails on cross sleepers. Signalling was probably to the Brighton company's standard — i.e., semaphore stop signals and double-disc 'turnover' distant signals (this pattern was introduced in 1846).

NOTE

1. Herapath's Railway & Commercial Journal, VI (27 January 1844), 96.

CHAPTER TWELVE

Extensions to the East

IT WILL be recalled that the London & Brighton Railway's Act authorized the construction of a line from Brighton to Lewes and Newhaven as well as the main line and a line from Brighton to Shoreham.

The reason for the lines to Lewes and Newhaven, and to Shoreham, was as already mentioned briefly, to serve the harbours of the two latter places, since Brighton itself has never had a harbour. Despite this, as early as 1792 there was a fleet of sailing ships trading regularly between Brighton and Dieppe, and a steamer *(Rapid)* was put on the service from 15 May 1824, sailing alternate days in each direction.

In June 1825, the General Steam Navigation Company's steamer *Eclipse* was put on the Newhaven-Dieppe service, sailing twice weekly in each direction and 'weather and circumstances permitting' calling at Brighton pier. In 1842 the G S N company started a service between Shoreham and Dieppe, connecting with trains on the Shoreham line.[1]

Protagonists of the line down the Adur valley to Shoreham and thence along the coast to Brighton, had stressed that that general route put Shoreham in direct communication with Brighton (and with London), thus avoiding the construction of a railway from Brighton to Shoreham which would be needed if the line from London used one of the 'direct' routes. Protagonists of an approach to Brighton from London by a course to the east of a 'direct' route, had in mind the possibility of a line to Newhaven. Factors of considerable importance in the choice of route from London to Brighton were therefore the respective advantages of Shoreham and Newhaven as sources of traffic. The people of

213

Brighton expected to derive benefit from the development of trade with the Continent and hence were considerably concerned with the outcome. A line of packets had already been established between Shoreham (Kingston Wharf) and France, calling at Brighton. On Mondays, Wednesdays, Thursdays, and Saturdays, the service was to Dieppe: on Tuesdays and Fridays it was to Havre. Support for Newhaven came from those who pointed out that the sea passage from there to Dieppe was shorter than that from Shoreham. A railway from Shoreham to Brighton was easier to construct than one from Newhaven to Brighton.

In the event, of course, a 'direct' route was chosen for the railway from London to Brighton, and this meant that both Shoreham and Newhaven could only be reached by branch lines. The Act of 15 July 1837 allowed both to be built, but only that to Shoreham was proceeded with initially. In the meantime, proposals were afoot in France for the construction of a railway from Paris to Dieppe, which would certainly facilitate trade with the British Isles. Hence the Mayor and President of the Chamber of Commerce of Dieppe sent a communication to the London & Brighton board inviting interest in the French proposals. The London & Brighton board passed a resolution in support of the proposals, and the Committee of Works had its meeting on Saturday 26 May 1838 delivered to the French consular agent at Brighton a list of parties requiring 350 shares in the proposed Paris-Dieppe company.[2]

Although, as already stated, construction of the line from Brighton to Newhaven did not proceed and trade with France was built up at Shoreham, the benefits of Newhaven harbour were still canvassed. Additionally, it was felt that Lewes, the county town of East Sussex, should be in railway communication with Brighton. As the London & Brighton Railway had not built such a line, a new concern was formed under the title of the Brighton, Lewes & Hastings Railway. There were two London & Brighton directors, and Rastrick was the Engineer. This concern had the blessing of the London & Brighton company, whose directors undertook (subject to the approval of their proprietors) to guarantee 4% per annum to the Brighton, Lewes & Hastings shareholders on the proposed capital of £475,000 for 10 years after the line was opened, together with a moiety of the profits which might be realized over and above such 4% . The capital was to be raised in 9,500 shares of £50 each, and was intended to cover the provision of works suitable for double track throughout, but with double track laid only as far as Lewes (beyond which a single road was to be laid initially).[3] In the meantime, the Rouen — Paris line was opened, bringing added emphasis to the question of trade with the Continent.

The London & Brighton company held a special meeting on 7 February 1844 at which the proposals were approved and matters then went ahead. The Brighton, Lewes & Hastings company received its Act on 29 July 1844 (7 & 8 Vic. Cap. 91), Section 328 empowering the company to sell their concern to the London & Brighton and authorizing the latter company to purchase the former. The Brighton, Lewes & Hastings company was, in the event, one of those forming the London Brighton & South Coast Railway in 1846 (see Chapter XVI).

The route required considerable engineering works, since it involved going across the deep valley in Brighton down which ran the turnpike road from London (later known as Preston Road), and then going over the high ground to the east of Brighton before descending to the Ouse valley at Lewes. In this area chalk predominates but there is some sand. After Lewes, the line ran for some 12 miles at the foot of the northern slopes of the South Downs (which end at Beachy Head) and then went along a flat plain close to the sea past Pevensey (where the Normans landed in 1066) until, at Bexhill some 4 miles before Hastings, a further range of hills approaches the sea. At this point the line had to climb to reach its terminus some 1½ mile short of Hastings. Temporarily, the terminus was at Bulverhithe.

The line commenced at Brighton and made a junction, trailing for trains from London, some ¼ mile from the stops in the station platforms. It turned sharply right from the junction (Figure 27), on a curve ranging from 17 down to 10 chains radius, which then eased to 70 chains and then sharpened to 50 chains. This initial right-hand compound curve extended for some 50 chains, and brought the line to an east-north-east direction. It will be recalled that the station area at Brighton had been levelled off on the east

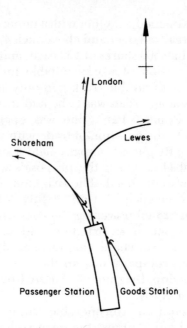

Figure 27. Lines at Brighton, 8 June 1846.

slope of a hill, and hence as soon as the Lewes line left the London line it had to be carried over stëadily falling ground whilst curving to the east. The first major work was therefore encountered here — the London Road viaduct over Preston Road, which started where the curve sharpened to 10 chains radius, and extended nearly to the end of the 70-chain section. On leaving the viaduct, the alignment continued for a short distance on the right-hand 70-chain curve, which then ran into a left-hand curve. At this point, the line was taken beneath Ditchling Road by an overbridge 63 yds long, which is officially called Ditchling Road tunnel. The left-hand curve succeeding the tunnel ranged from 68 to 62 chains for a total distance of almost a mile. The line was level until nearly at the end of the viaduct, but then started to rise at 1 in 258 for some 2¼ miles, after which it steepened to 1 in 101 for a mile to reach the summit some 4 miles from Brighton. Curvature up the bank was mainly to the right, and mostly at some 90-100 chains radius, but with a ½-mile straight and a ¼-mile left-hand 72 chain curve.

The summit level was some 35 chains long, and on this

216

was situated Falmer tunnel, 495 yds. long and straight (Plate 15). Beyond the summit the line descended at 1 in 88 for 3¼ miles, and then at 1 in 120 for about 30 chains, before becoming level approaching Lewes, some 8¼ miles from Brighton. The descent from Falmer tunnel past Falmer station (later resited west of the tunnel) was virtually all on a series of reverse curves, many of which were of compound design. The minimum radius was 80 chains except near the foot of the bank where there were two curves of 44 (to the right) and 46 (to the left) chains radius respectively, with an intervening length at 74 chains to the left. A tunnel 103 yds long and known as Kingston, was situated on the 74-chain curve on the 1 in 88 descent. Approaching Lewes, the route lay through the remains of Lewes Priory which had been founded and endowed by the first Earl de Warenne and his wife Gundreda, a daughter of William the Conqueror. The Priory eventually became one of the largest religious establishments in the south of England. It may be of interest at this point to note that, during construction of the line, the remains of de Warenne and Gundreda were discovered.[4]

At Lewes a most unusual layout was adopted, the approach from Brighton being passed through platforms known as Southover or Ham and then towards a facing junction, the line to the left going into a terminal station adjacent to Friars Walk and the line to the right curving sharply in that direction and continuing towards Pevensey and Hastings (Bulverhithe temporarily). Hence a train from Brighton towards Hastings running right into Lewes, had to be propelled out again before resuming its journey towards Pevensey (Figure 28).

Shortly after leaving Lewes the Hastings line was carried over the river Ouse at Southerham by an opening bridge, the general alignment curving to the left at radii of over 1 mile with the exception of one short length of 74 chains once clear of the bridge. Some 1¾ mile beyond Southerham bridge, there was a right-hand curve over ½ mile long at 90 chain radius. After this the line was virtually straight for some 21 miles, such curvature as was needed being mostly at 220 chains with long lengths of actual tangent between them. At the end of this stretch there was ¾ mile of curves down to 20 chains, to the terminus. From Lewes, the line

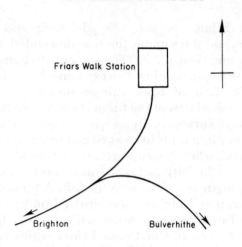

Figure 28. Lines at Lewes, 27 June 1846.

was nominally level for some 3¼ miles, and then rose mostly at 1 in 220 for a further 3¾ miles. Glynde, near which was a lime works, was the first station after Lewes. It was built about ½ mile before the start of the incline, and on the 90-chain right-hand curve before the long length of virtual straight. Berwick, the second station, was placed a short distance beyond the top of the rise and some 15¾ miles from Brighton; it was situated where the line crossed the road from Hailsham to Seaford.

Beyond Berwick, the line followed a slightly switch-back course in order to save earthworks, the steepest gradient being 1 in 176 for some 65 chains rising for trains going towards Hastings. This gentle switch-back extended past Polegate station for some 7¾ miles to Pevensey, the fourth station beyond Lewes and some 23¾ miles from Brighton, after which there were nearly 3 miles of dead level. The remainder of the route was gently undulating, the fifth station being at Bexhill some 6¾ miles after Pevensey, and the next one at Bulverhithe (St. Leonards), a temporary terminus a short way before the end of the line. Bulverhithe was 2¾ miles beyond Bexhill, this length involving a small amount of cutting and filling.

London Road viaduct consisted of 26 semi-circular arches of 30 ft. span, with one elliptical arch of 50 ft. span over Preston Road itself. The piers of this arch are stated to have been 22 ft. thick at the base, and 19 ft. 6 in. at the springing level: the piers of the ordinary arches are stated to have been 7 ft. thick at the base and 5 ft. at the springing level.[5] The viaduct being on a curve and the piers being normal to the curve, it follows that the piers were thicker at the outer side (i.e., the 'to Lewes' side) than at the inner side. The dimensions quoted were probably the nominal ones, taken along the longitudinal centre-line of the double track laid over the viaduct. The structure had a maximum height to rail level of 67 ft. and was 400 yds long. Each pier contained a jack arch with a semi-circular soffit and invert, so as to reduce the number of bricks required as compared with a solid pier.

Ditchling Road tunnel has already been mentioned, and the next work to be referred to by name is Hollingdean Road underbridge, which was followed by Lewes Road underbridge, some 2 miles from Brighton. Lewes Road bridge consisted of three arches each 60 ft. on the skew, the track being carried 46 ft. above Lewes Road. There was then a footpath crossing some ½ mile east of Lewes Road bridge, and two further underbridges before Falmer tunnel, the latter constructed through chalk with sand veins and involving one shaft.

Falmer station was situated in the cutting east of the tunnel, the buildings being on top of the cutting with steps down to platform level. After the line emerged from the cutting, it was carried for a considerable distance on a high embankment, through which there were eight underbridges before Kingston tunnel. The third of these was known as Newmarket bridge, because it crossed over the road to Newmarket Hill, and the Newmarket inn was situated to the north of the railway; the fourth underbridge was known as Ashcombe bridge. Kingston tunnel had no shaft, being only 103 yds long. There followed four underbridges close together, the third one being over Cockshot Road, and an overbridge carrying Ham Lane over the railway.

Eastwards from Lewes there was only one work of importance — Southerham bridge. The latter had to be constructed as an opening bridge in order to preserve the navigable rights on the river Ouse. The structure consisted of three spans of which the middle was pivoted at the west or Lewes end and was capable of being raised on its pivots so as to leave an opening for river traffic*. (The Author has been unable to substantiate a suggestion that a telescopic form of construction was adopted for this bridge as originally built).

After Southerham bridge, there were four level crossings before Glynde — the first one near the east end of Southerham bridge, and the others (Ranscombe, Cow, and Beddingham) farther east. There were nine crossings between Glynde and Berwick, the first being Ripe and the eighth Selmeston, and sixteen further ones on to Pevensey — the first immediately east of Berwick, the fifth and sixth being called Milton and Wilmington, the eighth Polegate, the ninth Ditton Farm, and the sixteenth immediately west of Pevensey. Beyond here, there were a further ten crossings on to Bexhill (Wallsend, one unnamed, Havensmouth, Pevensey Sluice, Grovers Field, Gilham Wood, two unnamed, Braggs Lane, and a footpath). Finally, there were three more between Bexhill and Bulverhithe (Manor Road, Dorset Road, and the third unnamed). There were also some 30 bridges of various types between Southerham bridge and Bulverhithe.

The contract was let after direct negotiation with George Wythes, who, in his earlier partnership with John Hale, had built a number of lines for the Brighton and associated companies. The absence of open tendering was the cause of criticism at one of the companies' meetings, allegations being made that Wythes' acceptance of shares in part payment implied an unsatisfactory state of affairs. The explanation by Mr. Nash, the Brighton, Lewes & Hastings chairman, that the arrangement had been entered into because South Eastern opposition had depressed the standing of the Lewes & Hastings company, and that the contractor's action was timely, did not eliminate criticism of the proceedings. Mr. Troup, one of the shareholders, in fact went so far as to say that 'the works can be executed in a superior manner by respectable local contractors for £100,000 less than the sum required by Mr. Wythes.'[6] Mr. Fabian, of Brighton, was the contractor for the permanent station at Lewes.

Construction of the line as far as Lewes started in September 1844, within two months of the company receiving its Act, and to begin with proceeded steadily except for occasional

*The illustration on p. 118 of Clark, R. H., *A Southern Region Chronology and Record 1805-1965*, (Oakwood Press, 1964) does *not* show Southerham bridge.

difficulties with landowners. Herapath records at least one instance of the latter.[7] The contractor found no major difficulties, although the sand veins in the chalk through which Falmer tunnel had to be made, caused construction of that tunnel only 495 yds. long to take 10 months.

The method employed by the contractor (Wythes) for excavating the cuttings approaching Falmer tunnel was referred to, with a very clear artist's drawing, in a contemporary issue of the Illustrated London News. Wythes' procedure was to drive a heading into the hillside along the line of, and at the level of, the floor of the finished cutting, this heading thus forming, in effect, the approach to the tunnel itself. Wythes then sank a shaft above the heading until it broke into the latter, enabling gangs of men to fill wagons brought along the heading to the bottom of the shaft. No doubt the material originally excavated in forming the shaft, was then got rid of by tipping it down the shaft.

As soon as the loose material had been cleared away, a second shaft was sunk a short distance beyond the first, the procedure being repeated as necessary up to the place where the tunnel was to start. The chalk between each shaft was then broken up and was also allowed to fall down the shafts, to be cleared as before. Finally, the slopes on either side of the cutting were trimmed back to the required angle and the whole work then completed.

It will be seen that by this method there was a minimum amount of lifting of chalk, which reached the loading position by gravity, and that the filled wagons were already on rail for delivery to wherever the chalk had to be deposited (usually it was required to form an embankment). The procedures for tipping down the shafts must, however, have involved danger to the navvies.

The Author considers it reasonable to assume that a similar method had probably been used to form the very large chalk cuttings north of Merstham tunnel and south of Clayton tunnel on the main line to Brighton, but as stated in Chapter VII, he has not found any evidence to that effect.

Rastrick was the Chief Engineer for the line, George Meredith being the Resident Engineer. While the work was proceeding action was in hand in three different quarters which had important consequences for the line to Hastings.

In the meantime, operations east of Southerham commenced in December 1844.

The first of the developments referred to was that the South Eastern company was itself pressing for a line from Ashford to Hastings, whilst the Brighton, Lewes & Hastings company sought to extend its line eastwards beyond Bulverhithe via Rye to Ashford.

The second was that the Brighton, Lewes & Hastings company sought powers to construct a line from Lewes to join the London & Brighton company's line south of Haywards Heath, so as to enable Lewes and Hastings to be reached direct from the London direction.

The third step was a move by the South Eastern to build a line from Tunbridge Wells to Hastings, to join, near Hastings, the proposed Brighton, Lewes & Hastings' extension to Ashford.

Two results of these moves occurred in 1845.

The first was that the 'direct' line from Lewes (Southover) to Keymer, just over 3 miles south of Haywards Heath, was authorized on 30 June 1845 (8 & 9 Vic. Cap. 5); and the second was that the Brighton, Lewes & Hastings company was authorized on 8 August 1845 (8 & 9 Vic Cap. 200) to build their extension from Bulverhithe to Ashford. This latter Act had itself a number of very important provisions, of which the chief were:

Section 38 — Power to sell or lease the line to the London & Brighton company;

Section 39 — Power, if required, and with the consent of the London & Brighton company, to transfer a portion of the line to the South Eastern company;

Section 43 — Power, if the option allowed in Section 39 were taken up, to sell to the London & Brighton company the rights transferred to the South Eastern company.

The Lewes company in the event decided to take up the option given to it by Section 39 of the Act, and transferred the ownership of the line from Bulverhithe to Ashford, to the South Eastern company whilst retaining running powers through to Hastings only.

Finally, on 18 June 1846 the South Eastern company was empowered (9 Vic. Cap. 64) to build their line from Tunbridge Wells (then its terminus, on the site of the present goods yard) to join the line from Bulverhithe to Ashford some little distance east of Bulverhithe. This Act provided (Section 15) that the line from Tunbridge Wells was not to be opened for public purposes until the Hastings to Ashford line was completed.

In the meantime, the line between Brighton and Lewes was completed and was opened on Monday 8 June 1846, after reported troubles with London Road viaduct, Lewes Road bridge, and other bridges.[8] The extension on to Bulverhithe was opened on Saturday 27 June 1846 as a single line, and the further extension to St. Leonards (near the later West Marina station) was opened on 7 November 1846. Bulverhithe was then closed. On the first Sunday of the opening between Brighton and Lewes, 14 June 1846, some 1,800 passengers used that line.[9]

Lewes (Friars Walk) station was, as already stated, a terminus on a short spur, the line onwards to Bulverhithe leaving the line from Brighton just outside the station. The Author has not seen any proper plan of this station at Lewes, but it had two platform roads, one parallelled with a run-round loop, together with a siding into the goods shed to the east of the passenger station and another siding to a wharf on the river Ouse. The two passenger roads ended in turntables. Figure 29 has been prepared from a published diagram,[10] which however can hardly have been complete in that a trailing crossover, at least, must surely have been provided. Such a crossover has therefore been added to the diagram, but the Author is solely responsible for suggesting its position. Southover (or Ham) platforms were on the approach from Brighton.

It seems that it was originally intended to make a triangular layout at Lewes, so that trains could work into and out of Friars Walk direct to and from the Hastings direction as well as to and from the Brighton direction, in addition to through running without entering the terminus. However, the eastern arm of the triangle (to give direct running between Lewes and the Hastings line) was not covered by the Act authorizing the line, and was never subsequently constructed. The station buildings at Friars Walk were not finished when the Brighton line was open on 8 June 1846, and a temporary wooden booking office was used until after

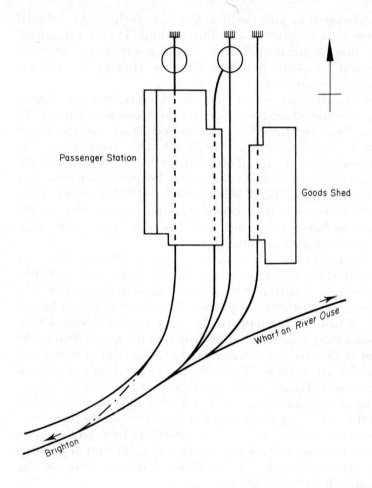

Figure 29. Lewes Station: Conjectural Layout as at 8 June 1846.

business on Friday 28 August 1846, the permanent building being opened on 29 August. The platform roofing does not seem to have been finished until early in February 1848. Lewes inhabitants who expected reasonable railway facilities in their town could therefore hardly have been impressed by the temporary accommodation provided at Friars Walk and by the platforms at Southover (Ham). Financial stringency was no doubt the reason for the poor facilities offered to the public at Lewes.

224

Intermediate stations on the Brighton-Hastings line had two platforms, those on the single-line section east of Lewes being arranged as passing places. Bulverhithe probably had two platforms. The permanent way is stated to have included bridge rails on transverse sleepers. Signalling was undoubtedly by means of semaphores, but 'auxiliary' or distant signals may well have been of the double-disc 'turnover' type introduced by the main Brighton company in 1846.

The Keymer Junction and Lewes line left the main line about 3 miles south of Haywards Heath by means of a 14-chain left-hand curve some 20 chains long, on a rising gradient now recorded as 1 in 298. At the end of the curve the line ran straight for over 1¼ mile, near the end of which the rise changed to an almost unbroken fall to the outskirts of Lewes in the Ouse Valley, nearly 7 miles away. Initially the fall is now recorded as 1 in 145, but much of it was easier until the last length of about 1¾ mile which eased to 1 in 543. Finally, there was a ½-mile rise at 1 in 598, and a short fall at 1 in 318 before the line joined the line from Brighton prior to entering the terminus at Lewes. Much of the Keymer line was straight, but at the end of the rise from Keymer Junction there was a mile-long left-hand compound curve, starting at 230 chains and reducing to 190 chains. Other curves ranged from 170 to 95 chains, in each case to the right, until the last 1¾ mile where curves down to 50 chains radius were found. A very sharp left-hand curve leading into the line from Brighton started in Lewes tunnel, just before the exit. The commencement of this curve within the tunnel mouth was later to be a source of trouble, as will be explained in due course. There were no intermediate stations on the line, but trains seemed to have called at the present Junction Road crossing, Keymer.[11] After that crossing, a few chains beyond the junction with the Brighton line, there were others at One O'Clock, 49 chains beyond the junction; Spat Horn Lane, later Spatham Lane, nearly 2 miles beyond Keymer Junction; Plumpton Green, nearly 1¾ miles farther on; East Chilington, a mile beyond Plumpton Green; at what is now Cooksbridge, a further 1¾ miles; and at Hamsey, ¾ mile beyond Cooksbridge. Additionally there were eleven occupation crossings and three footpath crossings. Those worth mentioning by name were Gallops

Homestead, Riddens, and Ashurst between Spatham Lane and Plumpton Green; and North Barns, Chapel No. 1, and Chapel No. 2 beyond Plumpton Green. The line was in cutting for a short distance after Keymer Junction, but after that was mainly on low embankments. In consequence there were only four overbridges, but thirteen underbridges until, near Lewes, the line went under a further overbridge and then through Lewes tunnel (397 yds, and straight except at the Lewes end) before going under yet another bridge to join the line from Brighton. There were no features of interest in the bridges or in Lewes tunnel, and the permanent way and signalling appear to have been in accordance with practice on the rest of the lines dealt with in this chapter. The Keymer line was opened for passenger traffic on Friday 1 October 1847; freight services had started in the previous month.

About the same time as the Keymer line was brought into use, down and up through platforms, 310 ft. and 200 ft. long respectively were provided at Pinwell on the Hastings line just east of the junction into Friars Walk.[12] Although these platforms were at an appreciable distance from those at Southover (Ham), and were some little distance from the terminal facilities at Friars Walk, the absence of any distinguishing names (e.g., Pinwell) from train service announcements probably implied that the scattered platforms were all officially regarded as part of an entity.

It may here be noted that the South Eastern company's line from Ashford to Hastings, and on towards St. Leonards, was opened on 13 February 1851, the Brighton-owned and built line as an extension eastwards to meet this some 1½ miles west of Hastings being brought into use on the same date, with Brighton running powers through to Hastings. There were no special features of interest on the Brighton company's extension line. 'Political' difficulties at Hastings will be referred to in Volume II. However it must be recorded that, when first opened, the two companies each had separate station masters and staff at Hastings, a joint staff not being formed until December 1854. Under the latter arrangements, the South Eastern company appointed the station master and the Brighton company appointed the local goods manager.[13] The line from Lewes to Bulverhithe had been doubled early in February 1847, and the extension line to join the South Eastern company west of Hastings was double track from the start.

While the line to St. Leonards was under construction, an Act was obtained for a line from Lewes to Newhaven and Seaford. Authority was given by 9 Vic. Cap. 63 dated 18 June 1846, the line commencing immediately east of Southerham bridge over the Ouse. The junction, as well as the bridge, were officially called Southerham. That part of the line from Newhaven to Seaford was not built immediately and the powers were revived under an Act of 1862 (Volume II).

The Newhaven line continued straight for a short distance after the junction at Southerham whereas the Hastings line curved left at 74 chains radius. The Newhaven line then involved successive curves of 91 chains left-hand and 76 chains right-hand to take the alignment towards the south. From the junction there was a fall at 1 in 529/218 for some 70 chains, and then some ⅓ mile of gentle switch-back (1 in 308 up, followed by 1 in 338 down). The rest of the line, over 4 miles to Newhaven harbour was virtually level as it ran near the left bank of the Ouse. There were various left-hand and right-hand curves, ranging from 72-120 chains radius with intervening straights, nearly as far as Newhaven, followed by several short curves down to 10 chains radius approaching the harbour station. The total length of the line was 5 miles 47 chains. Wharf facilities were provided at the terminus, and a station to serve the town—which was centred on the west bank of the river—was built a short distance nearer to Lewes. There was one underbridge about 1½ mile beyond Southerham Junction and there were level crossings at Itford and at Newhaven over the Newhaven-Seaford road. This latter crossing (known as Denton) was immediately north of the town's station. Earthworks on the line were negligible. The line was opened on 6 December 1847 for passenger traffic,[14] but freight traffic had commenced a short while previous to that date.

Brief mention must now be made of the legal position of cross-Channel services in relation to the powers of the three companies then concerned—the South Eastern Railway, the Brighton, and the South Western. Until the 1840's the general attitude of Parliament and the Government was that the granting of an Act to construct and operate a railway did not include authority to carry on any trade or enterprise which could effectively be conducted by individuals, private partnerships, or unincorporated companies. For a railway company to own and run steamers would therefore be contrary to this understanding. By 1847/1848 certain railways thought that it would be in their interests to run steamships; two of these were the Brighton and the South Western, who deposited Bills in Parliament accordingly. The South Eastern had already entered into arrangements with shipping companies to provide services from Folkestone and Dover, and so did not seek authority to run its own vessels.

The Select Committee which had been appointed on 26 November 1847 to decide what procedure should be adopted for dealing with the large number of railway Bills then before Parliament, considered these steamship Bills, and eventually concluded that:

(A) the South Western should be granted steamship powers for a limited period, subject to the following provisions:

   (i) the services should only be to Havre, the Channel Islands, and the parts of France immediately adjacent thereto;

   (ii) there should be arbitration on fares;

   (iii) the railway company was not empowered to lend money or subscribe to any other steam-vessel company; and

   (iv) passengers who used the steamers only, without travelling by rail, should not be treated disadvantageously.

(B) the Brighton was already authorised by its Act to subscribe, advance, or guarantee, up to £100,000 towards the establishment of steam communication with any port served by the Brighton company and any port or town in France.

Hence the Brighton company should be granted similar powers, under similar regulations, to those authorised for the South Western, but limited to voyages to Dieppe and possibly to Havre.

The Brighton company, having previously been unable to

conclude satisfactory arrangements with the authorities at Shoreham, had decided to make Newhaven their base for Continental operations. As the Keymer line, putting Lewes in direct communication with London, had already been brought into use when the line to Newhaven was opened, the way was then clear for a direct London-Newhaven service to be instituted. This clearly enabled the Brighton company to be a serious competitor to the South Eastern company for the Continental trade, as the latter's routes were via Folkestone Harbour and via Dover, access to which from London involved the South Eastern company running south to Redhill and then east to Folkestone and Dover.

Within its existing powers, the Brighton company had formed an independent concern in 1847, under the title of The Brighton & Continental Steam Packet Company, and the latter started to operate vessels as soon as possible after the line was opened to Newhaven on 6 December in that year. A hotel was built on the wharf at Newhaven, since the steamer service was tidal.

The South Eastern Railway had not invested any of its money directly into the shipping companies providing the cross-Channel services from Folkestone and Dover, but the Brighton company had put some of its money into the Brighton & Continental shipping Company. The South Eastern took exception to this, and commenced an action against the Brighton. The Brighton lost the case, and the Brighton & Continental Steam Packet Company had to be dissolved in 1848. There was then an interruption in the service from Newhaven to Dieppe for three years until 1851, when an arrangement was made by the Brighton company for Messrs. Maples & Morris to run steamers on the route.

The Act for the Newhaven line (9 Vic. Cap. 63 dated 18 June 1846) also authorized lines from Polegate to Eastbourne and from Polegate to Hailsham.

The Eastbourne branch was 4 miles 23 chains long, and commenced with a right-hand curve with a falling gradient away from Polegate; there was a gradual easing of the fall until it became negligible some 3 miles from Polegate. There was a final rise at 1 in 521 into the terminus (then the only station on the line — Hampden Park was not built until 1888), the rise steepening to 1 in 267 along the length of the platforms. Much of the line was straight after the initial right-hand curve from Polegate but there was a further right-hand curve over ½ mile long and of 40 chains radius approaching Eastbourne. There were nine underbridges and two overbridges (both the latter close to Eastbourne), but earthworks were light. There was a level crossing at Lockbridge Drove (later called Willingdon Crossing). East Bourne was a village about a mile from the coast, and was concerned with farming. At the coast, some fishing took place but bathing was growing in popularity. The latter was added to by the frequent presence of Royalty and by the development of property by the Duke of Devonshire and the Cavendish family. The railway (single) was opened on 14 May 1849.

The Hailsham branch started at the east end of Polegate station and curved left on a falling gradient of 1 in 100/116 before starting to climb towards Hailsham, first at 1 in 330 for some 35 chains, followed by a length falling at 1 in 1,320 and then ending with ¾ mile rising at 1 in 98 before the gradient eased off to 1 in 440 at the terminus. There were two overbridges and six level crossings over roads (Oltham Court Road, Sarah Land Road, and Mowbrook Farm Road), with several other crossings but the earthworks were not heavy. The foregoing crossings were later known as Otham Court Road, Sayerland Road and Mullbrook Farm Road respectively. Hailsham has always been a market town of some importance and the prospective traffic justified building the branch; this was about 2⅞ miles long and was always single track. It was opened on 14 May 1849, the same date as the Eastbourne line.

In passing, it may be noted here that it was not until 1881, as will be recorded later, that the present Polegate station was built about a ¼ mile to the east of the original one, and the two branches were realigned in order to give through running between them by entering Polegate station from opposite ends. With the opening of the Eastbourne and Hailsham branches in 1849 new railway construction by the Brighton company ceased for some years in territory to the east of their main line to Brighton.

The opening dates for the various lines referred to in this chapter were as follows:

Brighton-Lewes	8 June 1846
Lewes-Bulverhithe	27 June 1846
Keymer Junction-Lewes	1 October 1847
Southerham Junction-Newhaven ...	6 December 1847
Polegate-Eastbourne	14 May 1849
Polegate-Hailsham	14 May 1849

NOTES

1. Sekon, G. A. 'The Evolution of a Popular Railway.' *Railway & Travel Monthly*, 3, 184.
2. Original Minutes held by Public Records Office at 66 Porchester Road, London, W.2.* local reference LBR 1/26.
3. Herapath's Railway & Commercial Journal, VI (27 January 1844), 95.
4. *Ibid.*, VII (1 November 1845), 2389.
5. Contemporary account of unknown origin.
6. Herapath, VI (28 September 1844), 1138 and 1147.
7. *Ibid.*, VII (29 November 1845), 2625.
8. *Ibid.*, VIII (27 June 1846), 826.
9. *Ibid.*, (20 June 1846), 807.
10. Catchpole, L. T. 'Traffic Centres and Their Work—No. 5 Lewes.' *Southern Railway Magazine*, 1937, 342.
Present author's note: Since there are various errors and unsubstantiated statements in this article, it is commended only for its general data, and not as a source of historical information.
11. *Southern Railway Magazine*, 1935, 228.
12. *The Sussex Advertiser*, 31 August 1847.
13. *Southern Railway Magazine*, 1929, 281.
14. The Railway Record, 11 December 1847, 1266. The date of opening of the line to Newhaven has been generally, but wrongly, given as 8 December 1847.
Note: General data on the East Coast line, and a review of developments at Lewes, will be found in two articles in *The Railway Magazine:*
Sekon, G. A. 'The LBSCR East Coast Section,' 94 (1948); 146 and 260.
Lee, Chas. E. 'The Lewes Station Mystery,' 96 (1950); 35, 44, and 135.

*Correct at going to press.

CHAPTER THIRTEEN

Extensions to the West

TWO lines to the west of the main line must now be considered. One of these was to Horsham, and the other was an extension from Chichester to Portsmouth.

Horsham, an important market town in the northern part of West Sussex, would have been served by the various 'Dorking route' proposals which were considered among the alternative lines to Brighton, as already recounted in Chapters I, II, V, and VI. The final choice of route to Brighton, however, carried the line some 7 miles to the east of Horsham as the crow flies. Hence consideration was given to building a line to serve it. The revival of one of the 'Dorking route' proposals (Chapter XV) was an important incentive in this matter. The western Brighton road ran north to south between Horsham and the Brighton main line and passed through Crawley. The latter was a small coaching town where a road from Horsham crossed the Brighton road and continued towards East Grinstead. Its importance had waned with the opening of the London & Brighton railway. South of Crawley the Brighton road commenced a long drag up to Pease Pottage in Tilgate Forest, on the intermediate Wealden ridge of ground between the North and South Downs. The main railway line to Brighton ran through this ridge by means of Balcombe tunnel, as explained in an earlier chapter.

There were therefore really only two practical ways of reaching Horsham from the main line without incurring heavy engineering works. One was to keep to the south of the Tilgate Forest ridge and the other was to run to the north of it. A southerly route could have been found by starting south of Balcombe and turning west up the Ouse valley, the line probably being about 9 miles long, but serving nowhere of importance on the way. A northerly route could start at Three Bridges, and proceed west through Crawley and then south-west via Faygate to reach Horsham, a distance of about 8½ miles. The commercial advantages of the northerly route were clear and hence this route was chosen, although it involved a level crossing over the main Brighton road at the south end of Crawley and a second level crossing a short distance to the west over the Horsham road, as well as various others. The London & Brighton Act for the construction of the line to Horsham (8 & 9 Vic, Session 1845) was dated 21 July 1845.

Leaving Three Bridges immediately to the south of the station, the Horsham line curved to the right at 17 chains radius for ½ mile so as to run almost due west for about 1½ mile to Crawley, approaching which was a further right-hand curve of 80 chains radius. The level crossing over the High Street (main road to Brighton) was immediately west of the station, and the line then continued straight for over a mile before entering a 40-chain left-hand curve some 35 chains along which brought it round to a south-westerly direction nearly 3 miles from Three Bridges. Three further level crossings occurred on this length, the first over Horsham road close to Crawley, and the others over less important roads: the first of the latter was called Gossops Green or Goffs Lane, crossing and the second Lion Farm crossing (later Ifield crossing). Short give-and-take gradients occurred on this section, the steepest being at 1 in 225. The next 4¼ miles were virtually straight but included a summit about half-way, with gradients as steep as 1 in 100, passing Faygate crossing and station and then two more crossings (Roughey, late Roffey Road, and Rusper Road). The last mile into Horsham was mainly on an 80-chain left-hand curve, the latter part falling at 1 in 100 into the terminus at Horsham. One further crossing (Wimblehurst Lane) was needed near the start of this last curve. There was also a considerable number of occupation and footpath crossings on the line, About 18 bridges were needed, nearly all of them under the line, and a timber viaduct over Ifield mill-pond west of Ifield crossing. The line, which was 8 miles

38 chains long and was single from the start, was opened on 14 February 1848. The intermediate stations had two platforms. Horsham station, as opened, is shown in Plate 16.

The proposal for a line along the coast from Chichester to Portsmouth had its origin at Portsmouth itself, the desire being for a route to London of a less roundabout nature than was entailed by crossing to Gosport and then proceeding north-west to Bishopstoke (now Eastleigh) over the L S W Rly and thence to Nine Elms, itself a relatively long way from London. Herapath reported on 3 August 1844 that a meeting was 'shortly to be held' in Portsmouth and that, as might be expected, there was L S W Rly opposition to, and London & Brighton support for, such a scheme. This meeting had in fact been held on the previous day, but no doubt Herapath had gone to print by then.

Before there was any tangible outcome of this meeting, a rival scheme, itself a development of an earlier one, was announced. This was for 'The Direct London and Portsmouth Railway (Atmospheric Line)'. A subsequent chapter is devoted to the various proposals for atmospheric working on lines covered by this history, so all that is necessary to record here are three salient points: first, the London & Croydon had reached the conclusion that its line would benefit from atmospheric working; second, a nominally independent company, the Croydon & Epsom Railway, which had always intended to work in conjunction with the London & Croydon and which had received its Act on the basis of atmospheric working, had come firmly under the wing of the London & Croydon (over which the atmospheric working would extend); and third, proposals had for some time been canvassed for extensions, on the atmospheric principle, to Chatham and to Portsmouth. The 'direct' London & Portsmouth atmospheric line was, in fact, based on part of these earlier proposals, and involved a line from Epsom through or near Ashtead, Leatherhead, Mickleham, Dorking, Godalming, Haslemere, Liphook, Petersfield, and Havant, and thence to Portsmouth. The prospectus was dated 3 September 1844 and was published in Herapath for 7 September; it envisaged the construction of commercial docks at Portsmouth and, as a result, a lucrative traffic, but little other revenue could reasonably have been expected as the line would serve intermediate places which were then of only limited importance.

As atmospheric working was alleged by its promoters to results in considerable economies in operation as compared with steam working, and was receiving support from renowned engineers such as James Walker and I. K. Brunel, it undoubtedly had an appeal to investors. Hence the 'direct' London & Portsmouth was at once a serious contender as compared with a conventional line from Chichester to Portsmouth (for which Owen was the Engineer)—especially as a line from Chichester entailed running via Brighton, where a reversal was involved in order to reach London. Both proposals were, of course, opposed by the L S W Rly, which put forward a line from Fareham, on its Gosport line, around the harbour area to enter Portsmouth from the north.

Eventually the coast line from Chichester was sanctioned to be built by the Brighton & Chichester company, the Act (8 & 9 Vic. Cap. 199, 8 August 1845) also authorising a branch westwards to Fareham to join the L S W Rly there unless the L S W Rly built its own line—which in the event it did, although later than the line from Chichester.

The Brighton & Chichester's line commenced as an extension of the Shoreham-Chichester line, then still under construction, and continued on the 80-chain right-hand curve and 1 in 330 down gradient by which the Shoreham entered Chichester. This curve was some 65 chains long and was followed by about 20 chains of left-hand 40-chain curve. At the end of this, the line ran virtually straight for over 8 miles, a rise at 1 in 880 for over 2 miles being succeeded by undulations, mostly at that inclination or easier but with lengths of 1 in 293, 1 in 528, and 1 in 660. Earthworks were negligible, the line largely following the contours of the ground. Following the long length of near-straight there was a left-hand 65-chain curve about 45 chains long, followed by another length of almost straight, over 2 miles long; most of this section was on easy falling gradients, with however over ½ mile down at 1 in 240. Farlington Junction (to be referred to again later) was situated at the end of the straight. Double line appears to have been laid from the start.

The original stations were at Bosham, about 3 miles beyond Chichester, and almost at the top of the 1 in 880 rise after that station; Emsworth, 4 miles 9 chains beyond Bosham and on a short length of 200-chain left-hand curve on the long almost-straight section, where the road was rising towards Portsmouth at 1 in 1760; and Havant, about 1¾ miles beyond Emsworth and nearly at the end of the long straight, the road now falling at 1 in 1056. All were simple side-platform stations with small yards. Farlington Junction was some 3¼ miles beyond Havant, and at this point the line forked. The right-hand spur entered a 42-chain right-hand curve followed by a straight, and in a distance of about 44 chains all rising at 1 in 381 came to Cosham Junction. The left-hand spur at Farlington Junction entered an 85-chain left-hand curve some 45 chains long, on a rising gradient of 1 in 310, and came to Portcreek Junction. The triangle was completed by a line 38 chains long from Cosham Junction to Portcreek Junction, much of it on a 20-chain right-hand curve from Cosham Junction coming towards Portcreek Junction; this spur was almost level.

The line formed by the two spurs coming together at Cosham Junction continued for just under ½ mile to Cosham station, and then for 5¾ miles in a westerly direction to Fareham. There it joined the Gosport line, with the junction facing for trains coming from Bishopstoke (Eastleigh). The line formed by the two spurs coming together at Portcreek Junction crossed an opening bridge over a tidal waterway to obtain access to Portsea Island, and then entered a compound left-hand curve over ½ mile long, starting at 160 chains and sharpening to 80 chains, Beyond this curve, the line ran nearly south on a generally straight alignment for some 2 miles, before entering a compound right-hand curve almost ½ mile long and varying in radius from 30 chains down to 12 chains. This curve took the line into a westerly alignment, to which it held for about ½ mile to the terminus at Portsmouth. The gradients from Portcreek Junction to Portsmouth were negligible. The terminus abutted what is now called Commercial Road and was convenient for the north end of the town, but was a considerable distance from the older parts of Portsmouth. Only one platform was provided[1] (this was however double-faced).

The line from Fareham to a few chains short of Cosham was owned by the L S W Rly; that from just west of Cosham right through to Portsmouth was Joint Chichester & Portsmouth/L S W Rly; and that from Havant to Farlington Junction and onwards both to Cosham Junction and Portcreek Junction, was Chichester & Portsmouth only—as of course was also the length between Chichester and Havant.

The formation of all lines east and south of the triangle was virtually at ground level, so that there were few under-bridges (and those mostly over streams), a small number of overbridges, and a considerable number of level crossings over roads. The first crossing was a footpath and then came Fishbourne, about ¾ mile west of Chichester and situated where the 80-chain right-hand curve ran into the 40-chain left-hand one. Then came, apart from occupation and foot-path crossings, Clay Lane, New Fishbourne, Black Boy Lane, and Brook Lane. Immediately to the west of Bosham station was Bosham crossing, followed by Funtington, Green Lane, Drift Lane, Broad Road, Inlands Road, Stein Lane, and Emsworth, followed at once by the station of that name, and then by South Leigh Road crossing. At Havant there were New Lane and Leigh Road, followed by Stockheath, Bed-hampton, and Bedhampton Mill, the latter 2 miles 13 chains before Farlington Junction. There were also numerous occu-pation and footpath crossings. Beyond Portcreek Junction there were Dutton's Lane (later renamed Straight Lane), Green Lanes, Salterne, Moneyfield, Copnor, Cemetary, Stevens, Jolliffes, and Blackfriars Road. Chichester Station had a short overall roof.

Although the line was joint with the L S W Rly from just west of Cosham station, where there was another level crossing, to Portcreek Junction and then to Portsmouth, constructional work seems to have been in line with Chichester & Portsmouth practice, and hence similar to that adopted by the Brighton & Chichester company. The Brighton & Chichester company was one of those which formed the London, Brighton & South Coast Railway in 1846, before any of the lines now under review were opened to traffic. The opening dates were as follows:

Chichester — Havant ...   . 15 March 1847
Havant — Portsmouth   ...   . 14 June 1847
Farlington Junction — Cosham   ... 26 July 1848
   (for goods)[2]

Portcreek Junction — Cosham Junction
   (for goods) ... ... 1 September 1848
   (for passengers) ... ... 1 October 1848
Cosham — Fareham ... ... 1 September 1848
   (L S W Rly)

A daily service of seven trains each way was provided when the line was opened from Chichester to Havant, with three each way on Sundays.

Yapton station on the Shoreham-Chichester line, which had been opened when the line was brought into use on 8 June 1846, was closed in October 1847 but reopened in June 1849. Doubling of the line westwards from Shoreham as far as the Arun bridge took place in 1847, but as that bridge was only designed for one road the doubling had to cease there. Doubling west of the bridge, to link up with the two roads almost certainly provided at opening westwards from Chichester, seems to have been delayed for 10 years to 1857. Finally, complete reconstruction of the Arun bridge in 1862, enabling a double line to be carried over it, removed in that year the remaining length of single line between Brighton and Portsmouth, as will be covered in more detail in Volume II.

NOTES
1. Fay, Sam. *A Royal Road.* Kingston-on-Thames, 1882, 70
2. Opened for passengers on 2 January 1860

CHAPTER FOURTEEN

The London and Croydon's atmospheric phase, and the line to Epsom

THE working of the London & Croydon Railway was becoming increasingly difficult in the early 1840s. The financial position of the company was unsatisfactory, whilst their own traffic, and that of the London & Brighton and the South Eastern, was building up. The problem of working was in essence that there were two different traffic flows over the line — the local service, stopping at all stations and run by the Croydon itself, and the 'main line' services to and from the Brighton and S.E. companies and run by those companies. The mixing of the two flows was obviously not conducive to good operation, and the latter was in any case expensive due to the difficulty of working up the steep bank from New Cross to Dartmouth Arms. Moreover, the heavy expenditure in constructing the line meant that a large capital had to be serviced from revenue, after a considerable slice of the latter had gone as tolls to the Greenwich company. As has already been explained, the Greenwich company found itself unable to reduce the tolls because it was also in a similar position of being a short and over-capitalized line.

The Croydon board therefore explored the possibility of attracting extra revenue by extending their line to places which had good traffic potential but which would not entail heavy construction costs. At the same time they supported the South Eastern company in promoting the Bricklayers Arms branch as a means of forcing the Greenwich company to reduce their tolls. The Act for the Bricklayers Arms branch was passed on 4 July 1843, as recorded in Chapter X, and this not only achieved its object regarding the Greenwich tolls but was also seen to be only the first move to improving the

239

finances of the Croydon company.

Several other steps were now considered. The first was that it was decided to encourage traffic by reducing fares and by improving the stock used for second-class and third-class passengers; this being a complete change from the serious consideration being given earlier to ceasing to provide what was really an unremunerative local service and merely continuing in existence on the basis of tolls from the Brighton and South Eastern companies. The extra traffic could be handled when the Bricklayers Arms branch was opened. The second step was to consider extending the line from Croydon to Epsom to bring in more revenue, the area having worthwhile traffic potential. The third was actively to explore means of reducing working expenses. In this chapter attention is given to the two latter steps.

Various proposals for mechanical alternatives to steam locomotives had been made since George Medhurst had published a pamphlet in 1810 entitled 'A new method of conveying Letters and Goods with great certainty and rapidity by Air', using a small tube.[1] Medhurst extended his idea to include the carrying of goods in vehicles running on rails in an iron tube,[2] and after further theoretical studies made more precise proposals in 1827, in his pamphlet entitled 'A new system of inland conveyance for Goods and Passengers, &c, without the aid of horse or any animal power'. Medhurst never patented any of his ideas, and the first patent for any form of atmospheric working seems to have been by John Vallance in 1824. Other inventors followed, but it was patent No. 7920 granted on 3 January 1838 to Samuel Clegg and to Jacob and Joseph Samuda, that was to lead to practical results.

In essence, Clegg's and Samudas' principle was that a train was propelled by normal atmospheric pressure acting on the rear of a piston in a circular tube, as a result of a vacuum being created in front of the piston. The tube had a slot along its top through which projected an arm (or 'coulter'), attached at its lower end to the piston rod at a point in rear of the piston itself; that portion of the arm which was outside (and therefore above) the tube being attached to a special vehicle known as a piston carriage. The slot along the top of the tube was normally covered by a flap so as to make the tube airtight, the flap being moved aside just ahead of the piston arm but in rear of the

240

piston itself, and being closed again behind the latter. Leather packing, the equivalent of piston rings, sealed the mechanical clearance that was necessary between the piston and the tube. The latter was laid in the '4 ft', between the normal running

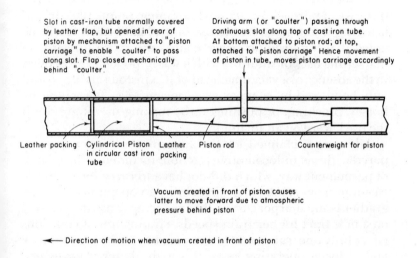

Slot in cast-iron tube normally covered by leather flap, but opened in rear of piston by mechanism attached to "piston carriage" to enable "coulter" to pass along slot. Flap closed mechanically behind "coulter".

Driving arm (or "coulter") passing through continuous slot along top of cast iron tube. At bottom attached to piston rod; at top, attached to "piston carriage" Hence movement of piston in tube, moves piston carriage accordingly

Leather packing   Cylindrical Piston   Leather   Piston rod   Counterweight for piston
                   in circular cast iron   packing
                   tube

Vacuum created in front of piston causes latter to move forward due to atmospheric pressure behind piston

◄—— Direction of motion when vacuum created in front of piston

Figure 30. Atmospheric Principle: Arrangement of Piston in Tube, and Method of attachment of Piston Rod to Piston Carriage.

rails. The principles are illustrated in Figure 30. This shows that the 'coulter' was attached to the mid-point of the piston rod, the rear end of the latter carrying a counterweight for the piston.

On creation of a vacuum ahead of the piston, as a result of exhausting air by means of a mechanically-driven pump, normal atmospheric pressure behind the piston caused the latter to move forward, taking the piston carriage with it. The latter therefore represented a locomotive, normal rolling stock being formed behind it, to make up a train. The piston carriage was in charge of a 'driver' and was provided with a handbrake, but the piston carriage could not, of course, move unless a vacuum was created ahead of it. The latter action took place shortly before a train was due to leave a station, and the train would then start as soon as the 'driver' released his handbrake. Vacuum was created at pumping (exhausting) stations beside the line, normally situated at distances ranging up to 3 miles apart. A separating valve in the tube divided one vacuum section from the next, the separating valve being operated by the arrival of the piston carriage at that point. It was intended that pumping (exhausting) would cease while the train was approaching its next stopping point, the 'driver' bringing it to a stand by the use of his handbrake. It will be noted that the piston carriage could only move forward, so that setting back or shunting with it was impossible. Moreover, in the absence of a vacuum ahead of it, a piston carriage could only be moved by some external means (e.g., towroping by horses, pinching, or pushing, or by making use of gravity if the track were on an incline).

Advantages claimed for the atmospheric system as compared with steam locomotive traction, included reduced cost of permanent way, which did not have to carry locomotives; freedom from smoke and dirt; ability to operate on steeper gradients and sharper curves, thus reducing construction costs on a new line; higher train speeds; elimination of collisions (since only one train could be between two pumping stations); and reduced operating costs. It was the latter claim which caused the atmospheric principle to attract the greatest interest.

Clegg (primarily a gas engineer) and the Samudas (shipbuilders at Blackwall) realized that extended practical experience was necessary to establish the technical details of their invention (apparently tried in France in 1838, the year in which it was patented). Only after considerable experience could it be offered as a worthwhile alternative to steam traction. Trials were therefore made on part of the West London Railway, starting in June 1840, and were considered to be successful. Hence as early as 4 August 1840 Messrs. Samuda Bros. approached the chairman of the London & Croydon Railway suggesting that adoption of their system on New Cross bank would bring about more economical working than with the Croydon's locomotives. The Croydon company sought the opinion of Cubitt, their Engineer, and of Rastrick, the Brighton's Engineer, and as a result of their views the Croydon's reply must have been such that no further approach was apparently made to the Croydon company by the inventors themselves.

In Ireland, however, it was decided in 1842 that a 1½ mile extension of the Dublin & Kingstown Railway, going on to Dalkey, should be operated on the atmospheric system, and the first train on the system ran on 18 August 1843. The public opening was on the following day, and trains ran successfully, although not, as yet, to a regular timetable. Hence the inventors' claim could now be put to commercial test. This was followed by proposals for entirely new atmospheric lines in England, the first prospectus that the Author has traced being for the Gravesend, Rochester & Chatham Railway in January 1844, for which line Isambard Brunel (who had seen the Dalkey line) was Engineer. Shortly afterwards the Samudas suggested that the proposed Chester & Holyhead Railway should be operated atmospherically, but Robert Stephenson, that company's Engineer, was not enthusiastic over what he saw at Dalkey.

Although the Gravesend, Rochester & Chatham proposals were unable to proceed because of a legal issue, the interest of the London & Croydon was aroused by an atmospheric scheme near London. In consequence Cubitt (originally, as already explained, not impressed by the system) suggested to W. A. Wilkinson, the Croydon chairman, that if the Epsom extension from Croydon were to be operated on the atmospheric system, and the latter were to be continued over an independent third road to London, an excellent method would be provided of reaching a reliable assessment of the merits of the system for a frequent local service.

One development led to another, and at a meeting of the Croydon's shareholders on 7 March 1844 it was decided that the company should build an independant atmospheric line from London to Croydon. The Chairman's statement that 'The relaying of the line will at a future period, be rendered necessary unless the atmospheric principle is adopted', of course indicates muddled thinking. Further, the Croydon board agreed on 1 April that the Croydon & Epsom line should be built by a separate company as an atmospheric line, the formation and bridges being constructed for double track but only a single road being laid. This latter decision was taken on the basis of the Samudas' claim that an hourly atmospheric service could be run provided that there was a crossing loop at Carshalton; if crossing facilities were also provided at

Sydenham, a half-hourly atmospheric service could be run[3]. The Act (7 Vic Session 1844, dated 29 July 1844) therefore included a clause (No. 313) to the effect that the Croydon and Epsom company were desirous of adopting the atmospheric principles of traction.

The Croydon terminus of the London & Croydon company was on the east side of the London Road, which was at a higher level than the railway and under which the Epsom line had therefore to pass. Approaching the south side of the former canal basin at Croydon, there was the site of the former canal company's branch to the Croydon, Merstham & Godstone Railway referred to in Chapter I. This branch had been closed on 22 August 1836 when the Croydon canal had been stopped (see Chapter IV); the London & Croydon Railway had taken over the land on which the branch had been laid when they had purchased the canal company. Traffic over the 'main line' of the Surrey Iron Railway between Croydon and Wandsworth did not cease until 31 August 1846. Tamworth Road now occupies the site of this branch.

The route therefore selected for the Croydon and Epsom line started at a junction with the London & Croydon a short distance to the east of the latter's terminus, and involved a continuation of the existing left-hand curve of about 25 chains radius by which the London & Croydon approached the station before the alignment of the latter line became virtually straight into the terminus. As soon as the new line was clear of the junction it began to fall at about 1 in 106 and 1 in 90 in order to pass under London Road, the fall including a short length of straight before a right-hand curve of 42 chains radius, some ¼ mile long. This latter curve was necessary in order to clear the Pitlake area, and took the alignment to the north of the old Croydon Merstham & Godstone Railway branch. The right-hand curve was followed immediately by a short 40-chain left-hand curve, this in turn being succeeded by about 25 chains of straight and some 50 chains of right-hand compound curvature (230/58 chains radius). The 1 in 90 descent leaving Croydon extended about as far as the middle of the reverse (42/40 chains) curve, after which a nearly level length occurred until about half-way round the compound right-hand curve, some 1¼ mile from the start of the new line. Beyond this point, the line rose fairly steadily for some 3¼ miles until it went under King's Lane on the outskirts of Sutton. The alignment over this section was straight except for a right-hand/left-hand reverse curve of 39/42 chains radius, nearly a mile long in all, on the approach to Sutton. The 3¼ mile rise was at very broken gradients, but appreciable lengths were little easier than 1 in 100.

Once clear of Croydon, the line was largely at ground level for over 1½ mile, but then ran along the north side of the North Downs and so involved some cut and fill in chalk. The levels were naturally so arranged as to reduce this to a minimum, but there was nevertheless a cutting through a low eminence known as Bandon Hill, another shorter one near the start of the 39/42 chain reverse curve, and a third approaching Sutton. After King's Lane bridge at Sutton, the line fell at 1 in 82/94 in order to pass under Brighton Road, which had itself to be raised in order to give sufficient clearance. From this point the line was straight to Epsom except for two left-hand cruves; approaching Epsom there was a ¼ mile long right-hand curve at 42 chains radius into the terminus. There was a general fall from Sutton towards Epsom, broken by three short rises, the ruling downward gradient being at 1 in 100. Leaving Sutton the line was in a chalk cutting about 20 feet deep, this being succeeded by about a mile of low embankment. There was then a succession of embankments and cuttings as far as the entrance to Epsom station, which was itself at ground level.

At the Croydon and, Pitlake Road had to be diverted over a bridge, to the east of its former alignment, which was at ground level. Immediately to the west of the new bridge, the Surrey Iron Railway had also to be raised and taken over the Croydon and Epsom Line by a bridge, and there were further diversions and lifting of roads over the next mile, past Duppas Hill ('Dowbers Hill' in 1543, and 'Dubbers Hill' in 1548). Beyond this point, work was of a more routine nature, roads being raised or lowered where necessary where they were crossed by the new railway. In all, some 35 bridges were needed in a length of about 8¼ miles. Several of the overbridges were constructed with a central pier, so that when a double line came to be laid the pier would be in the '6ft' space. The Author has not found any particular reason for this practice being followed so regularly on the Croydon and Epsom line. One underbridge, about a mile on the Croydon side of Sutton, was formed as a short viaduct of three brick arches.

At Croydon, the alignment entailed the provision of separate platform accommodation on the Epsom line. Beyond Croydon, stations were provided at Carshalton (renamed Wallington on 1 September 1868), Sutton, Cheam, Ewell (renamed Ewell East on 9 July 1923, shortly after the Grouping brought the Southern Railway into existence), and Epsom. Extensions beyond Epsom were made later, as will be recorded in due course. The station at Epsom was renamed Epsom Town in 1870, but later reverted to its original name; the suffix 'Town' was again added by the Southern Railway in 1923, and that station was finally closed to passengers on 3 March 1929 on opening of the present station on the site of the former London & South Western Railway station, some way to the west.

Since the railway was to be operated as a single line with a passing loop at Carshalton (Wallington), as already recorded, two platforms were planned for that station. A single platform, on the up side, appears to have been planned at Ewell. At Cheam the single platform was probably on the up side; at Epsom it was almost certainly on the down side. At Croydon it is thought that a single platform was provided on the down side. The Author has not been able to ascertain where the platform was to be provided at Sutton.

Carshalton (Aweltune in A.D. 880) served an area where there were mills turned by the Wandle (which rose near Croydon) and also had traffic potential from various farms and large houses. Sutton station was well sited, beside the Brighton Road near where it crossed the Croydon — Epsom road by the Cock inn; the area was becoming residential, and the railway considered that it was commercially attractive. Cheam and Ewell served villages (known respectively as Cegeham and Euuelle in A.D. 675), the former station being fairly well sited with respect to the centre of the community but Ewell station being some distance away from the centre of population. Epsom (former name Ebbisham or Ebba's Home) was a town of some antiquity, and the station was near the east end of the High Street. The traffic potential therefore being quite good for the line as a whole, and there being no heavy capital outlay in construction costs because of the easy route, the line was expected to bring in a good return to the London &

Croydon, who planned to take it over. The purchase of the Epsom line by the London & Croydon, in fact, was decided upon on 22 August 1844 under 7 & 8 Vic cap 97 of 6 August 1844 — a step not taken immediately. Equally, operating conditions appeared to favour atmospheric traction, on the data put forward by the Samuda brothers and the results so far achieved on the Dalkey line in Ireland. This was, of course, the basis for Cubitt's suggestion to Wilkinson, as already stated. The Croydon & Epsom company was, in the event, one of those forming the London Brighton & South Coast Railway in 1846 (see Chapter XVI).

Earlier in this chapter it was recorded that Cubitt had proposed that the atmospheric system should be extended from Croydon to London, using an additional road specially constructed for it. The reason for this was of course that it would enable the Croydon company's trains to be kept clear of those of the London & Brighton and the South Eastern companies, thereby separating the all-stations (atmospheric) trains from the fast 'long distance' services. Action was accordingly initiated to provide for this third road, which would only be necessary from the London end as far out as the junction with the Brighton line south of Jolly Sailor (beyond which the Croydon's line was used only by their own trains). In actual fact, the plans went further, in that it was appreciated that, should the proposed atmospheric railway to Portsmouth (Chapter XIII) be built, a single line would be inadequate for the likely (or at least hoped-for) traffic. Hence the plans for widening, and the powers sought, were such as to enable a second atmospheric line (i.e., double track atmospheric) to be laid as far as Croydon. This would give four roads (two atmospheric and two steam) as far out as the Brighton line junction south of Jolly Sailor, and three roads (two atmospheric and one steam) on to Croydon. Beyond Croydon there would have been the two atmospheric roads, only.

Authority for the work was granted by 7 & 8 Vic cap 97 of 6 August 1844, under the same Act which empowered the Croydon to take over the Epsom line — itself only authorized a week previously, on 29 July. Hence, for all practical purposes, a virtually new railway was to be built on the atmospheric principle from London to Epsom. The atmospheric line was to be single at this stage.

Whilst preparatory work for the London — Epsom line was in hand, experience of atmospheric working was accumulating on the Dalkey line in Ireland. Although there were continuing reports of defects and troubles, promoters in other areas were very active and new atmospheric lines were being proposed for various routes. The most ambitious scheme, for a line to Portsmouth, has been mentioned in Chapter XIII, whilst another was floated for a line from Newcastle-upon-Tyne to Berwick; developments also occurred in France. These schemes were the forerunners of others. The Samuda brothers must have had some influential friends!

On the other hand, the atmospheric principle received no support at all from Robert Stephenson, who condemned it as of no real practical value; Herapath's Journal and Railway Magazine (issued weekly and, having a financial bias, appealing to investors) opposed it from the start, and continued to do so consistently both and before the Croydon was empowered to adopt it. John Herapath himself was a mathematician and physicist, and hence was able to analyse the results of working and to ask awkward questions on the costs and effectiveness of the whole principle.

Clegg and the Samudas continued to base their case on reduced construction and installation costs for a new atmospheric line as compared with a new steam-locomotive line, and on reduced working costs as compared with those of a conventional steam line. These claims were impressive, and the Croydon company continued with its plans for its London-Epsom atmospheric line, which it had decided to carry out in four stages:

Stage 1	Dartmouth Arms to Croydon
Stage 2	Dartmouth Arms to New Cross
Stage 3	New Cross to London Bridge
Stage 4	Croydon to Epsom

The Epsom line was scheduled as the last stage because in this case the entire railway, including all earthworks and construction, were new, and had to be well forward before any atmospheric equipment was installed.

Between Croydon and the junction with the Brighton's line south of Jolly Sailor, this junction then being known as Brighton Junction, the requirements for a separate atmospheric line could be met by appropriating one road for the purpose, leaving the other to be operated as a single line with steam locomotives as necessary (e.g., for freight). North of the junction, however, an entire separate atmospheric line was, as already explained, needed.

From the operating point of view it would have been desirable for the atmospheric line to be on the up (or west) side of the two existing roads, so as to run parallel with the Brighton and South Eastern traffic without crossing the latter, although this would have entailed crossing the Bricklayers Arms line. However, it would also have involved a widening of the Greenwich company's viaduct on the south or Croydon side, and this would have entailed the purchase of land for the purpose. This was because the 1842 widening of the viaduct has been on the south side, which had therefore taken over the land originally forming the southern 'boulevard' of the London & Greenwich Railway. The land forming the northern 'boulevard' was still available, however, and hence a widening on that side would be cheaper to carry out than one on the south side. This factor was decisive, and hence the Croydon's planning went ahead on the basis of the atmospheric line being on the down side from Corbett's Lane southwards.

The main work arising from arranging the atmospheric line on the down side was that involved in crossing the Down and Up Brighton company's roads south of Jolly Sailor, and it was decided to do this by building a flyover — the first in the World. Due to the limited axle weights that would be involved, since locomotives would not normally be using the line, a timber trestle form of construction was adopted, with gradients of 1 in 50 on each slope — one of the claims for the atmospheric system was that it enabled steep gradients to be climbed with comparative ease.

At the Croydon end of the flyover the road would be connected to the existing Down line to Croydon, which would then become the atmospheric (single) line onwards to Croydon.

Pumping-engine houses were planned for the stations at London Bridge, New Cross, Dartmouth Arms, Jolly Sailor, Croydon, Carshalton, Cheam and Epsom. Bridges were to be rebuilt as necessary. At New Cross, where the station building was on the road overbridge, the existing Down platform was to be made into an island. Up New Cross bank retaining walls were constructed at the foot of each cutting side. At Dartmouth Arms, the station buildings were on the up side, so the Down platform was made into an island. At Sydenham the Up platform appears to have been moved back, necessitating the construction of a retaining wall behind it, the two existing roads then being slued over to enable the third (atmospheric) line to be on the site of the existing Down line and thus to serve the existing Down platform with its buildings. At Penge (already closed — see Chapter VIII) the station buildings were on the down side, and hence the widening was on the up side with appropriate sluing; this also applied to Anerley and at Jolly Sailor.

Because, with the exception of the flyover, the length from Dartmouth Arms to Croydon was virtually level without heavy earthworks, it was decided that this should be equipped as Stage 1 in order to act as a good proving ground for the atmospheric system on the Croydon company's line. Hence arrangements for the engine-houses at Dartmouth Arms, Jolly Sailor, and Croydon were given priority and Messrs Maudslay, Son & Field, of Lambeth, were awarded the contract for the supply of the exhausting equipment. A 15 in. diameter traction pipe was decided upon for the line, the Coalbrookdale company receiving the contract.

At each site power was to be provided by pairs of single-cylinder beam engines of the condensing type, supplied with steam by three Cornish boilers, each engine being rated at 50 horse-power. An atmospheric pump or exhauster was to be operated off each beam, the air being discharged up the engine-house chimney along with the boiler flue gas. The boilers were to be fired with a mixture of coal and coke, brought by rail to an adjacent siding. The flywheel of one engine of each pair was to be adjacent to its fellow, so that by coupling the two flywheels together by means of a locking pin the two engines could be operated as one two-cylinder engine. The two engines were, in fact, intended to be normally coupled, but could be separated and one, only, worked while the other was under repair. The performance of the installation would obviously be halved when one engine, only, was used. It was claimed by Herapath (a consistent detractor of the system) that each pair of engines, although rated at 100 horse-power, could develop 200-400 h.p.[4]

Herapath's figure may be considered to be high, but hard driving would no doubt have enabled them to have exceeded their nominal rating by a considerable amount.

Communication between engine-houses was to be by means of an electric telegraph circuit, to the design of Cooke & Wheatstone. The telegraph clerk at each engine-house was to give orders to the pumping engineman by means of an electric bell. An 18 in vacuum was expected to be created 2 minutes after the signal to start was given, and the clerk would signal ahead to get the next engine working before the train reached his own station. Hence when the train arrived the vacuum ahead would already have been partly created.

The engine-houses and chimneys (or 'stalks') were to be given architectural treatment in view of the objections on the score of unsightliness. A sketch was made by Thomas Noakes about 1854 (i.e., after atmospheric working had ceased), of the engine-house at Norwood. Noakes was then a pupil at Ewell Academy, but lost his life at sea in 1856; he was the grandson of William and Lucy Killick of Whitehall, Cheam. Their descendants, Commander F. S. Stewart-Killick, R N, and Mrs. Doris Mills, have lent the original sketch to British Railways, and it is now at the National Railway Museum at York. The Author has the permission of Commander Stewart-Killick and Mrs. Mills to include a reproduction of the original in this book, as Figure 31.

The South Eastern Railway, since 1st January 1845 in control of the Greenwich, obtained an Act in that year (8 & 9 Vic Cap 186) for widening the Greenwich viaduct on the north side to take one extra road (making 5 in all), it being the intention that the new road would be used for down Greenwich traffic; the existing Down Greenwich would then become the Up Greenwich and the existing Up Greenwich (the middle road of the 5) would be used as the Croydon company's atmospheric line. Clause 12 of the Act stipulated that, when the road was available to the Croydon company, the latter should pay £25,000 to the South Eastern Railway for the privilege of having the free use of the line on payment of tolls. That Clause in addition required the South Eastern to execute the works within 2 years on penalty of the powers lapsing, and also recited that the Croydon company had a Bill in Parliament in the same Session, for the same widening works, if the South Eastern

Figure 31. Atmospheric Working: Norwood Engine House (from sketch by Thomas Noakes).

failed to carry them out.

The Croydon company's Bill was also passed, as 8 & 9 Vic Cap 196, Clause 12 reciting the South Eastern's Act and stating that the Croydon's powers would come into operation if the South Eastern Railway did not at once commence the Works or failed to complete them within 2 years. The Croydon obviously did not have much confidence that the South Eastern would undertake the work, and hence drew up its own Bill; and Parliament, by granting the Croydon its Act, would appear to have held a similar view. The Croydon's Act also empowered that company to widen its line from Croydon to Corbett's Lane, in extension of the authority given by 7 & 8 Vic Cap 97 of 6 August 1844. The South Eastern's estimate for the work on the viaduct, prior to its Bill becoming law, was £66,500.[5]

In the event, neither the South Eastern nor the Croydon exercised its powers to widen the Greenwich viaduct, since a financial panic in 1845, which heralded the end of the 'Railway Mania', would have made it very difficult to have raised addition capital. Hence the viaduct was not widened under either company's Act. Widening of the Croydon's own line proceeded, however, and it was also decided in 1845 that the Croydon and Epsom line should be built as a double line from the start. On 3 July in that year Dartmouth Arms was renamed Forest Hill, and Jolly Sailor became Norwood (later, Norwood Junction).

It will be seen, from the description earlier in this chapter, that atmospheric traction could only take place as long as the piston of the piston carriage was in the traction tube and a vacuum was created ahead of the piston. A further point was that, as the piston arm or 'coulter' was joggled to facilitate opening and closing of the longitudinal leather valve along the top of the traction pipe, the piston carriage was, in effect, 'handed'; that carriage could not, therefore, be turned at the end of each journey in readiness for the return trip, although it had to be transferred to the other end of its train. At terminal stations the tube had therefore to end in order that the piston carriage could be run out of the tube, and the piston had then to be detached from the leading end of the piston rod and exchanged with the counterweight at the other end of the rod (in order that what was the back of the carriage on arrival might become the front for the return journey). The piston carriage had then to 'run round' its train in order to be ready for its next trip.

In order that the piston carriage could 'run round' its train, it was obviously necessary for sets of points (turnouts) to be installed unless recourse were made to turnplates (turntables), fan or sector tables, or traversers. As the tube was mounted at sleeper height in the '4 ft', ordinary turnouts could not be used because the piston would foul one of the rails of the diverging route, between the switch and the common crossing. The use of turnouts would, however, save some time as compared with that needed to operate turntables, fan or sector tables, or traversers, in what was at best a most unsatisfactory operation. Cubitt therefore designed a special form of turnout with only one switch, the heel of which was pivoted adjacent to the crossing nose and the toe of which was planed both sides and was moved right across from one stock rail to the other. Hence whichever way the turnout was set the piston carriage only encountered, in effect, plain road.

The Author has unfortunately not found any detailed drawings of the crossing assembly, which must have been of great interest as it will be noted that wheel flanges ran on either one side or the other of the single switch rail, depending upon which stock rail the switch was laying against. Several drive rods, linked together, must have been needed in order to 'change' the points, and the operation of setting the road must have been slow and heavy.

It is possible that, by making use of gradients or by introducing artificial inclines, gravitational help may have been given to the movement of piston carriages at termini, but towroping by horses or man-handling were probably the normal methods of 'shunting' and of getting the piston into the pipe at the start of a journey. In the Author's opinion, such slow and complicated terminal working, which must have been anathema to practical railway operating staff and those in command of them, must sooner or later have brought an end to atmospheric working on a busy line, no matter how reliable and effective train running on plain road might eventually have become.

By the late summer of 1845 it was possible to start trial running between Forest Hill and Croydon, and the first was made on Friday 22 August. According to Jacob Samuda, the trial train exceeded 60 m p h. In later trials 70 m p h was reached with 6 vehicles, and 30 m p h with 16 on.[6][7] Trials over the next few weeks showed that the pumping (exhausting) engines at Norwood were not needed, successful working being possible by using only the engines at each end of the 5-mile length from Forest Hill to Croydon. Herapath was not, however, impressed by newspaper accounts of good running.[8]

The hopes raised by the successful running so far, were soon dashed as mechanical failures started to occur with the pumping equipment. In some instances engine crankshafts (which had been made of cast iron) broke, and there were other troubles. The public opening was delayed while efforts were made to improve reliability, but failures continued to occur. Much has been written, in numerous accounts, of the failure of the longitudinal valve along the traction-pipe to work properly, but the Author wishes to emphasize that this was *not* the main source of difficulty in the early stages: mechanical breakdowns with the pumping (exhausting) equipment were the real trouble.

Very prudently, the public opening continued to be postponed as a policy, until reliable working could be assumed, and in consequence 1845 closed without commercial atmospheric operations. The death of Jacob Samuda on 12 November 1845 as a result of an accident to one of his steamships on the Thames, left Joseph Samuda to face mounting criticism without the support of his brother. Nevertheless the hopes of the supporters of the atmospheric system were buoyed up by the knowledge that causes of failures were gradually being eliminated.

In the meantime, a company was formed to offer the use, under licence, of James Pilbrow's atmospheric system. In the latter, there was no direct connection between the 'piston carriage' and the piston in the main tube, the movement of the piston in the tube under vacuum conditions causing external gears to rotate and so drive the piston carriage along by means of toothed racking. There were two main advantages as compared with the Clegg-Samuda system:

(a) once the 'piston carriage' was in motion, its toothed rack could, under appropriate circumstances, run clear of the last gear wheel before a turnout or crossing in the track, and the piston carriage could, by its momentum, engage with other gears operated by another piston farther on. In other words, the main tube need not be continuous, and normal switch and crossing work could be used;

(b) the whole tube assembly was intended to be airtight, so that there was no leakage of air, and hence reduced pumping.

The Author has not found any record of the adoption of Pilbrow's system, probably because of the cost and complication of the system against the background of mounting disillusion about the whole conception of atmospheric traction.

NOTES

1. 8vo Tract, London, 1810
2. 'Calculations and Remarks tending to Prove the Practicability, Effects, and Advantages of a Plan, for the Rapid Conveyance of

Goods and Passengers on an Iron Road, through a Tube of 30 feet in Area, by the Power and Velocity of Air.'
8vo Tract, London, 1812
3. Lewin, H. G. 'Early British Railways.' Locomotive Publishing Company, 1925, 170.
4. Herapath's Railway and Commercial Journal VII (29 October 1845), 2359
5. *Ibid.*, (5 July 1845), 1092
6. Hadfield, Charles 'Atmospheric Railways.' David & Charles. 1967, 118-119
7. Herapath, VIII (28 March 1846), 435 This reference hinted that the speed of 70 m p h might have been when descending the flyover.
8. *Ibid.*, VII (25 October 1845), 2311

Important contemporary accounts of atmospheric railways and their principles include:

Samuda, Jacob	'The Atmospheric Railway.' Minutes of Proceedings Inst.E.C, 1844
Berkeley, George	'The Peculiar Features of the Atmospheric Railway System', *Ibid.*, 1845
Barlow, Peter W.	'Comparative Advantages of the Atmospheric Railway System.' *Ibid.*, 1845
Harding, Wyndham	'On the Resistance to Railway Trains at Different Velocities.' *Ibid.*, 1846

Herapath's Railway and Commercial Journal.

CHAPTER FIFTEEN

General developments, 1844-45

TWO of the matters which particularly concerned the Croydon company during the period 1844-45, were of such importance that they have been made the subjects of individual chapters in this history; the Bricklayers Arms branch (joint with the South Eastern) was dealt with in Chapter X; whilst the start of the work on the Epsom extension, and the policy to adopt atmospheric working on one section of its original line, were covered in Chapter XIV. It is now necessary to record many other matters which had significant repercussions on future events, and which, over all, made the years concerned some of the busiest and the most important in the histories of the Brighton and Croydon companies.

The first factor to be recorded was the more or less continuous dissatisfaction of both companies' shareholders, because of the low dividends that they received. The Croydon's decision to try to reduce their working expenses by adopting atmospheric traction, may have impressed a percentage of the Brighton's shareholders, but some of the latter undoubtedly felt that their own company's finances could best be improved in other ways. A letter from 'A Brightonian' to Herapath in August 1844 is worth reproducing in full:[1]

> As much is said, and said wisely, on the small dividend of 12s., can it be otherwise as long as there are 13 stations with their expenses on a line of 50 miles: it is appalling. A station every six or seven miles is ample. Other Companies have closed several stations and why not the

Brighton; but to let any train stop at every station is neutralizing speed, which is the object of every railway. As to the expense of working the line it is frightful, and it is hoped that the new Directors will attend to it. Brighton and London should be done in an hour and 40 minutes.

There had been changes in the Brighton's directorate before this letter was written, but there was little or no action in the way suggested. The 13 stations included New Cross, Dartmouth Arms, and Jolly Sailor on the Croydon line; the Croydon company had itself closed Penge as early as 1841, as already recorded. 'Brightonian's' views were very forward-looking—over 110 years were to elapse before the closing of lightly-used intermediate stations on main lines, and a great increase in the overall speed of long-distance trains became general policy on British Railways.

Regarding the working expenses, the South Eastern's chairman said that his company's costs under this heading were 50 per cent (of their revenue) whilst the Brighton company's costs were 56 per cent.[2]

The shareholders' troubles on both the Croydon and the Brighton companies, arose of course not because the working expenses were really excessive, but necause the net revenue had in each case to service the high capital involved in building the lines. The South Eastern cost considerably less per mile to build than the Brighton, because of the much easier terrain involved for most of the distance, and hence the former company had better opportunities than the latter to pay reasonable dividends to the shareholders. Moreover, the South Eastern's policy of low fares was undoubtedly increasing its traffic; fares for comparable distances from London were:

London Bridge to:		Brighton (L & Bn Rly) (50½ miles)	Marden (S E Rly) (50 miles)
		s. d.	s. d.
First class	Fast trains	14 6	8 0
	Slow trains	12 0	
Second class		8 0	5 6

The journeys, by slow trains, took in each case 2¼ − 2½ hours.

At this stage (July 1844) there were train services on the Croydon and Brighton lines as follows:

258

Croydon Company
Hourly between Bricklayers Arms and Croydon, leaving at 08 05 to 12 05, and again between 13 20 and 21 20, with services from London Bridge at 09 05, 11 05, 14 20, 16 20, 17 20, 18 20, and 20 20. On Sundays the service was slightly reduced. There was a similar pattern of up trains.
Presumably the London Bridge services involved attachments to, and detachments from, Bricklayers Arms services. However, Bradshaw gives no clue and there might only have been a shuttle service between London Bridge and New Cross.

Brighton Company
Slow trains (all stations) from London Bridge to Brighton at 08 30, 12 00, 15 00, and 18 30; and fast trains (Croydon, Reigate, Three Bridges, Haywards Heath, and Hassocks Gate only) at 10 30, 14 00, and 16 45. The up service was similar, and there were three slow trains (all stations) each way on Sundays.
The Shoreham service consisted nine trains each way between Brighton and Shoreham. Normally these called at all intermediate stations, but the 14 45 from Shoreham was not booked to call intermediately to Brighton. Some of the Shoreham trains included through first-class vehicles to and from London Bridge, but the Shoreham trains concerned did not necessarily work in conjunction with fast trains on the London service: for example, the 15 00 train from Brighton to Shoreham conveyed first-class vehicles off the 12 00 all-stations train from London Bridge.

Another matter which must now be referred to concerned potential Continental traffic. It will be recalled, from Chapter XII, that the local authorities at Dieppe had, as early as 1838, sought the Brighton company's support for the railway then being actively considered from Paris to Dieppe, and that prior to that the Brighton company's Act in 1837 had authorized the construction of a line from Brighton to New-haven via Lewes. In the event, as has also been recorded (Chapter XII), the line to Newhaven was not constructed until a second Act was obtained on 18 June 1846. In the intervening period dissatisfaction had been growing (see Chapter IX) with the unreliable steamer service from Brighton to

France, that was run by a shipping company which apparently
withdrew its vessels in winter. With the building of the South
Eastern Railway to Dover, and their branch to Folkestone
Harbour, support mounted in France for a railway from Paris
to Boulogne and Calais. As this would clearly result in an
alternative route from London to Paris, with a short sea
crossing, the Brighton company's attention was called to their
neglect of the French traffic by a letter in Herapath for 13
July 1844.[3] The Brighton company did not, however, react
with any urgency, as almost 2 years elapsed before that
company got its new Act for the branch to Newhaven.

In other directions, however, matters were extremely active,
and there were schemes for a considerable number of lines
which, if built, would have had a very important effect on the
fortunes and developments of the companies being dealt with
in this book. The more important of these proposals from the
point of view of this history are dealt with hereunder.

The first to be considered would, in effect, have given an
entirely new line from London to Brighton. It will be recalled
from earlier chapters in this history that G. P. Bidder, under
the direction of Robert Stephenson, had drawn up a detailed
scheme in the 1830s for a line to Brighton via Shoreham,
starting from the London & South Western Railway (then still
under construction as the London & Southampton Railway)
near Wimbledon, and proceeding through Dorking and
Horsham to run down the Adur valley. This scheme, one of a
number of proposals which made use of this general route,
had of course been ultimately set aside in favour of Rennie's
final 'direct' route. Supporters of the Dorking route continued
to be active behind the scenes, however, and Herapath reported in September 1844[4] that it was expected that the broad
Stephenson/Bidder scheme would shortly be revived in a
different form. The prospectus appeared on 12 October 1884[5]
for a London and Portsmouth Railway, with an independent
London terminus at the south end of Hungerford footbridge.
The line was intended to proceed via Epsom, Leatherhead,
Dorking,· and Horsham to Arundel, beyond which it was
planned to join the Brighton & Chichester Railway. A line
would run down the Adur valley from Horsham to Shoreham,
and it was also intended to make a branch from Capel (beyond
Dorking) to Reigate to join the South Eastern Railway.

This scheme had little public support, and Herapath reported that there were considerable doubts in some quarters whether Stephenson had consented to his name being shown on the prospectus.[6] The Brighton company naturally issued a statement giving relevant history and firmly denying the necessity for the proposals; but the Brighton did say that they proposed to seek authority for the construction of lines to Dorking and to Horsham.[7] The London and Portsmouth scheme came to nothing, and the Horsham line has already been dealt with in Chapter XIII.

As regards the Brighton company's line to Dorking, which would have run westwards from Reigate, it is appropriate to refer here to a proposal by the Croydon company to extend their Croydon to Epsom line (to be worked atmospherically) on to Dorking as, in effect, part of the proposed London and Portsmouth atmospheric line (Chapters XIII and XIV). Nothing came of the atmospheric line to Portsmouth, and so the Croydon's atmospheric extension west of Epsom was not pursued. As the Brighton company did not go ahead with their line from Reigate to Dorking, the latter town remained without railway facilities for a few more years.

The next scheme to be mentioned was for a line from the Bricklayers Arms branch to Nine Elms (L S W Rly), with lines to the south ends of Waterloo, Hungerford, and Westminster bridges.[8] This was, in effect, a scheme for extending the Bricklayers Arms branch as close as possible to the West End of London without involving a new bridge over the Thames. If constructed, it would clearly have had an influence on the traffic of the South Eastern company, and also on that of the Croydon company (which was one-third owner of the Bricklayers Arms branch until late in 1844), as well as on the London & South Western Railway (who would have been able to exchange traffic with the Croydon and the South Eastern Railways). The Brighton would almost certainly have also been affected. The line never materialized, although the South Eastern company sought to build a similar one from Hungerford bridge to Bricklayers Arms and then to extend that branch under the Croydon's line down to Tonbridge.[9] A proposed South Eastern extension of the Bricklayers Arms branch into North Kent did eventually come about, but is outside the scope of this book.

Another line which came to nothing was the Grosvenor Junction. This was to start on the north side of the Thames near the entrance to the Grosvenor canal, and to join the Brighton line near Godstone Road (i.e., the present Purley). There was to be a connection to the L S W Rly.[10] This line, if constructed, would have enabled the Brighton company to reach the West End — as broadly envisaged by Rastrick in 1842 and referred to in Chapter IX.

Yet another attempt to establish a railway across what is now South London, was made with the South Eastern and Richmond Junction line. This was to make a line from Bricklayers Arms station over the L S W Rly.[11]

The Croydon company itself planned a grandiose system of lines in Kent, all of which were expected to be able to be built relatively cheaply and to have good traffic potential. The main line of the new system was to commence at Sydenham and to run through Lewisham, Bromley, Chislehurst, Farnborough, Sevenoaks, Maidstone, and Charing, to Ashford. Another line was to leave the main line at Lewisham and to run via Northfleet to Rochester and Chatham, with a branch from Northfleet to Gravesend. Lewisham was also to be the junction of other lines to Maidstone (by a separate route from that of the line to Ashford) and on to Tonbridge; and to Chilham by a separate route from that to Ashford. There were also to be several subsidiary branches, including one from Lewisham to Orpington, and connections to the S E Rly. These developments eventually came to nothing, but the scheme as a whole remained active for a considerable time.

Other schemes involved variants on some of those already referred to: these included a South Eastern Railway extension from Bricklayers Arms to Waterloo,[12] a line from Croydon to Wandsworth,[13] and a Direct West End and Croydon line which had more than one phase and which was re-launched in the autumn of 1845.[14]

A proposal for railway communication with East Grinstead involved discussion at that town on 18 April 1845 of such schemes as the Central Sussex. This line would have commenced at Bishopstoke (later Eastleigh) on the L S W Rly, and would then have proceeded via Bishops Waltham, Petersfield, Midhurst, Petworth, and Billingshurst, to Horsham; from Horsham to Three Bridges use would have been made of the Brighton company's Horsham branch authorized 3 months earlier on 21 July, and the Central Sussex would then have proceeded to East Grinstead. From there it would have gone on to Tonbridge and thence to Rochester (joining there another line under discussion and so ultimately reaching Chatham and Sheerness). The promoters held that there was a need to establish railway communication between Portsmouth, Chatham, and Sheerness.[15] It may be noted here that certain parts of the proposed route were shortly afterwards adopted for new lines by the Brighton and South Eastern companies (see below).

There were also proposals for lines from Dorking to Brighton via the Adur valley and Shoreham,[16] for a S E Rly branch to Dorking from Reigate,[17] for a S E Rly line to East Grinstead from near Tonbridge,[18] and for a Brighton company's line to East Grinstead from Three Bridges[19] (i.e., similar to part of the Central Sussex scheme outlined above).

Farther afield, lines to serve Littlehampton[20] and Bognor,[21] in the former case via a branch off the Worthing and Chichester line, and in the latter case from the proposed L S W Rly — sponsored line via Chichester to Portsmouth, were proposed.

Reverting to the London area, there were schemes to connect the Croydon line with the London & Blackwall Railway by means of the Thames Tunnel,[22] and for a line from New Cross to the docks and wharves at Deptford.[23] This latter was an old idea being put forward again (see later).

Another proposal to be mentioned here concerned a Metropolitan Junction railway, to start at Red Hill or Reigate and to proceed through Dorking, Leatherhead, Weybridge, (i.e., along the Mole valley), Egham, Datchet, Slough, Uxbridge, Rickmansworth, Watford, St. Albans, Hertford, Ware, Chelmsford, and Billericay, to Tilbury (from which there would be a ferry to Gravesend). Junctions would be made with lines to be crossed. Such a line might have been of some benefit to the Brighton but little, apparently, to the Croydon, and might have had South Eastern support. Farther along its route it would have had to depend on sources of traffic other than from the southern companies.[24]

Yet another concern floated at this period was the South London railway. This was to have left the Greenwich line about

1 mile from London Bridge, and then to run through Peckham, Camberwell, Brixton, Clapham, and Tooting, to Mitcham. An extension would have continued to Ewell and Epsom. Branches would have gone to Norwood and Dulwich, and to join the L S W Rly at Wandsworth.[25]

Additionally, record needs to be made of a proposed Reading and Reigate atmospheric line,[26] and of the Southern Junction railway joining the Great Western at Slough to the South Eastern at Reigate.[27] There were various others that need not be noted here.

Nothing materialized directly from these schemes that affected the Brighton or Croydon companies, although some parts of the proposed routes were afterwards used for lines that were constructed — see later in this history.

Apart from the firm proposals referred to above, there were suggestions by various shareholders and others. One such idea which merits attention in this account was for a line from Lewes to Tunbridge Wells, which appeared in the course of a letter to the editor of Herapath.[28] The writer proposed that, 'at some convenient point', a branch should leave a suggested Lewes — Tunbridge Wells line and then curve round to meet the then proposed S E Rly line from Tunbridge Wells to Hastings (Chapter XII). The object of the line was thus to save the independent Brighton, Lewes & Hastings, from building 'an unnecessary' route beyond Lewes, and also to put Brighton into direct communication with Tunbridge Wells. Later, as will be recorded, such a line from Lewes to Uckfield was extended to join a then-existing line on to Tunbridge Wells.

Aside from schemes for new lines, consideration was also given to the conversion of the Surrey Iron Railway from a horse-worked plateway into a locomotive-worked railway, and to make a connection at the Wandsworth end with the Richmond line. Extension from Nine Elms to Hungerford bridge would be an entirely new line. This scheme was a joint proposal of the Brighton and South Western companies, working with the Richmond company.[29] The scheme came to nothing, but some years later part of the old Surrey Iron Railway road bed was used for the construction of the West Croydon and Wimbledon line.

Finally, mention must be made of a scheme for a line from

Wimbledon to Epsom. An independent company, the South Western and Epsom Junction Railway, proposed to build the line, and then to sell or let it to the L S W Rly. This scheme came to nothing, although a broadly similar line was built later.

The schemes referred to above were all proposed during the period that became known as the 'Railway Mania', and their hopes of gaining support from investors were shattered with the downward trend in the value of railway shares in the autumn of 1845 which, in retrospect, may be seen as the start of the end of the 'railway mania'.

An extension to the South Eastern company must also be mentioned. This was the opening on 24 September 1844, of a line from Maidstone Road (renamed Paddock Wood at the same time) to Maidstone, the terminus being on the site of part of the present Maidstone West station. The line was opened as a single line and was provided with the electric telegraph from the start. The branch was doubled in 1846. It was 10¼ miles long and the cost was only £10,000 per mile.

A signalling installation similar to that at Bricklayers Arms Junction was installed at Brighton Junction (Norwood) where the Brighton line joined the Croydon. This was brought into use in the summer of 1844, the work being done under the orders of Mr. C. H. Gregory, the Croydon's Engineer.[30]

The South Eastern seems to have been earlier in the field than the Brighton in making general use of the electric telegraph. By November 1845 it was installed between Edenbridge and Dover (as well as on the Maidstone branch), and the decision had been taken to extend it from Edenbridge to London Bridge and also from Bricklayers Arms Junction to Bricklayers Arms station. The first public telegraph line had been opened in February 1845, between London and Gosport.[31]

There was a serious fire in a store over the engine house at New Cross used by 'pool' engines, on 14 October 1844. The damage was estimated at some £25,000, not all of it covered by insurance. The cause of the fire was thought to be spontaneous combustion.[32]

Earlier that year, on Sunday 14 July, a fatality had occurred on the Croydon, due to the stupidity of a young man named Robert Cattermole. He was travelling third class, and tried to climb on to the rave of the open-topped vehicle in order, apparently, to sit on the top of the bodyside. He fell out of

265

the train. A labourer on the line, Charles Hill, was run over early in October 1845, and died. There was another fatality on the Croydon line near Sydenham on Sunday 26 October 1845, when a man, thought to have been a trespasser, was run over by a steam-worked ballast train.[33] Shortly before this event, the piston came off the piston-rod under a piston carriage on one trial atmospheric trip, the piston then travelling forward so rapidly that it smashed the chamber at the end of the section of tube concerned.

A further incident, on the opening day of the extension from Shoreham to Worthing (24 November 1845), caused delay at Lancing. The 12 55 train from Worthing to Brighton, worked by a locomotive running tender first, hit a horse as the train was entering Lancing station. It will be recalled that this railway was opened as a single line but that the formation had been built for double track, and the horse was the leading animal of two which were pulling some ballast wagons on the road not yet in use as a running line. The horse driver had failed to keep his charge from moving foul of the running line, and the tender and engine were derailed. The horse was killed by no injuries to persons occurred.[34]

In proportion to the numbers of passengers conveyed, railways were already a very safe means of travel. Partly for this reason, but undoubtedly also owing to lingering antagonism to railways in certain persons' minds, any report of an accident on the railway was given prominence. It may help to restore perspective by referring briefly to a coaching accident on the Preston New Road on Saturday 8 November 1845. A coach capsized, and all eighteen passengers received injuries, some of them very severe.

The troubles incurred by the Croydon in trying to make the first stage of the atmospheric system reliable enough to be used commercially have been already referred to (Chapter XIV). Meanwhile, work was proceeding on the other stages, taking account of experience already gained. The most important decision was that the pumping equipment should be obtained on a competitive basis rather than going again to Maudslays. Messrs Boulton & Watts put in the lowest tender, and their bid was accepted for the supply of pairs of single-cylinder horizontal engines, arranged with flywheels adjacent to one another to facilitate coupling; working pressure was to be 50 lb per square inch. The orders were for Stages 2, 3, and 4 (see Chapter XIV). Each pair of engines was rated at 100 h p except for the pair for Carshalton (Wallington), which were to be rated at 165 h p.

Construction of the Croydon and Epsom line was not moving as quickly as had been hoped, due to difficulties in acquiring certain parcels of land. Messrs. William Hoof & Sons of Kensington put in a tender and schedule of prices in July 1845, but no contract was then let. Messrs. Charles Penfold of Croydon's tender was accepted on 11 June 1846. It was clear that the line would not be opened that year. Incidentally, consideration was given to resiting Croydon station on the Epsom line, to the west of London Road bridge, but in the event this proposal was dropped.

Work on Stage 2 progressed steadily, however, the extra road being laid on the down side from New Cross to Forest Hill. The down platform at New Cross was made into an island, in the same manner as the down platform at Forest Hill. Associated works included the provision of a footbridge at Forest Hill, over the two 'steam' lines. It was reported on 1 November 1845 that the 'steeple' on the Croydon engine-house was to be removed as it had become unsafe, due to vibration from 'the violent and desperate working of the engines' in order to get acceptable train working.[35]

In the meantime, the South Eastern company had, as already explained in Chapter X, exercised its right and had purchased the Croydon's share of the Bricklayers Arms branch, the latter thus becoming purely a S E Rly line. Earlier, in December 1844, William Cubitt had resigned from his position of Engineer to the South Eastern Railway.

NOTES

1. Herapath's Railway and Commercial Journal, VI (24 August 1844), 1000
2. *Ibid.*, (14 September 1844), 1079
3. *Ibid.*, 825
4. *Ibid.*, (28 September 1844), 1157
5. *Ibid.*, 1229
6. *Ibid.*, 1251
7. *Ibid.*, (26 October 1844), 1289
8. *Ibid.*, (9 November 1844), 1350
9. *Ibid.*, (7 December 1844), 1462

NOTES—*continued*

10. *Ibid.*, 1459
11. *Ibid.*, 1462
12. *Ibid.*, VII (6 December 1845), 2651
13. *Ibid.*, (19 November 1845), 2562
14. *Ibid.*, (15 October 1845), 2139; and (15 November 1845), 2540
15. *Ibid.*, (22 October 1845), 2277
16. *Ibid.*, (29 November 1845), 2619
17. *Ibid.*, (6 December 1845), 2651
18. *Ibid.*, 2651
19. *Ibid.*, (27 December 1845), 2757)
20. *Ibid.*, (19 November 1845), 2564
21. *Ibid.*, (11 October 1845), 2103; and (19 November 1845), 2562
22. *Ibid.*, (29 November 1845), 2620
23. *Ibid.*, 2620
24. *Ibid.*, (6 December 1845), 2650
25. *Ibid.*, (Supplement to 18 October 1845), 2243
26. *Ibid.*, 2650
27. *Ibid.*, 2650
28. *Ibid.*, VI (7 December 1844), 1450
29. *Ibid.*, (21 September 1844), 1125
30. Rapier, R. C. On the Fixed Signals of Railways. Proceedings Inst. C. E., XXXVIII (1873-74), 204-205
31. Prescott, George W. *Electricity and the Electric Telegraph.* D. Appleton & Co., New York, 1877, 549
32. *British Railways Magazine, Southern Region* 3 (1952), 230
    This article gives a detailed account, quoting lengthy extracts from *The Illustrated London News.*
33. Herapath, VII (29 October 1845), 2364
34. *Ibid.*, (26 November 1845), 2613
35. *Ibid.*, (1 November 1845), 2407

CHAPTER SIXTEEN

Events in 1845-46, and the formation of the L B S C Rly

FROM what has already been recorded, it will be clear that the decision to adopt atmospheric traction on the London and Croydon Railway was involving that company in considerably greater expenditure than had been envisaged, as well as giving what would now be called a poor public image. The Croydon's shareholders became more and more disgruntled, but the directors, and in particular the Chairman (Mr. W. A. Wilkinson), still had faith that the atmospheric system would be commercially viable on their line, and hence pressed on with it. Wilkinson seems to have had great powers of persuasion and hence to have been able to continue to obtain considerable support for his unswerving advocacy of atmospheric working on the Croydon. Eventually, in fact, it appeared that Wilkinson himself was the main supporter of the scheme, and carried the directors and the shareholders with him. This became so pointed that Herapath—always against the atmospheric system, for any railway—on more than one occasion suggested in print that he (Wilkinson) was a partner of the Samudas. No denial of this insinuation apparently appeared in Herapath, from which it is very difficult to avoid at least a passing thought that there might have been some justification for such a damning remark—which must surely have been actionable if it had been a complete fabrication, and which Wilkinson would presumably have hotly denied if his conscience had been clear. To have ignored such an allegation, twice made,[1] had it been completely false, can hardly have improved Wilkinson's stature among either his fellow directors or the Croydon's shareholders; nor, for that matter, have enhanced the standing of Herapath if it had been found to have been untrue.

Be that as it may, there is no doubt that opinion among certain sections of the Croydon shareholders was hardening against the way in which the company was working. Some of the Brighton's company's shareholders were equally restive. Moreover, the latter company's desire to reach the West End in London, which had been alluded to by Rastrick in 1842 (Chapter IX) and had been the reason for the proposed Direct West End and Croydon line previously mentioned, had also been opposed by the London and Croydon company. Hence the Brighton and the Croydon companies were not on good terms.

Ever since the outstanding financial success of the Liverpool and Manchester Railway, considerable numbers of investors in the north of England had been prepared to put money into lines which they felt had a future, and hence many railways had, for example, 'Liverpool Parties' among their shareholders. Dissatisfaction with the lack of financial progress of both the Croydon and the Brighton companies finally came into the open when on Wednesday 15 October 1845 a party of influential shareholders travelled from Leeds to London to try to effect an amalgamation of the two companies.[2] Discussions were held on the next two days, but the move was defeated by Mr. Wilkinson. However, the two boards met on 27 October 1845, and reached general agreement on amalgamation, but the minutes of the meeting were not confirmed. However, a Special General Meeting of the shareholders in the London and Brighton company, took place on 6 November 'to consider the expediency of amalgamating with the Croydon company'. At the meeting the Chairman, Mr. Rowland Hill, after general discussion, reminded those present of their defeat by the Croydon during one of the Brighton's attempts to reach the West End. (In fairness, it must be pointed out that the Croydon could hardly have looked with equanimity at a proposal which would, if carried out, have very considerably reduced its (the Croydon's) tolls from Brighton traffic.) Rowland Hill went on to admire George Hudson's method of taking over small companies, by driving very hard bargains, and then asked the Brighton shareholders to pass the resolution to the effect that amalgamation should be pursued. This the shareholders did, leaving their directors to negotiate details.[3]

Later on the same day, 6 November 1845, there was a meeting of the Croydon shareholders to authorize the proposed amalgamation. This company's shareholders also agreed to the proposal, and left their board to arrange details.[4] Mr. Wilkinson announced, at that meeting, his decision to retire from the Croydon's chairmanship and directorate, into private life, but in the event he did not do this.

Despite the companies' shareholders' decisions that their boards should negotiate detailed terms for amalgamation, things did not go forward smoothly. Herapath had been outspoken in drawing attention to the fact that the suggested terms (on the basis of £50 for each £50 Brighton share and £18-10 for each £20 Croydon share) was a triumph for Wilkinson and a disaster for the Brighton, who as a consequence would be saddled with the Croydon's expensive and unsatisfactory atmospheric system.[5] Additionally, the Brighton had made a prior agreement with the London & South Western, concerning the latter's proposal to make a line to Portsmouth via Chichester; the South Western had undertaken to accept half the Brighton's liability under their guarantee to the Chichester and Brighton company (then under construction), and had offered the Brighton a share in the South Western's line from Guildford, prior to their (the South Western) making their plans public. This was none other than a case of the L & S W Rly buying off the Brighton's opposition before matters became generally known. Yet another factor in the Brighton-Croydon discussions was that Wilkinson tried to insist that the Direct Portsmouth, a proposal that would have been linked with the Croydon, had also to be included in the amalgamation; Wilkinson in addition continued his opposition to any line from the Brighton to Wandsworth.

However, the Croydon shareholders were no longer in sympathy with Mr. Wilkinson, and as a result the amalgamation was finally agreed, to take effect during the following year (1846) after all necessary authority had been given to the decision. In the meantime, the Croydon and Brighton companies continued to function separately, and attention must now be given to operating and engineering matters.

In the Autumn of 1845 the Croydon was still struggling to make atmospheric working sufficiently trustworthy that public traffic could be contemplated. Reliability increased gradually, and the date for public opening was finally fixed for Monday 19 January 1846, over Stage I of the project (i.e., Forest Hill to Croydon). For the first hour or two all went well, but at 11 00 hours one of the Croydon engines broke down; hence the other engine had to operate on its own, and was no doubt driven very hard in order that there should not be too much diminution of performance. Whether or not the likely overloading was responsible, the second Croydon engine failed at 19 20 hours, and locomotive working had to be introduced between Croydon and Norwood until 11 00 hours on the following morning, when atmospheric working was resumed.[6] According to Herapath, the second day's working was also ruined by a crank failure, and repairs had not been effected by Wednesday.[7] The public image was thus spoilt on the opening day.

Breakdowns of the pumping (exhausting) engines continued. Both engines at Croydon failed again on 10 February, whilst some two months later the beam of one of the Forest Hill engines fractured. Although Maudslays (the engine builders) had to shoulder the responsibility for such events, for which hard driving may well have been a contributory factor, the public as a whole not unnaturally put the blame on Joseph Samuda (the surviving brother and the one chiefly concerned with the system on the Croydon line) for the atmospheric railway as a whole; and critics of the system inevitably made great play with its continuing unreliability. Samuda's Report to the Half-Yearly meeting of the Croydon shareholders, held on 10 March 1846,[8] is of sufficient interest to be reproduced as an Appendix to this chapter. Experiments on the resistance of trains formed the subject of an important paper before the Institution of Civil Engineers.[9]

By about Easter 1846, further modifications to the pumping equipment were resulting in reasonably satisfactory performance, and the service began to run more reliably than previously. The traffic built up steadily, and at last it seemed that the faith of the system's supporters might yet be justified. Two unconnected matters however, one already in the past and the other soon to come, shortly began to play an increasing part in the chain of events. The factor which was already history by Easter 1846, was the impending amalgamation of the Croydon with the Brighton, in which the Brighton would inevitably have the major voice. In the immediate future lay the hitherto unappreciated effects of Nature.

Taking these two factors in order, the Croydon board gave consideration to the facts that, after the amalgamation, the atmospheric system would no longer have the untrammelled enthusiasm and support of Mr. Wilkinson, but that on the other hand success now appeared to be possible and also that a considerable amount of money had been committed to Stage 2 (Forest Hill to New Cross). Additionally, the Croydon and Epsom line was going ahead on atmospheric principle and financial commitments had been entered into for tubes and pumping plant for that line. The Croydon therefore decided to continue with the system, and matters went ahead actively on Stage 2, as already recorded in Chapter XV.

Hitherto, the main trouble with the atmospheric system had been due to mechanical breakdowns of the pumping plant, possibly accentuated by hard driving as already explained. Just when the pumping plant itself had been made reasonably reliable, the hitherto unrealized effects of Nature began to make themselves felt as the weather started to warm up at the start of an unusually hot summer. This brought into play an entirely new cause of trouble: the longitudinal leather flap or valve along the top of the tube became partly ineffective because the mixture of beeswax and tallow intended to seal the flap melted, and allowed the leather itself to become hard.

The resulting leakage of air caused bad working and occasional train failures on the Norwood flyover, as well as increased fuel costs by extra pumping. Further, rubbish, etc., and even rats, were drawn into the pipe and then sucked to the pumping stations where they choked the air valves — this again causing bad train working. The technical reasons for the unsatisfactory performance of the longitudinal valve are outside the scope of this account, and in any case have been described elsewhere,[10] but the result was that satisfactory operation was again no longer possible. Towards the end of May, in fact, atmospheric working had to be given up until a new leather valve and new sealant were developed and fitted. The Samuda principle included a weather valve, but it was not fitted on the Croydon line. Atmospheric working was resumed on 13 July 1846. However, instances of failing to stop properly at intermediate stations, and of buffer collisions at Croydon, also occurred from time to time when the rails were greasy.[11]

With the return of cooler weather in the Autumn, improved working was to be expected, but as the amalgamation of the Croydon and Brighton companies approached the atmospheric system was very much under a cloud.

Apart from problems affecting atmospheric working, a number of other matters must be recorded at this stage.

The Locomotive Pool finally came to an end on 31 January 1846, and the engines passed again into the direct ownership of the companies concerned—but were not always returned to their previous owners.

The South Eastern company opened their line from Ashford to Canterbury on 6 February 1846, and extended it from Canterbury to Ramsgate on Easter Monday 13 April 1846; this brought more traffic on to the Brighton line and hence on to the Croydon. The Easter traffic on the Croydon line was very heavy, and Herapath records that locomotives were employed to give rear-end assistance to atmospheric trains that were heavily loaded.[12] A summons against the Croydon company for allowing excessive smoke to be produced by the Norwood engine-house, was dismissed.[13]

The Surrey Iron Railway wished to dissolve itself in the Spring of 1846, and its Bill was considered in a Committee of the House of Commons, on Saturday 20 June. After amendments, approval in principle was given on Monday 22 June,[14] and the Act of Dissolution was passed on 3 August (9 & 10 Vic. Cap. 333). Final closure was on Monday 31 August 1846.

Having adopted semaphore signals in lieu of rotating discs (see Chapter IX), the London & Brighton decided that distant (or 'auxiliary') signals, when required, should be of a distinctive pattern. Hence in 1846 the company started using a double-disc 'turnover' signal for that purpose. The two discs were mounted at opposite ends of an horizontal rod carried through the top of the signal post, and were so weighted that the two discs were normally presented full-face to enginemen—and when so displayed indicated that the semaphore signal farther on was at that moment in the 'on' position. When the new type of distant signal was pulled 'off', the horizontal rod was rotated through 90 degrees so as to present the edges of the two discs towards enginemen—thus continuing with the principle that the absence of a signal meant 'proceed'. The working face of each disc was painted a red-orange colour, and the back was painted white with a black St. George's cross. A revolving lamp, operated by the movement of the signal discs, showed a red or a white light as appropriate. (see Figure 32.) The Author, in another capacity, arranged for a model of one of these signals to be made and placed on display at the National Railway Museum at York.

Early in 1846 the South Eastern Railway completed the installation of the electric telegraph throughout its system,

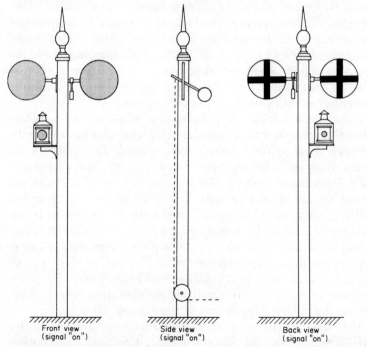

Front view
(signal "on")

Side view
(signal "on")

Back view
(signal "on")

Figure 32. London & Brighton Railway 'Turnover' Double — Disc Distant Signal.

in continuation of what has already been recorded in Chapter XV. Nominally, the South Eastern's telegraph circuits would have gone straight from Merstham to Bricklayers Arms and London Bridge, as the intermediate stations were all in other companies' hands. It is likely, however, that Croydon and New Cross—at both of which South Eastern trains called—would also have been provided with instruments, with South Eastern Railway staff to operate them. In any case, the Brighton and the Croydon companies soon followed the South Eastern's lead if they did not put their installations in simultaneously with those of the South Eastern.

Train services on the Croydon and Brighton companies' lines had settled down to a steady pattern, but one feature which must be mentioned was the elimination of normal second-class facilities on the Brighton company's 'express' services, with the exception of the 10 30 hours London Bridge 'express mail'—for which the single fare to Brighton was 10/-. On other Brighton 'express' services, second-class accommodation was only available for servants in attendance on members of the families concerned. This change was announced on 8 October 1845, and was presumably made on two accounts: to ensure that passengers requiring a speedy journey had to pay first-class fares; and to effect economies by reducing the weight of 'express' trains.

Passengers transferring from one platform to another normally crossed the line on the level, and this undoubtedly resulted in occasional narrow escapes from being struck by trains in an age when railways were still new and somewhat fearful to many people. An instance where there was no escape occurred at Balcombe on 30 June 1846. A woman, wishing to travel to London, started to cross the line to reach the up platform without seeing the approach of a down train. When the driver opened his whistle the woman was petrified and sank down in front of the train. The station clerk ran to her help and both were killed.[15] There were also near escapes, and one or two fatalities, on the atmospheric line, due to the relative quietness of the trains.

It is now necessary to notice the final steps leading to the amalgamation of the Brighton and Croydon companies, following the policy decision and subsequent discussions referred to earlier in this chapter. Both companies held shareholders' meetings on 31 March 1846 to confirm that the earlier decision to go ahead with the arrangements still had the proprietors' support, and therefore that they would agree to the Bills going forward to Parliament. The respective boards obtained their shareholders' support, and hence Parliamentary action was pursued.[16] This was taken to a successful conclusion, and the necessary Consolidation Act received the Royal Assent on Monday 27 July 1846 as 9 & 10 Vic. Cap. 283, to bring the combined companies into existence under the title of the London Brighton & South Coast Railway Company. The Croydon & Epsom, the Brighton, Lewes & Hastings, and the Brighton & Chichester companies were also brought into the L B S C Rly, whose authorized capital was £5,581,000.

The first meeting of the combined boards was held early in August 1846,[17] Mr. C. P. Grenfell (the Brighton's chairman) being elected chairman and Mr. W. A. Wilkinson (the Croydon's chairman) being elected deputy chairman. The first meeting of shareholders of the new company took place on 19 August 1846, under Mr. Wilkinson's chairmanship, Mr. Grenfell having 'been called out of town by important business'.[18] Presumably the latter referred to some domestic or vital private matter, as it seems strange that the chairman of the new company should have been absent from its first meeting.

Earlier in the year, the Brighton company's had active proposals in hand for new lines as follows:

Serial No:	Line	Approximate length: Miles	Estimated construction cost: £*	Layout: Lines
1	Wandsworth Branch	6⅝	140,000	Double
2	Dorking Branch	7¾	145,000	Double
3	East Grinstead Branch	6⅞	80,000	Double
4	Steyning Branch	4⅛	44,000	Single
5	Littlehampton Branch	1¼	10,000	Single
6	Bognor Branch	3⅝	35,000	Single

7	Newhaven and			
	Seaford Branch	8½	104,000	Double
8	Hailsham			
	Branch	2⅞	30,000	Single
9	Eastbourne			
	Branch	4⅜	40,000	Single
	Total 46 miles			

*Excluding stations and Parliamentary expenses.

At the same time the Croydon company had active proposals in hand for the following new lines:

Serial No:	Line	Approximate length: Miles	Estimated construction cost: £†	Layout: Lines
10	Thames Junction (New Cross to Deptford) (Freight only)	1	40,000	Single
11	The Kent group of lines	—	—	—

†Including construction of a wet dock at Deptford.

Of the foregoing, Serials Nos. 8 and 9 received their Acts before the L B S C Rly was formed, and Serial No. 7 did so for a line from Lewes to Newhaven only. Serials Nos. 1-6 were dropped for various reasons, largely financial, and as such followed in the wake of the many proposals listed in Chapter XV (and of others, less important from the point of view of this book, that have not been mentioned). Serials Nos. 3, 4, and 5, and the Seaford extension of the Newhaven line representing Serial No. 7, were revived later and received their Acts, as will be recounted in due course. Serial No. 6 was revived later in a different form and was, in that form, enacted. Serial No. 1 was, in effect, represented by a later development; whilst Serial No. 2 died, to be replaced by a South Eastern Railway line over much the same ground. These revivals and replacements will be referred to in greater detail at the appropriate stage in this history.

Going back to Serials Nos. 7 (as far as Newhaven) 8, and 9, these have already been referred to in detail in Chapter XII. Serial No. 10 was enacted on the day that the Croydon company was amalgamated with the others to form the L B S C Rly and hence will be dealt with in Volume II; and

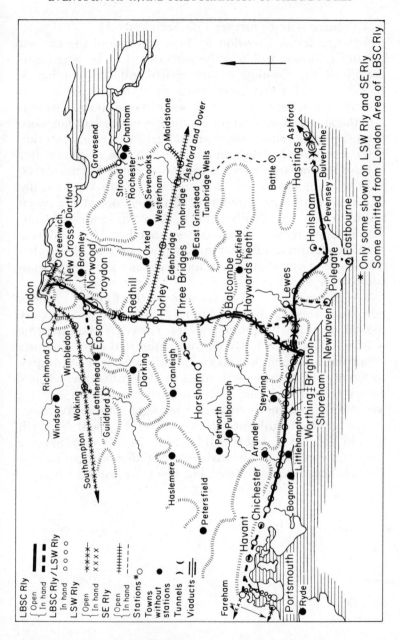

Figure 33. Map of London Brighton & South Coast Railway at August 1846 (immediately following formation of consolidated company).

that Volume will go further into Serial No. 11.

The London & Croydon Railway was one of the earliest serving London, and may be considered to be a contemporary of the London & Greenwich and the London & Blackwall. All these lines were short but expensive to construct, and hence all of them were in due course brought into the association of larger companies which had far more extensive territories to cover and far greater traffic potential.

The London & Brighton Railway was one of the earlier main-line companies serving London, and may be considered to be a contemporary of the London & South Western, the Great Western, the London & Birmingham, the Eastern Counties, and the South Eastern. As such, it was laid out with long straights and easy curves, together with moderate gradients (although Bidder and Stephenson considered that the Brighton's gradients were too steep, as will be clear from Chapters V and VI).

The South Eastern had taken over the Greenwich on a perpetual lease as from 1 January 1845, and it was only logical that the Brighton and the Croydon should come together. The L B S C Rly not only inherited the Croydon's atmospheric system, but also a considerable area of country in Surrey and Sussex (with some in Hampshire) which had as yet no railways and whose potential originating traffic was mainly passengers and dairy and agricultural produce.

The gradual build-up of the L B S C Rly will be dealt with in Volume II, but it will be useful at this stage to see a map of the system as already open, together with an indication of those lines still being built (see Figure 33).

APPENDIX

LONDON & CROYDON RAILWAY REPORT

by Mr. Joseph D. A. Samuda
on the Working of the Atmospheric System

Submitted to the Half-Yearly Meeting of London & Croydon
Shareholders on Tuesday 10 March 1846

In accordance with the instructions of your Board, I beg to report the progress and present state of the atmospheric works for the London, Croydon, and Epsom Railway. In addition to the Atmospheric line from Croydon to Forest Hill, which was opened for public traffic on the 19th January, the works up the New-cross incline, from the first bridge below New-cross to the Forest-hill station, are completed, and experimental trains have been run over this distance. Vacuum tubes and apparatus for a further portion (about 5 miles) are prepared and in readiness to be laid immediately the road is ready to receive them. The working of the public traffic has been regular and satisfactory, with some few exceptions; interruptions have arisen—1st. From the breakage of the crank axles and connecting rods of the steam-engines. 2nd. From the peculiar description of valves employed in the vacuum pumps. 3rd. From the temporary arrangements at the sideings. And, 4th. Some slight delay has in two instances occurred, from the line requiring more power than it could obtain; one-half of the engine power at two out of three of the engine houses being at the time unavailable. In this latter case, the only inconvenience that resulted was that a few trains proceeded at a decreased rate, and arrived from 10 to 15 minutes behind time. The engine-makers have now substituted wrought iron for cast in five out of six of the broken crank shafts, and they will make a similar change of material in the connecting rods, and such other parts of the engine as require it, as soon as the new work can be prepared. Air-pump valves, of the construction of which we have practically found to be efficient, are also in course of preparation, in lieu of the present ones. Some time must elapse before these alterations can be carried into effect; and until then I cannot but feel apprehensive that what has occurred may recur, though I hope that such may not be the case; for I believe the engine-makers will use every exertion to get them finished with as little delay as possible, and the regular working of the engines may be relied on when they are completed. With these exceptions, nothing can have been more satisfactory than the

APPENDIX – *continued*

results obtained. The men each day become better acquainted with their respective duties, and a manifest improvement in the execution of them is the result. The facilities of managing apparatus, regulating the speed of the trains, obtaining the power, exchanging the trains from locomotive to atmospheric traction, working a single atmospheric line (and that in conjunction with and in continuation of a double line of railway), have now practically been demonstrated to be in all cases equal to our expectations, and in some have surpassed the anticipations to which we gave expression. Express trains have now been put on in addition to the ordinary hourly trains. We have found no difficulty or inconvenience result from adopting this course, while the increased accommodation the Company thus afford the public cannot fail to augment considerably the revenue of the line.

JOSEPH D. A. SAMUNDA

NOTES

1. Herapath's *Railway and Commercial Journal,* VII (18 October 1845), 2180; and (12 November 1845), 2502.
2. *Ibid.,* (18 October 1845), 2179.
3. *Ibid.,* (8 November 1845), 2445.
4. *Ibid.,* 2446.
5. *Ibid.,* 2502.
6. Clayton, Howard *The Atmospheric Railway.* Howard Clayton, Lichfield 1966.
7. Herapath, VIII (24 January 1846), 119.
8. *Ibid.,* (14 March 1846), 362.
9. Harding, Wyndham *On the Resistances to Railway Trains at Different Velocities.* Minutes of Proceedings. Inst.C.E., 1846.
10. Clayton, Howard *The Atmospheric Railways.* Howard Clayton, Lichfield, 1966.
11. Herapath, VIII (11 April 1846), 497.
12. *Ibid.,* (18 April 1846), 521.
13. *Ibid.,* (25 April 1846), 551.
14. *Ibid.,* (27 June 1846), 814.
15. *Ibid.,* (4 July 1846), 856.
16. *Ibid.,* (4 March 1846), 461-462.
17. *Ibid.,* (8 August 1846), 987.
18. *Ibid.,* (27 August 1846), 1037.

CONCISE INDEX TO VOLUME I

*A Comprehensive Index to both Volumes
will be included in Volume II*

*General description of inter-mediate stations.

†General note on construction of line.

Accidents 152, 154, 160, 165, 265, 266, 274, 276
Alderson, Capt. Robert, R. E. 113
Amalgamation of Brighton, Croydon, and other Companies to form L B S C Rly 271, 277
Angmering 209, 210*
Annerley (sic) 51, 57
Anerley 250
Arundel (now Ford) 209, 210*
Atmospheric System
  Adoption of System by London & Croydon and Croydon & Epsom companies 243, 247
  Description of Basic Principles of System 240-242
  Pumping-Engines and Engine-Houses 249, 250-251, 266
  Train Working 253, 272, 273
  Troubles 254, 266, 272

Balcombe 121, 126, 127, 137, 183, 232-233
Berwick 218, 225*
Bexhill 218, 225*
Bidder, George Parker
  Brighton Line proposals 28, 68, 69
  Evidence in Parliament, 1836 83-86
  New Proposals for Line to Brighton 260

Bognor (later Woodgate) 209, 210*
Bosham 235, 236*
Bricklayers Arms branch 192-204
Brighton
  Goods Station 127
  Historical 20
  Lewes and Hastings, Line to
    See under Brighton, Lewes & Hastings Rly
  Passenger Station 123, 127, 128, 137, 138, 163, 215
  Proposals for Lines to 21, 28, 30, 65-114
  Shoreham, Line to
    See under Shoreham-Brighton line
Brighton & Chichester Rly (Shoreham-Chichester, and westwards) 205-212, 235-238
  Consolidation with other Companies to form L B S C Rly 277
  Permanent Way 212, 237†
  Signalling 212, 237†
Brighton Junction
  (at Norwood, earlier Jolly Sailor) 117, 248
Brighton, Lewes & Hastings Rly 214-227, 229-231
  Consolidation with other Companies to form L B S C Rly 277
  Permanent Way 225, 226
  Signalling 225, 226
Bulverhithe 215, 218, 222, 223, 225
Burgess Hill 122, 126

Carshalton (now Wallington) 246, 249
Cheam 246, 249
Chichester 209, 212, 235, 237

Chichester & Portsmouth Rly 235-238
Clegg, Samuel 240, 248
Coaches, Road, 20, 162
Continental Traffic 213, 227, 259
Corbett's Lane Junction 27, 36, 49, 63
Cosham 236, 237
Cosham Junction 236, 237
Crawley 233
Croydon
    Historical 1
    Proposals for Line to 21
    Stations
        Brighton Company (later East Croydon) 117, 126, 137, 138
        Croydon Company (later West Croydon) 52, 57, 244, 246, 249
Croydon Canal 3, 4, 7, 27, 45, 60
Croydon & Epsom Rly 243-248, 267
Consolidation with other Companies to form L B S C Rly 277
Croydon, Merstham & Godstone Rly 16, 19, 115, 125, 131, 244
Cubitt, William 126, 159, 171, 242, 243, 247, 253
Cundy, Nicholas 28, 66, 67, 68, 69

Dartmouth Arms (now Forest Hill) 50, 57, 148, 184, 249, 250
Doubling of Single Lines
    See under Widening Works
Drayton 209, 210*

Earth Slips
    See under Slips, Earth
Eastbourne 229, 230
Electric Telegraph, introduction of 265, 275
Elms, Mr. 66
Emsworth 236
Enginemen, appointment of on London & Croydon Rly 165
Epsom 240, 243, 246, 249
Ewell (now Ewell East) 246

Falmer 217, 219, 225*
Fares
    See under Financial Matters
Farlington Junction 235, 236
Faygate 233
Financial Matters
    including Fares and Toll Questions 150, 151, 156, 163, 172, 173, 174, 176, 185, 187, 199-204, 257, 271
Ford
    See under Arundel
Forest Hill (earlier, Dartmouth Arms) 50, 53
Friars Walk (Lewes) 217, 223, 224, 226
Fulton, Hamilton 66

Gas-Lighting in Tunnels 141
Gibbs, Joseph 27, 28, 47, 67, 68, 69, 113
Giles, Francis 21, 66, 67
Glynde 218, 225*
Godstone Road (later Caterham Junction, and now Purley) 117, 126, 137
Goring 208, 210*
Government Traffic, arrangements for 187
Greenwich, proposals for Line to 21
Gregory, Charles Hutton 165, 166

Hailsham 229, 230
Ham (Southover) 217, 223, 224, 226
Hassocks Gate (now Hassocks) 122, 126, 128
Hastings 222, 223, 226
Havant 236
Haywards Heath 121, 126, 127, 138, 163, 225
Head Signals, Train 149, 188
Hooley 136
Horley 120, 126, 127, 182-183
Horsham 232-234
Hove (original station) 129, 131, 161

Jago, Mr. 66
James, William 21
Jolly Sailor (now Norwood Junction)
52, 57, 249, 250

Keymer Junction 225
Keymer-Lewes line 222, 225
Kingston (West Sussex) 129, 130, 162

Lancing 208, 210*
Lewes 214, 217, 227
Lewes-Keymer line 222, 225
Littlehampton (original station at
Lyminster) 209, 210
Locke, Joseph: Evidence in Parlia-
ment, 1836 106-112
Locomotives, Pooling of 186, 204,
274
London & Brighton Rly
Choice of Route 65-115
Consolidation with other Com-
panies to form L B S C Rly 277
Construction of Line 130-139
Description of Line 117-128
Founding of 24, 33
General 33
Permanent Way 132, 139
Proposed Leasing by S E Rly
185, 192-193
Signalling 139, 167, 274
London & Croydon Rly
Atmospheric Working
See under Atmospheric System
Bricklayers Arms branch 192-204
Consolidation with other Com-
panies to form L B S C Rly 277
Construction and Description of
Line 45-64
Founding of 23, 26, 27
General 30, 152
Permanent Way 60, 62
Proposing Leasing by S E Rly
185, 192
Signalling 61
London & Greenwich Rly
Construction and Description of
Line 40 (brief note)

Founding of 21 (brief note)
General 150
Leasing by S E Rly 202-203
Permanent Way 43
Right-hand Running on 42
Signalling 61
London Bridge Station
Exchange of Sites as between
Croydon and Greenwich com-
panies 157, 178
Station (general) 28, 32, 36, 56,
138, 177-182, 204, 249
Station Committee (later, Joint
Board) 158, 175-177

Medhurst, George 240
Merstham 118, 126, 136, 165, 184
Military Traffic, arrangements for
187
Mocatta, David 124, 128, 137
Monson, Lord 119, 136, 165

New Cross (now New Cross Gate)
49, 56, 147, 249
New Cross Bank, assisting trains
up 148
Newhaven 213, 227
Norwood (earlier, Jolly Sailor, and
now Norwood Junction) 52, 249

Palmer, Henry 28, 67, 68, 69, 113
Penge (now Penge West) 51, 57, 166,
250
Permanent Way
Bricklayers Arms branch 196
Brighton & Chichester Rly (and
on to Portsmouth) 212
Brighton, Lewes & Hastings Rly
225, 226
London & Brighton Rly 132, 139
London & Croydon Rly 60, 62
London & Greenwich Rly 43
South Eastern Rly 172
Pevensey 218, 225*

Pilbrow, James 255
Pinwell 226
Polegate 218, 225*, 229, 230
Portcreek Junction 236
Portslade 129
Portsmouth 4, 65, 205, 234, 236, 247, 260
Purley
See under Godstone Road

Rastrick, John Urpeth 126, 130, 159, 160, 166, 182, 211, 214, 221
Red Hill (sic) & Reigate Road 119, 126, 137, 184
Reigate (Red Hill (sic)), S E Rly 171, 184
Renamed Stations
See under each name
Rennie, Sir John
Early Railway Work in Surrey and Sussex 21, 65
London-Brighton line
Basic proposals 28, 65, 66, 67, 69
Detailed scheme (later modified) 70-72
Evidence in Parliament, 1836 88-106
Final 'Agreed Plan' 113
Final Route 114
Road Coaches, conveyance of rail 162
Rolling Stock, Pooling of 186, 204

St. John's Common 122, 130, 137
St. Leonards (Bulverhithe) 215, 218, 222, 223, 225
St. Leonards (near the later West Marina) 223
Samuda, Jacob 240, 248
Samuda, Joseph 240, 248
Seaford 227
Select Committee of 1839 36, 152
Shipping, Cross-Channel: Legal position 227

Shoreham 130, 208, 210*
Shoreham-Brighton line 128-130, 134-135, 161
Signalling
Bricklayers Arms Junction 196
Brighton Junction (Norwood) 265
Corbett's Lane Junction 63, 149
London Bridge 63, 149
Semaphore Signal, first railway 166
Types of
See under Railway or Line concerned
Slips, Earth 165, 185
South Eastern Rly
Bricklayers Arms branch 192-204
Choice of Route for original line 28, 30, 33, 35
Founding of 24, 31
General 170
Leasing of Greenwich company 202-203
Permanent Way 172
Proposed Leasing of Brighton and Croydon companies 185, 192
Signalling 172, 196
Southerham Junction 227
Southover (Ham) 217, 223, 224, 226
Southwick 129
Spa Road, closing and reopening of 42, 183
Stations
See under name of Station
Stephenson, Robert
Early railway work in Surrey and Sussex 28, 66, 68, 69
London-Brighton line
Detailed scheme by G. P. Bidder 69-70
Evidence in Parliament, 1836 73-83
Final 'Agreed Plan' 113
New proposals for 260
Stoats Nest 118, 166
Surrey Iron Rly 3, 5, 18, 274
Sutton 246
Sydenham 50, 57, 250

Tarring Crossing, proposed station
    at 208
Telegraph, Electric
    See under Electric Telegraph
Three Bridges 120, 126, 128, 233
Three Bridges-Horsham line 233
Tickets, prices of (i.e., Fares)
    See under Financial Matters
Tolls
    See under Financial Matters
Tunnels, Gas-Lighting in 141
Turnpike Roads 2, 20, 150

Vallance, John 23, 240
Vignoles, Charles 21, 28, 66, 67, 68,
    69

Wallington
    See under Carshalton (not
        renamed until 1868)
Widening Works (including
    doubling of single lines)
    Brighton-Shoreham 136
    Croydon-Epsom 253
    Greenwich Viaduct 153, 155, 166
        249, 251
    Lewes-St. Leonards (Bulverhithe)
        226-227
    London & Croydon Rly 247, 249
    Shoreham-Chichester 238
Wilkinson, W. A. 159, 243, 269,
    271, 273
Woodgate (for Bognor) 209, 210*
Worthing 208, 210*

Yapton 209, 210*, 238